99.1% PURE
BREAKING BAD ART

TITAN
BOOKS
LONDON
AN INSIGHT EDITIONS BOOK

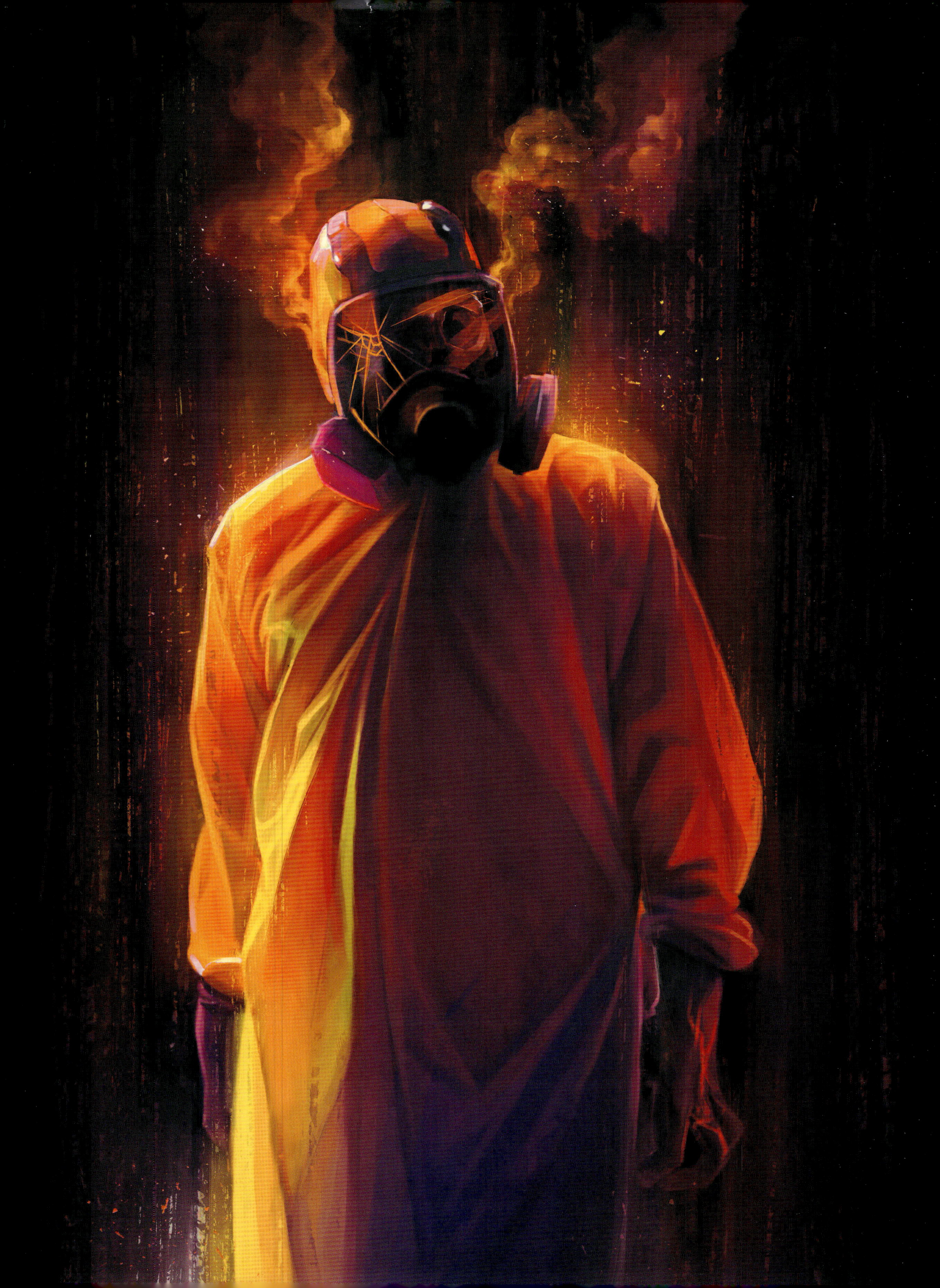

Contents

Introduction by Vince Gilligan 6

chapter 1
Say m**Y** n**Am**e 9

chapter 2
Yeah, **Sc**ience! 39

chapter 3
The em**P**ire **B**usiness 89

chapter 4
sa**N**gre **Po**r sang**Re** 129

chapter 5
Land **O**f en**C**hantment 163

Epilogue 227
Acknowledgments 232

PAGE 1: Joey Reinisch | *Just Add Walter* | Digital
Sherman Oaks, California, USA | 2013 | jreinisch

PAGES 2–3: Eric Guan | *Jesse Pinkman* | Digital painting | USA | 2013 | eman27

OPPOSITE: Xenia Shatova | *Fumes* | Digital painting
Yekaterinburg, Russia | 2014 | shatova_k

THIS PAGE: Lori Kay Farr | *Breaking Caps of ABQ* | Paint chip mosaic bottle caps
Hamilton, Ohio, USA | 2015 | www.lkfdesigns.net | LKFdesigns

The views and opinions expressed in this book are those of the authors and quoted individuals and do not necessarily represent the views and opinions of Sony Pictures Entertainment or any of its respective affiliates or employees.

Introduction

I can't tell you how tickled I am by this book. Its very existence makes me want to pinch myself.

After all these years, I'm still coming to grips with the world's reaction to *Breaking Bad*. It's so odd when people say, "You knew that show would be a hit, right?" The hell I did. None of us did. I was just praying for one full season on the air. I figured if we could squeak along that far without getting canceled, maybe I'd earn enough Hollywood cred to run some bigger, less-out-there-type series.

Never in my wildest dreams did I imagine *Breaking Bad* would inspire works by brilliant artists around the globe. Never did I picture a big, classy hardcover chock-full of such visions, destined for finer coffee tables everywhere.

Back in Farmville, Virginia, I used to be a fool for painting and sculpting. It's pretty much all I remember doing in our flying saucer–shaped elementary school (the keenly missed J. P. Wynne, whose name I borrowed for the high school in our show). There, my friend Kevin and I were the two best draw-ers, as Jesse Pinkman might say. Heady times!

In sixth grade I decided I'd make my living as a famous artist, seeing as I was so damned outstanding at it. Then came high school and cold reality. I briefly attended Interlochen, an excellent arts academy in Michigan. There, everybody—and I mean *everybody*, right down to the stoners and dipshit rich kids—was more talented than I.

This was a bracing kick in the butt. I'm grateful for it. It helped turn me to writing—where only 32.7 percent of my peers are more talented, a ratio I find acceptable.

Still . . . sometimes I wonder what life would have been like had I taken a different path. Because I was always at my happiest drawing, painting, and sculpting. Art was a place where the hours passed like minutes. In it I could lose myself, literally. Jesus, what's better than that? I haven't had that kind of escape in decades. I certainly never get it when I'm putting words on paper.

Shed no tears for me, however. This book massages my ego quite nicely. The sculptors, painters, and draw-ers herein are one exceptional bunch. They hail from all over the planet. Every one of them labored on their own time and dime—the creations you're about to see are theirs alone.

Do I covet their mastery? Does it stir in me a long-dormant envy dating back to my teenage years? Yeah, a little bit. But that's okay. For me, these works are a special gift. Through them, I get to see my own television show with brand-new eyes.

I thank every one of these artists, and I'm proud to share them with you.

Constance Harvey | *Cartoon Vince* | Digital painting | Montréal, Québec, Canada | 2015 | www.constanceharvey.com

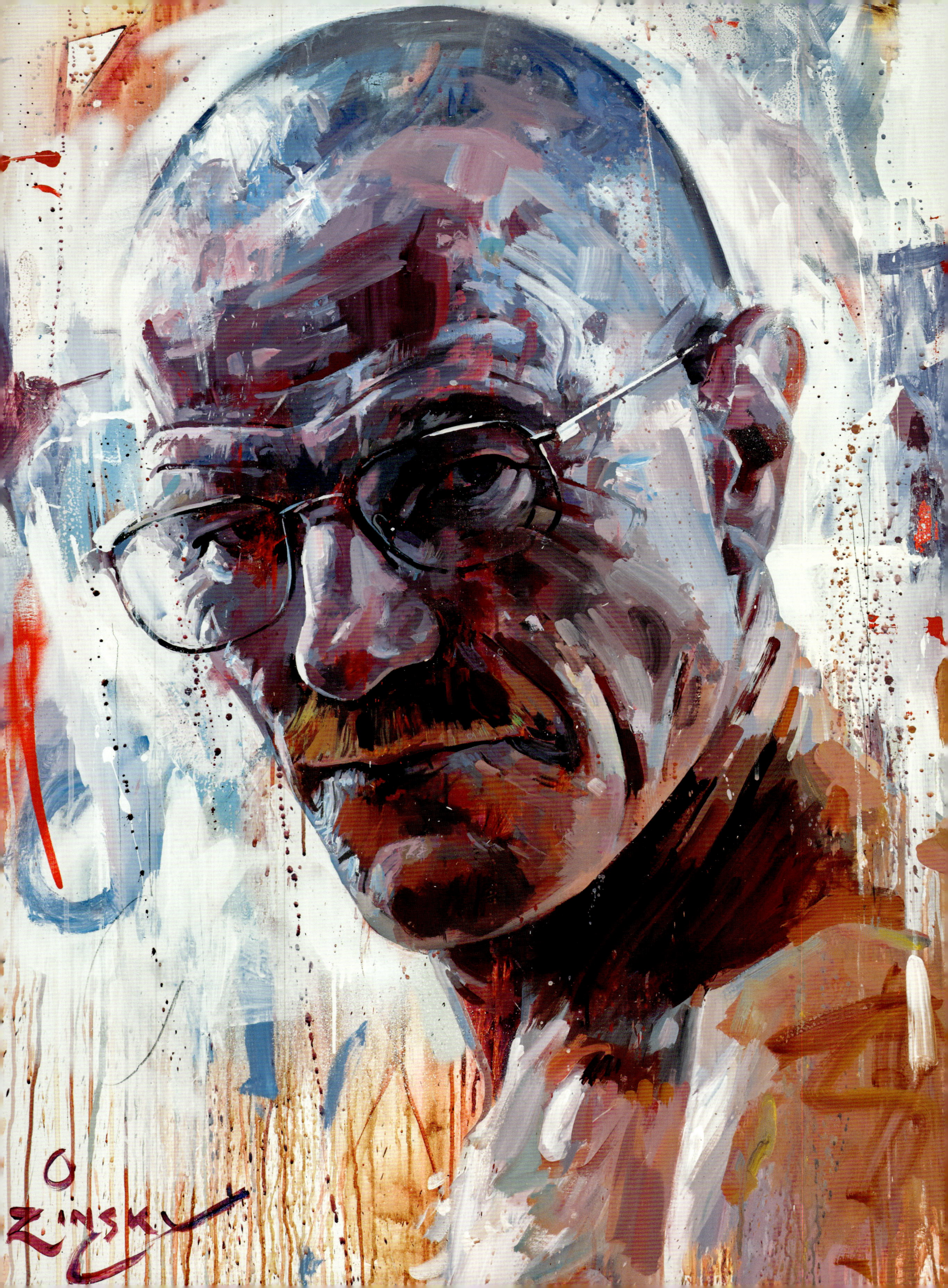

chapter 1

Say mY nAme

"My name is Walter Hartwell White." For fans of *Breaking Bad*, this line conjures the image of a panicked man in his green button-down shirt, tighty-whities, and Wallabees, a punishing desert expanse stretching into the distance behind him. Haunting cinematic moments like these abound in the series, inspiring viewers to adopt new ways of seeing.

Nowhere is the legacy of *Breaking Bad* more evident than in the proliferation of art celebrating the series—particularly pieces created by fans of the show, from professional artists to hobbyists. "When our show inspires extraordinary fan art, it means we made an impact, that *Breaking Bad* lives on inside the hearts and imaginations of talented people," reflects co-executive producer and writer Peter Gould. "What greater compliment can there be?"

Walter White's transformation from a down-on-his-luck chemistry teacher with a terminal cancer diagnosis to the ruthless meth kingpin known as Heisenberg has challenged creators around the world, leading them to evaluate how they relate to the character's moral descent through original works of their own.

OPPOSITE: Zinsky | *Heisenberg* | Acrylic on canvas | Segovia, Spain | 2015 | zinskyofficial | zinskyartist

FROM MR. CHIPS TO SCARFACE

From his first ride-along with DEA agent brother-in-law Hank Schrader to the last time he ever sets foot in a meth lab, Walt cycles through various personas. Some, like Heisenberg, are more enticing than others. Colombian painter Armando Mesías saw "an opportunity to explore portraiture through the different phases of Walt's character arc" in a multi-part series including Walter and Ozymandias, showcasing the stages of "Walt's evolution—or rather, decay." Similarly, in her piece The Evolution of Walter White, California-based Elba Raquel reimagined Rudolph Zallinger's The Road to Homo Sapiens to depict multiple versions of Walt—from a hunched-over Walt in his teaching attire to a fully upright Walt in his professional lab gear, finally ending on a bearded Walt from the series finale, again hunched over and clutching his fatal bullet wound. "From the very beginning," composer Dave Porter notes, the Breaking Bad team "made sure we kept our eye on the series-long view of the transformation of Walter White into Heisenberg." Raquel believes that only by taking on his alter ego Heisenberg did Walt "gain the confidence in himself to stand up tall." "What most fascinated me," she says, "was the ingenious weaving of the physical and psychological evolution of Walter White's character."

Brazilian illustrator Rustem Gomes ties the physical to the psychological in analogizing Walt's worsening lung cancer symptoms to the "degeneration in his character over the course of each episode." In his comic-book-style piece Bad to the Bone, Gomes portrays a meek Mr. White cowering in the shadows of a domineering Heisenberg. He views Heisenberg as Walt's disguise, "just like in the comics, where heroes and villains have disguises to hide who they really are." Chilean digital artist PerroBike – MOS cites this "transformation and empowerment" as his primary attraction to Breaking Bad. His piece Breaking Bike features Walt, clad in his Heisenberg porkpie hat, pedaling a tandem bicycle with a windblown Jesse hanging on for dear life. PerroBike – MOS slings a motorcycle lock around Jesse's neck as a nod to the Season 1 episode ". . . And the Bag's in the River," in which Walt wrestles with his morals and ultimately uses a lock to strangle rival drug dealer Krazy-8, but not before Jesse comically tries to fit the lock over his own head. When asked which moment stands out most to him in Walt's metamorphosis, Breaking Bad associate producer Andrew Ortner has only two words: "bike lock."

GRAY MATTER

Despite what his surname might suggest, Walter White exists in—at best—a gray zone of morality. It is an open question as to whether he is a good guy making a series of progressively immoral decisions or a bad guy whose true nature is revealed over time. Italian illustrator Alessandro Saiu leans toward the latter: "Totally empathizing with Walter White is difficult. From the beginning you admire his hard desire for emancipation and self-determination through his skills, but suddenly his deep, dark side shows itself." In his piece *Walter*, Saiu depicts the character clinging to his last barrel of money moments after the brutal execution of his brother-in-law Hank, whose long hunt for the mysterious Heisenberg has finally come to an end. Even then, Walt cannot let go of what Saiu identifies as his true motivation all along—"money and power." Artist Armando Mesías is less certain: "I think one of the main features of *Breaking Bad* is how someone can have a complete transformation, whilst planting a subtle doubt [as to] whether deep down he was always like that and it just flourished due to circumstances."

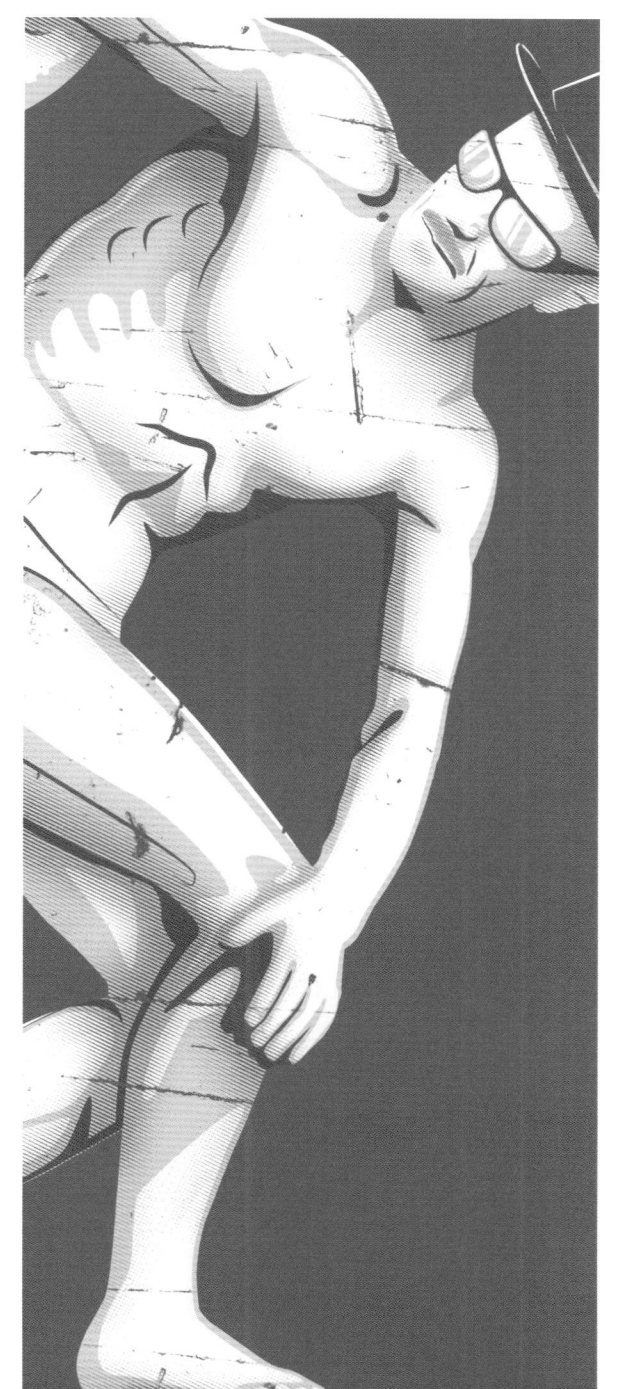

As the blood on Walt's hands thickens, audiences must grapple with their tolerance for his crimes. Artist Elba Raquel contemplates: "We all have that inner Heisenberg inside of us, and it comes out every once in a while. But being aware of when to pull back before our actions become destructive is what keeps us grounded in our core, our true Walter White." Raquel felt she could no longer root for Walt after he repeatedly manipulated Jesse, turning him into "a walking shell of his initial charismatic self." Spanish artist Victor Moral also experienced mixed emotions, finding it "heartbreaking" to watch Walt descend into Heisenberg territory: "There's no good choice, no good end. Bitter as life." In his piece *Discobolo / Pizzobolo*, Moral painted Walt wielding a pizza in the vein of Myron's *Discobolus* as a nod to the Season 3 episode "Caballo Sin Nombre," in which Walt, in a fit of rage, launches a pizza onto his roof. *Breaking Bad* executive story editor and writer Gennifer Hutchison muses that it is these "funny, absurd moments" that made Walt's character "feel like a real person."

Los Angeles–based digital artist Joey Reinisch, who created a series of pixelated renditions of Walt entitled *Just Add Walter*, maintains that "Walt is a monster," while acknowledging that "it's a testament to the writers that you still feel empathy for someone who has done so many horrible things." Perhaps Walt's actions are cathartic for viewers, a safe exploration of darker desires. Who hasn't wished they could throw off the chains of convention and do something wild to change their lot in life? Brazilian illustrator Felms identifies with Walt's appetite for danger: "*Breaking Bad* made me feel human and alive." Felms injected that potency into his piece *Out of Time Man*, which shows Walt blowing up an expensive convertible belonging to Ken Wins, the obnoxious loudmouth with a Bluetooth earpiece who swiped Walt's parking space in the Season 1 episode "Cancer Man." Chilean artist Plastivida, who sculpted Plasticine bars into a miniature Heisenberg, all from memory, is likewise invigorated by Walt's transformation: "I absolutely empathize with his anger and his desire to live life as he had never dared before."

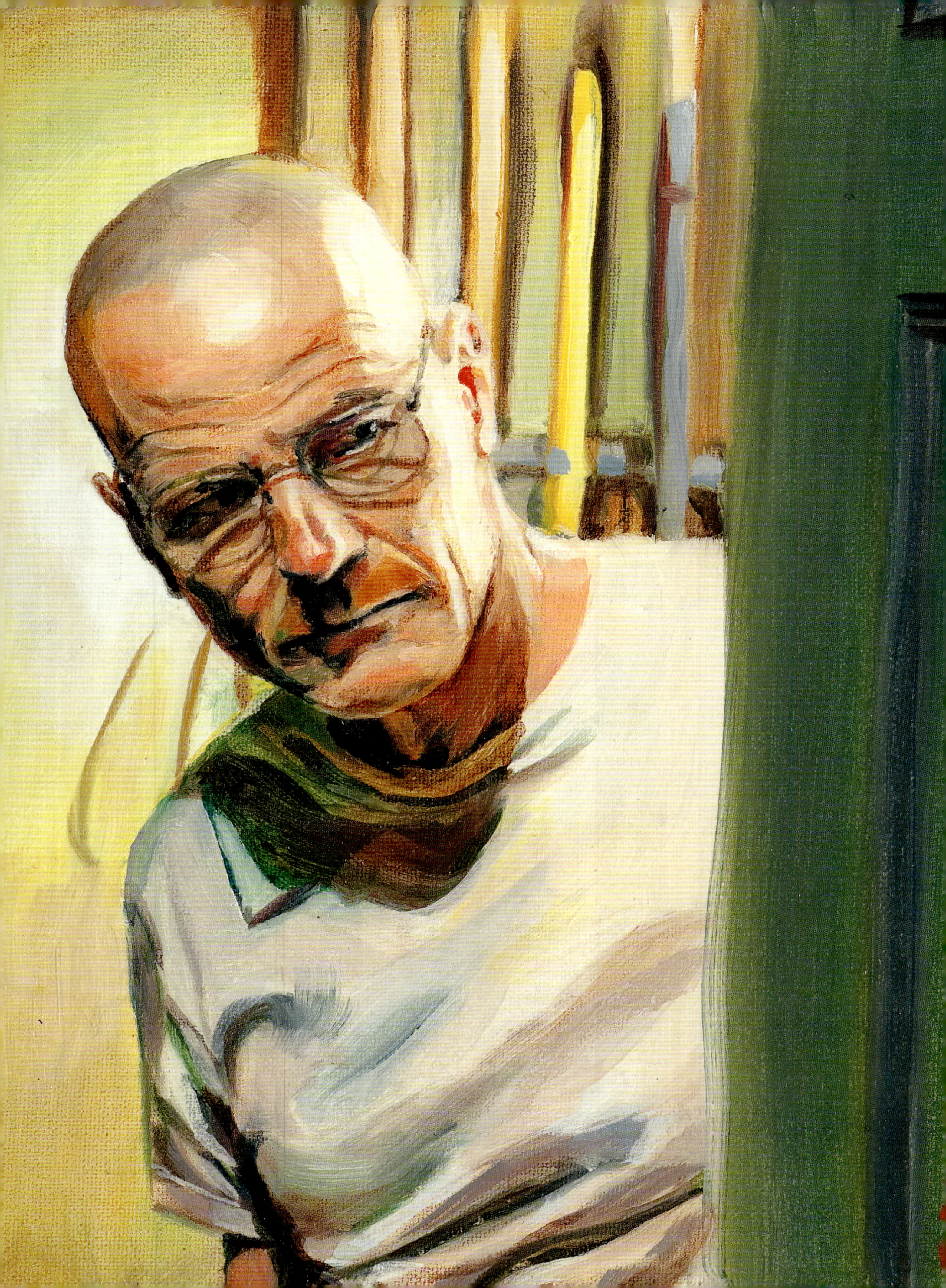

OPPOSITE: Adam Brooks | *Walter White Is Breaking Bad* | Oil on canvas | Winnipeg, Manitoba, Canada | 2009 | www.adambrooks.net | 📷 adambrooks79

ABOVE: Natalie Schnitter | *Tread Lightly* | Oil and digital painting | Vancouver, British Columbia, Canada | 2016 | 📷 nataliececelia

OPPOSITE: Leftdead (Leonardo Tassi) | *I Am the One Who Knocks* | Pen and ink | Guarulhos, São Paulo, Brazil | 2016 | ⌾ lftdead

Breaking

I AM THE ONE WHO KNOCKS

Dave Hopkins / Phosphorart.com | *Heisenberg for GQ Magazine, UK* | Ink on paper | Broadstairs, Kent, UK | 2014 | www.phosphorart.com/artist/dave-hopkins

Brian Reedy | *Walter/Heisenberg* | Linocut | Miami, Florida, USA | 2016 | brianreedy

ABOVE and OPPOSITE: Armando Mesías | *Walter* and *Ozymandias* | Oil, acrylics, spray paint, pencil, markers on paper and canvas | London, UK | 2014
www.armandomesias.com | armandomesias

"I met a Traveler from an Antike Land who said: Two vast trunkless legs of stone stand in the desert. Near them on the sand half sunk, a shattered visage lies, whose frown, and wrinkled lip, and sneer of cold command, tell that it's sculptor well those passions read, which yet survive, stamped on these lifeless things, the hand that mocked them and the heart that fed. And on the pedestal these words appear— "My name is Ozymandias, King of Kings, Look on my Works, ye Mighty, and Despair!" Nothing besides remains. Round the decay of that colossal wreck, boundless and bare the lone and level sands stretch far away."

A.M.

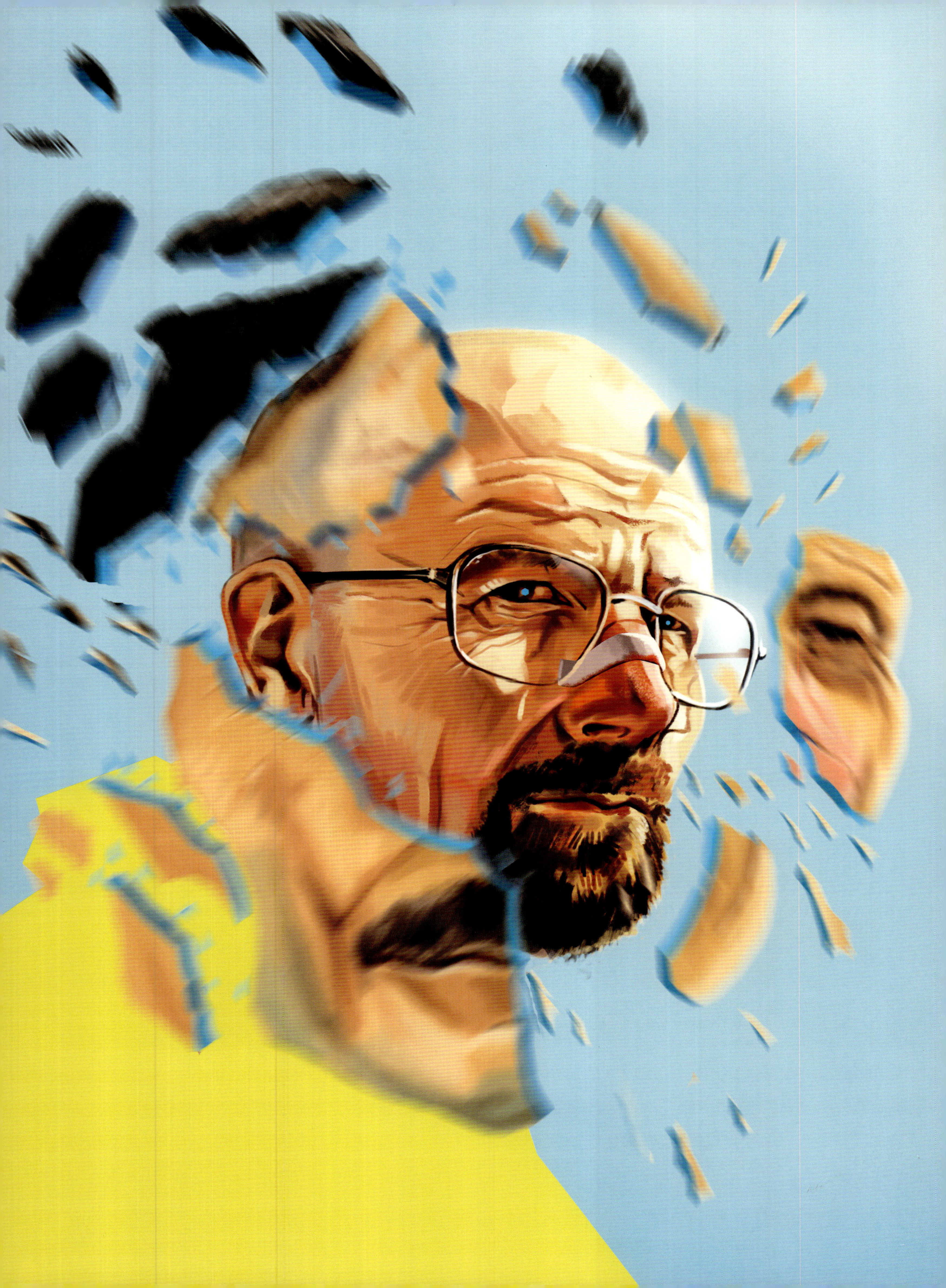

OPPOSITE: Mukuch Chanchanyan | *Knock Knock* | Painting and digital illustration | Yerevan, Armenia | 2014/2020 | 🅘 mukooch

ABOVE: Jonny Cookiee (Joseph & Sons Mosaic) | *Bad Crystals* | Mosaic glass, stainless steel, and stained glass | Los Angeles, California, USA 2009 | www.josephandsonsmosaics.com | 🅘 jonnycookiee

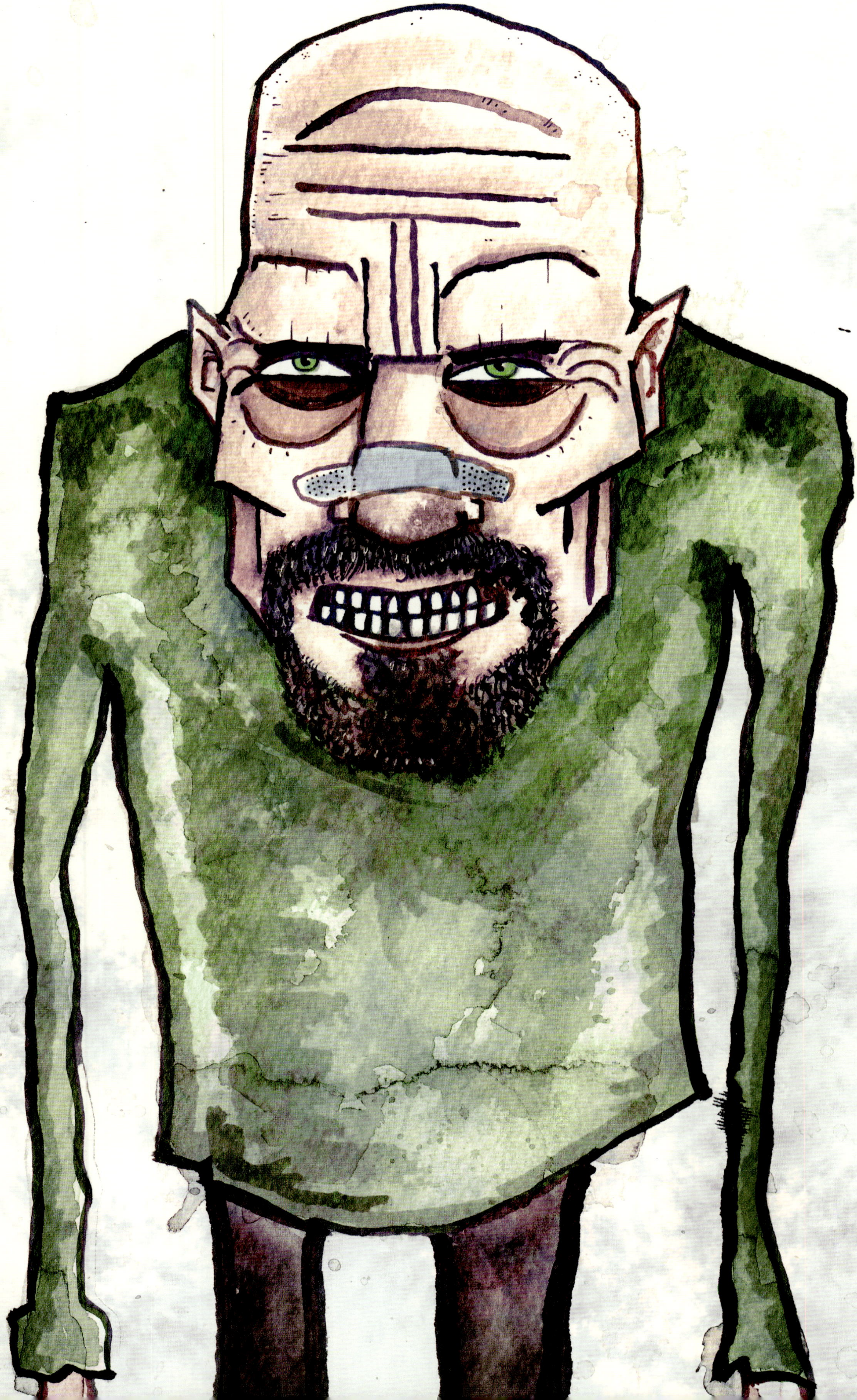

OPPOSITE: Grant Hunter | *Mister White* | Ink on paper and digital | Newcastle, Australia | 2014 | www.granthunter.net

ABOVE: Maks Andala | *Take It* | Mixed media | London, UK | 2015 | ⓘ maksandala

ABOVE: Felms | *Out of Time Man* | Digital art | São Paulo, Brazil | 2018 | 🅾 felms

OPPOSITE: Misura Mano | *Walter's Journey* | Digital 3D, cinema 4D | Barcelona, Spain | 2016 | www.elloboestudio.com | 🅾 misuramano

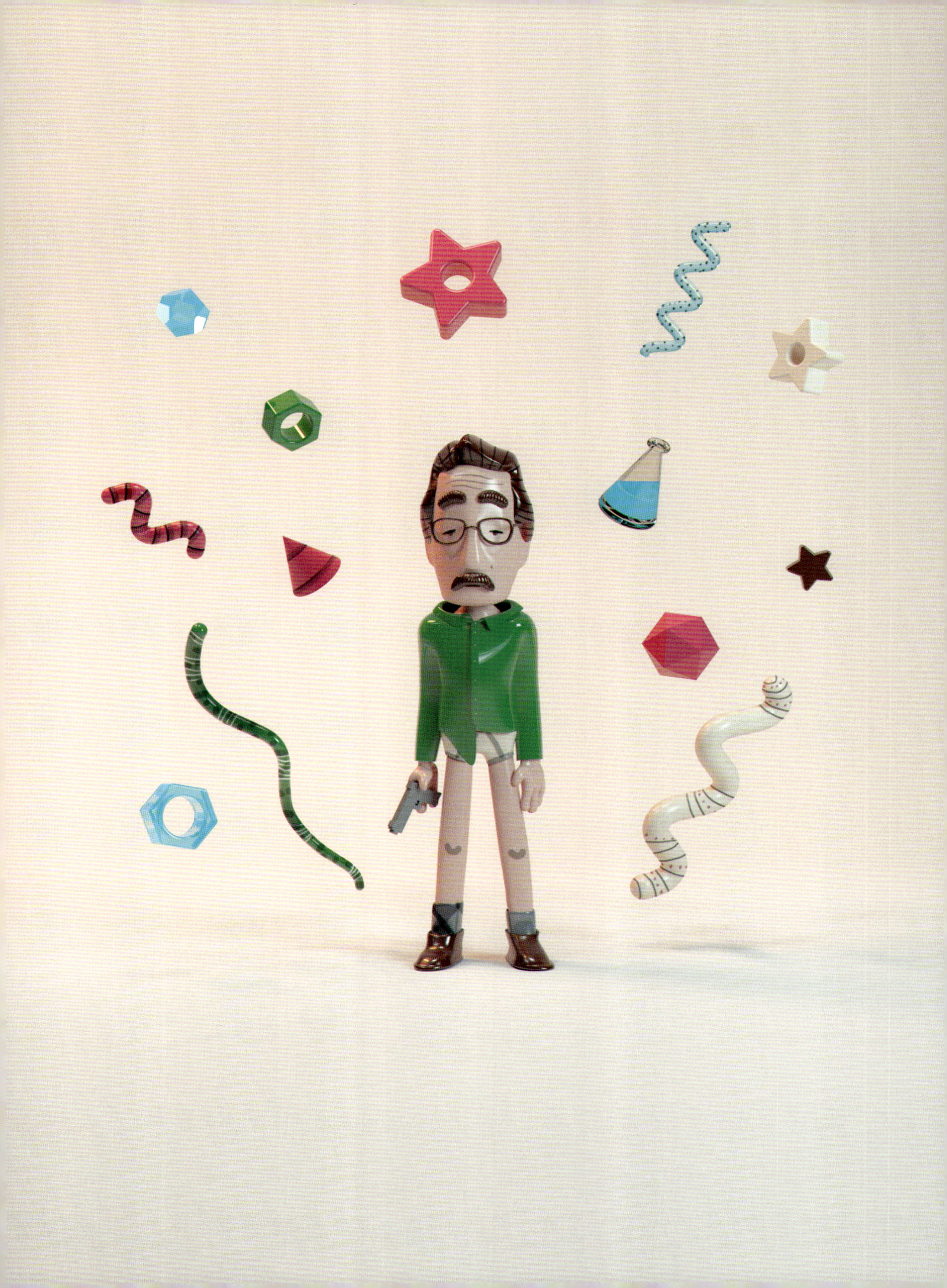

26

OPPOSITE: Plastivida | *Mr.PlastiWhite* | Photography and dimensional illustration in plasticine and crushed glass | Plaza Dignidad, Santiago, Chile | 2013 | www.plastivida.cl | 🅞 plastivida

ABOVE: PerroBike — MOS | *Breaking Bike* | Digital art | Santiago, Chile | 2016 | 🅞 perrobike.mos

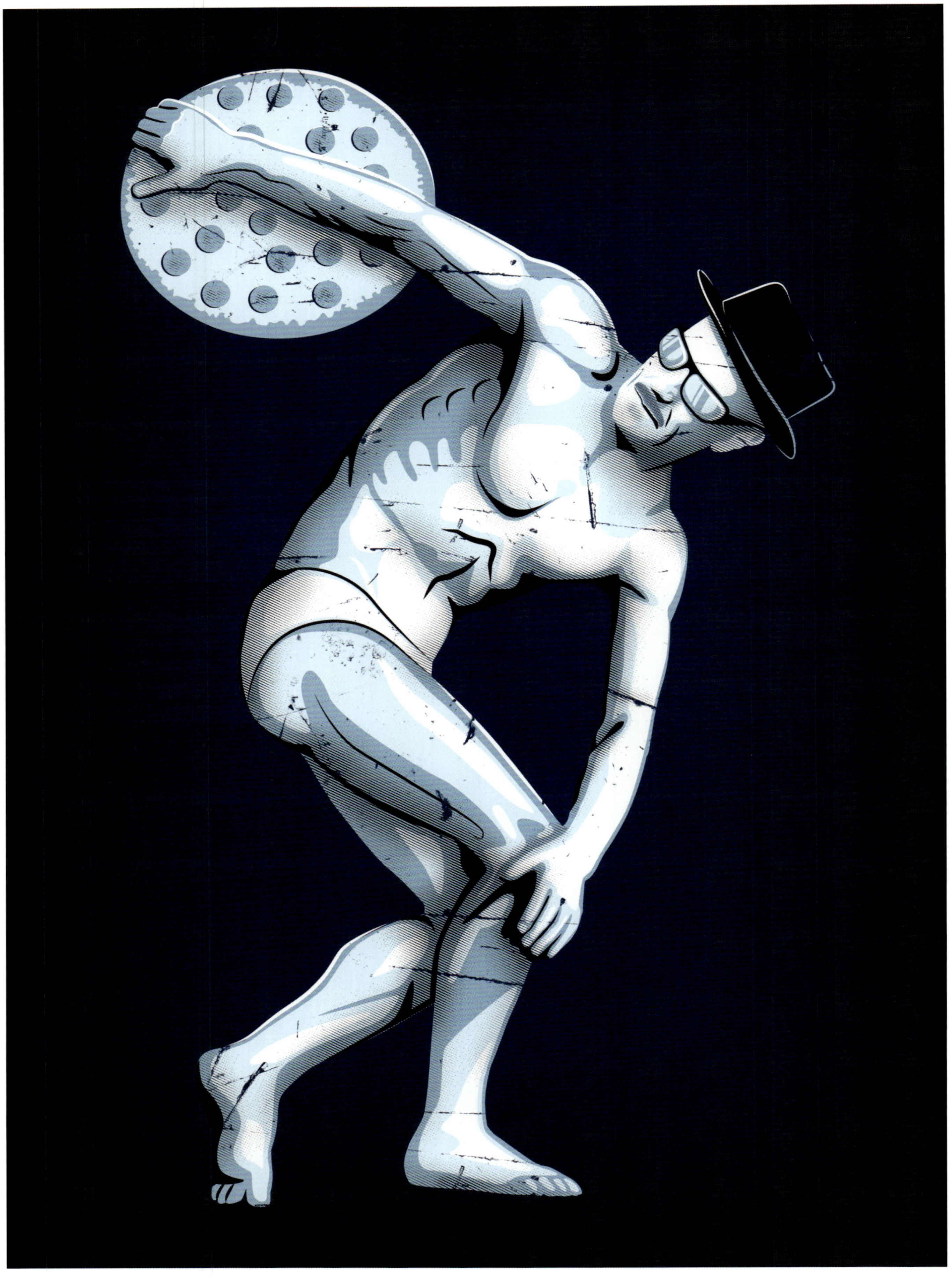

OPPOSITE: Victor Moral | *Discobolo / Pizzobolo* | Pencil sketch and digital art | Cartagena, Spain | 2015 | biticol

OPPOSITE: Cole Mitchell | *Hunt for Heisenberg* | Digital illustration | Atlanta, Georgia, USA | 2013 | raisedcreative

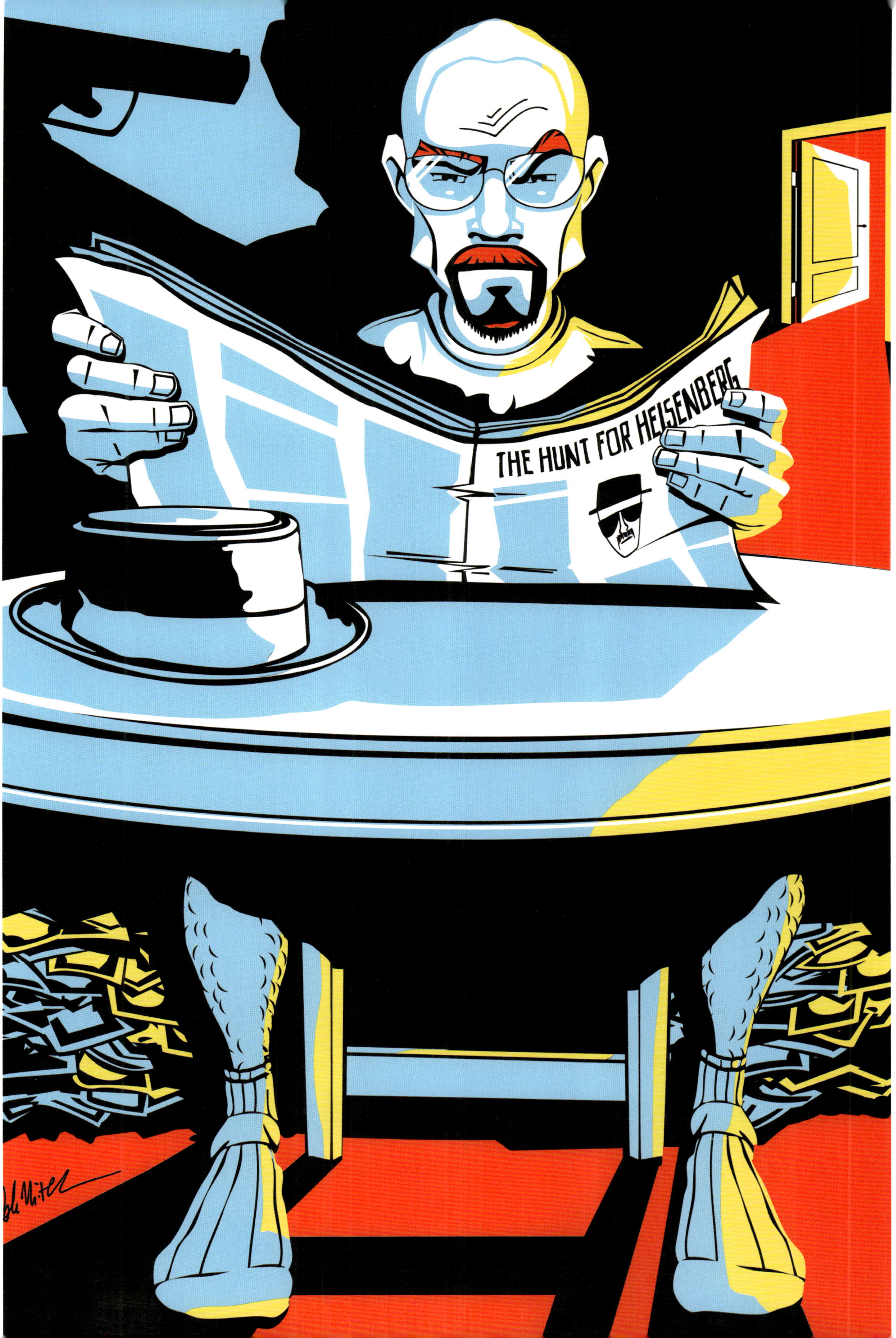
THE HUNT FOR HEISENBERG

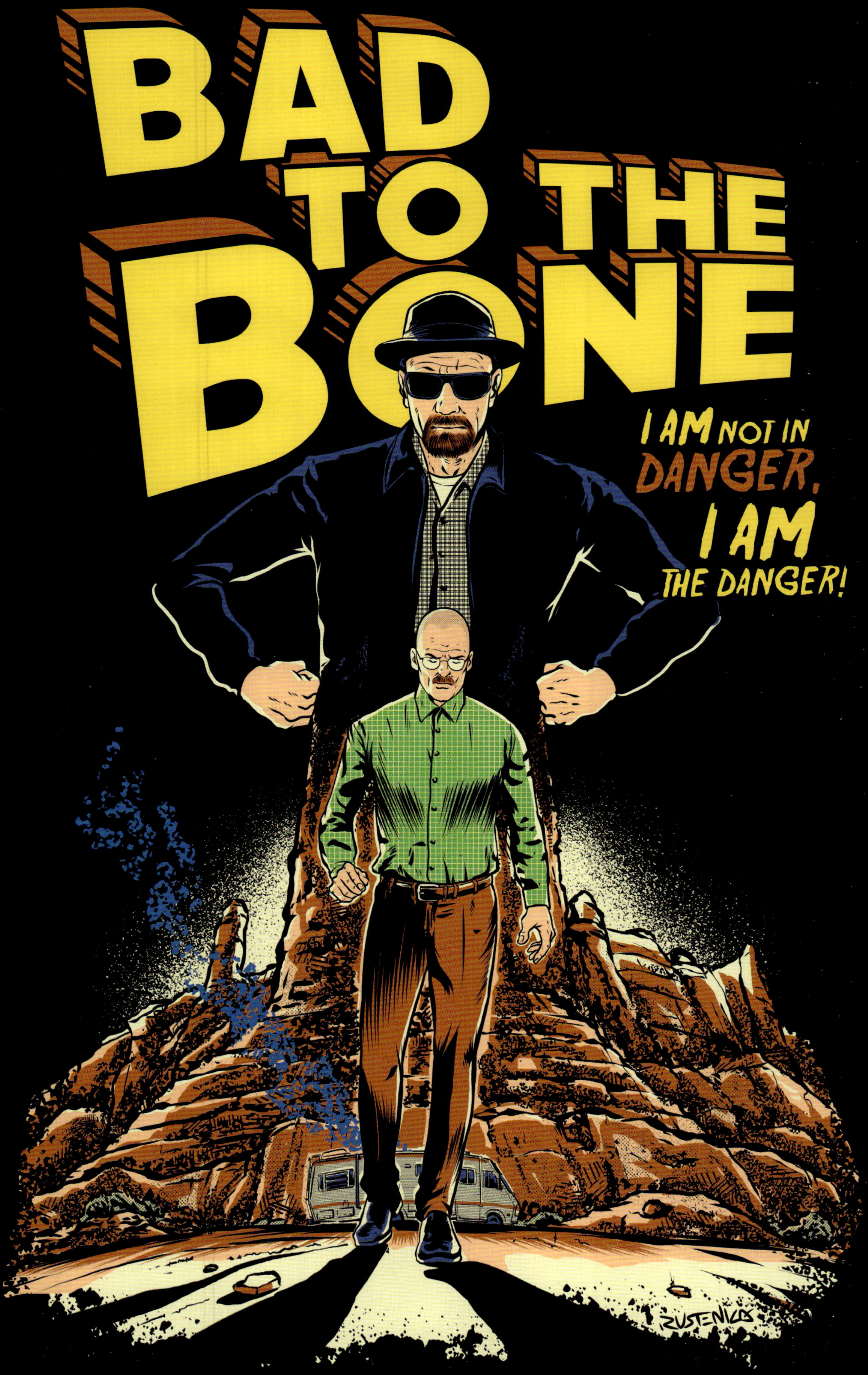
BAD TO THE BONE
I AM NOT IN DANGER, I AM THE DANGER!
RUSTENICO

OPPOSITE: Rustem Gomes (rustenico) | *Bad to the Bone* | Digital illustration | Rio de Janeiro, Brazil | 2018 | rustenico

ABOVE: Alessandro Saiu | *Walter* | Digital drawing | Turin, Italy | 2019 | a_s_a_i_v

Br Ba

OPPOSITE: Evan Kang | *Mr. Lambert* | Digital illustration | Portland, Oregon, USA | 2013 | www.evankang.com

TOP: Saryth Chareonpanichkul | *Walter White Transformation* | Digital painting (Photoshop) | Bangkok, Thailand | 2016 | toonyforyou4ever

ABOVE: Elba Raquel | *The Evolution of Walter White* | Digital painting | San Jose, California, USA | 2013 | www.elbaraquel.com | theelbaraquel

OPPOSITE: Matu Santamaria | *"Yo soy el que llama"* | Digital illustration, vector | Almería, Spain | 2016 | matusantamaria

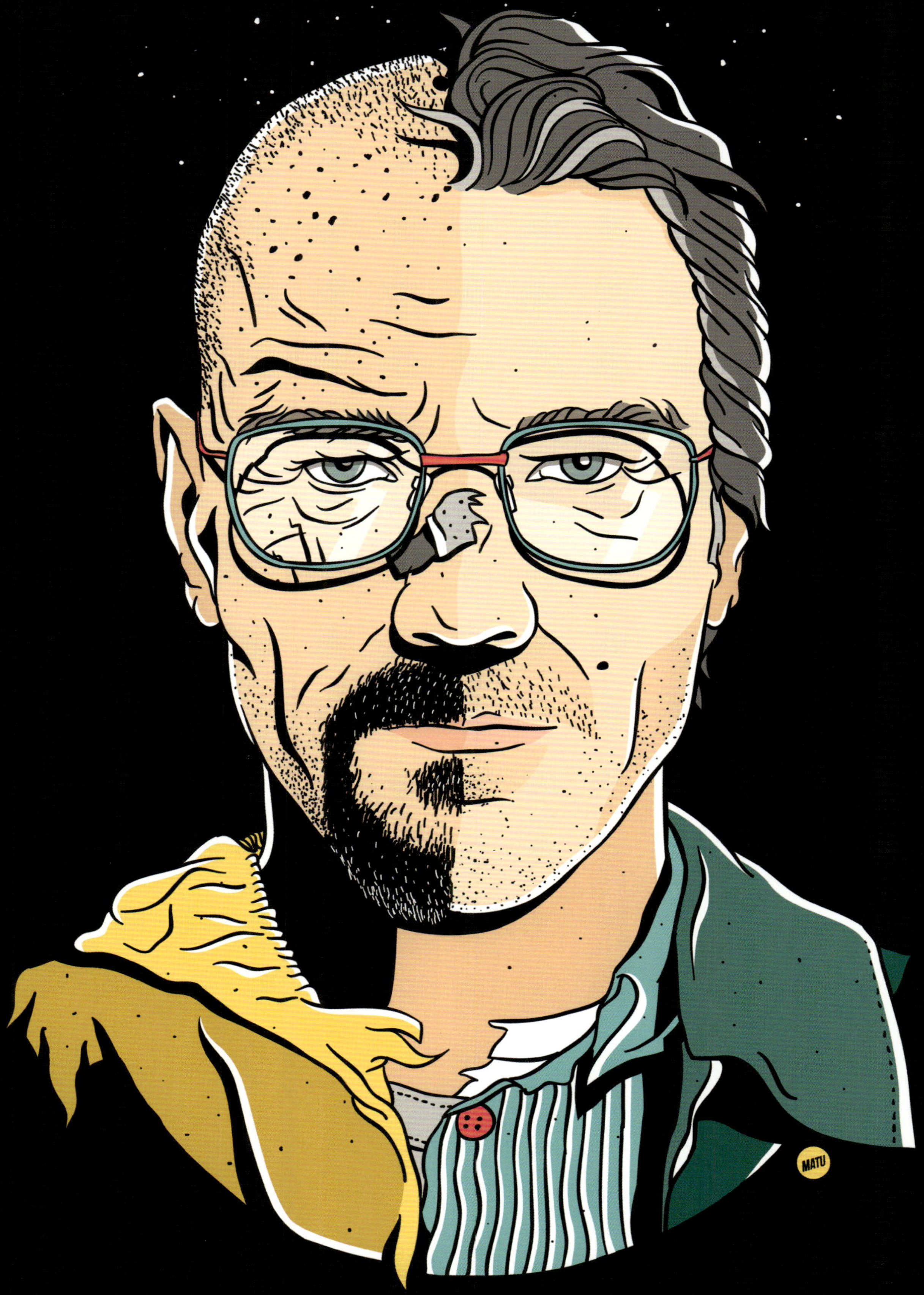
MATU

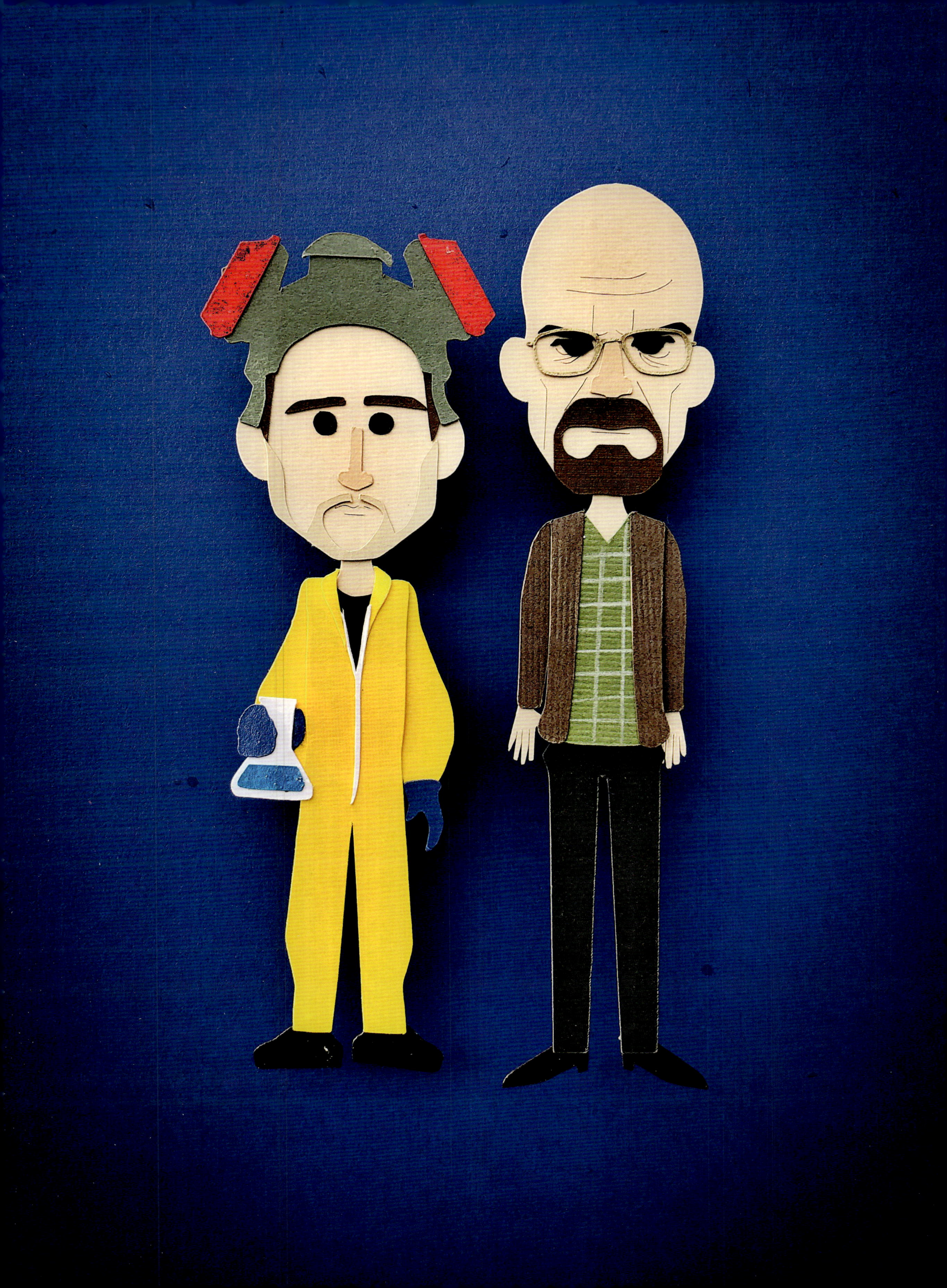

chapter 2

Yeah, **Sc**ience!

It's "the study of change," Walter White tells his high school students. Walt could be describing *Breaking Bad* itself, a show about the elasticity of human nature. In fact, he is talking about *chemistry*—his life's passion and a catalyst for the story. As a science, chemistry is essential to the cooking of methamphetamine, without which Walt could not have perfected his notorious 99.1 percent pure formula. In emotional terms, chemistry drives the love-hate bond between Mr. White and his favorite delinquent pupil, Jesse Pinkman.

ART AND CHEMISTRY

Walt and Jesse didn't always see eye to eye on the virtues of chemistry, especially when it came to the amount of rule-bending involved. As Jesse tells Walt in the "Pilot" episode: "This ain't chemistry. This is *art*!" In reality, it might be a little bit of both. In British illustrator Stuart Herrington's opinion, chemistry tends to follow strict rules, but artists prefer to get a little more creative: "That's why they put chili powder in their meth." Herrington set out to portray Walt and Jesse's pernicious dynamic, "a symbiotic relationship that also turns to conflict." His digital illustration, aptly titled *Breaking Bad*, features Walt in nothing more than a green cooking apron and tighty-whities, standing triumphantly on top of Jesse, who is trapped in a giant blue chrysalis of meth.

"*Breaking Bad* is like meth," surmises Jeff Ward, a graphic designer from Vince Gilligan's home state of Virginia. Ward's pieces, entitled *King Walt* and *King Jesse*, place Walt and Jesse in yellow Tyvek lab suits on separate playing cards, both kings. After sharing his art online, Ward received a few comments from fans of the series that Jesse should have been a jack or a joker, as opposed to a king, but he stands by his choice: "Some kings can be vulnerable and manipulated while other kings can be diabolical evil genius meth lords."

Many artists who drew inspiration from the show's use of chemistry developed a newfound appreciation for the subject. Mexican designer Nora Adame remembers: "I had never failed a subject until I got to chemistry. Now, as an artist, I see it like a kind of magic. I see the essence of life in the way energy is transformed." Adame repurposed textile waste, primarily clothing labels, to construct colorful portraits of Walt and Jesse with gas masks perched on their foreheads.

OPPOSITE: Kristy Edgar | *Un Papel Nuevo* | Paper craft | Houston, Texas, USA | 2018 | @ frompentopaperstudio

Plastic Cell, a team of Californians who created sculptures of Walt and Jesse wearing their signature yellow lab gear, considers the bright Tyvek suit "an iconic superhero-like costume." They credit *Breaking Bad* with giving them a new perspective on chemistry and have come to view scientists as artists. French illustrator Nancy Vanadia agrees: "*Breaking Bad* showed me how interesting science could be, as there is chemistry in everything." She used ballpoint pen to depict Jesse attentively weighing a tub of blue meth in her piece *Jesse at Work*, likening the alchemy of forming a chemical compound to that of creating a painting. Although Vanadia does not recall being attentive in chemistry class, "maybe," she speculates, "if I had a teacher like Mr. White, it could have been different!"

BEHIND THE SCIENCE

Getting the science right on the show was a science—and sometimes, an art—in itself. *Breaking Bad* writers' assistant Gordon Smith notes that research typically began with a simple internet search to see if "any science-related idea was within the realm of possibility." If so, it then progressed to consulting with experts. In particular, Dr. Donna Nelson, a chemistry professor at the University of Oklahoma, provided invaluable assistance and insight.

Not only did the science on the page have to pass muster, but it also needed to translate to the screen, most notably during the meth-making sequences in the outsize Superlab where Walt and Jesse churned out hundreds of pounds of "Blue Sky" a week. "The space is very well built," remarks Ecuadorian Carlos Valarezo, an architect by profession, who "did a whole study to understand the space and the distribution of the devices" in the Superlab. Valarezo considers Walt and Jesse's methodical torching of the Superlab in the Season 4 finale a "masterpiece." His ink and digital painting *The Destruction of the Superlab* portrays that scene in an intricate, stylized manner, with a flurry of abstract flames rising above the burning lab equipment. Production designer Mark Freeborn, who brought the medical-grade complex to life, sourced the lab equipment shown in Valarezo's piece using elements commonly found in the food processing and cosmetics manufacturing industries.

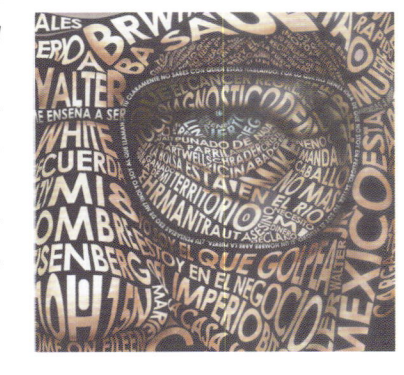

Vietnamese illustrator f.buffy, who paints Walt and Jesse in the Superlab carefully studying a shard of meth in her piece *Heisenberg and His Partner*, expresses amazement at how "super serious and focused" the pair become when making meth, "no matter how many times they have gone through the same process." UK-based illustrator Chris Sharples regards the Superlab as "the highest point" in Walt and Jesse's "cooking careers." Sharples's vector illustration *Time to Cook* features a cartoon-style Walt and Jesse adding chemicals to a giant vat. Sharples reflects: "The cooking montages always came across like something from *Willy Wonka & the Chocolate Factory*. . . . The camera and music create some whimsy that lets you know something magical is happening." *Breaking Bad* editor Skip Macdonald explains that he would initially assemble the clips of Walt and Jesse in the lab in accordance with specific steps in the recipe for cooking real meth, altered only slightly to foil copycats. Macdonald often worked with music supervisor Thomas Golubić early on in the editing process to select the accompanying music and would then refine the cuts until he achieved "the correct artistic feel."

WALT AND JESSE'S CHEMISTRY

The chemistry between Walt and Jesse extended far beyond their roles as meth cooks, of course. "They had a father-son feel to their characters, and also made a good comedy team," notes Illinois-based Rick Fortson, also known as "DrPencil." As writer Gennifer Hutchison observes, "The humorous moments ground those darker elements, invest us in the characters, and make the dramatic moments even more devastating." In his piece *Superlab*, Fortson used a variety of pencil grades to draw Walt and Jesse's focused expressions from the perspective of "the bottom of a 'batch of Blue'" being cooked in the industrial-scale lab.

Walt and Jesse's relationship was "rocky from day one," comments actor Aaron Paul. "I do love the odd-couple-shorthand partnership they have. It was beautiful to play within." Texas-based Kristy Edgar, who created a papercraft Jesse wearing lab gear and standing alongside a scowling Mr. White, appreciates their "yin-and-yang dynamic," noting that "they both need what the other has, and their personalities are strengths and weaknesses for one another." Edgar herself pursued a chemistry degree before changing course to become a middle school history teacher.

Walt and Jesse's history in the classroom contributed to the show's most memorable science-related moments, including the darkly comic scene in the Season 2 episode "4 Days Out" where Jesse asks Walt if he could build a robot to get them out of the desert. *Breaking Bad* co-executive producer and writer Thomas Schnauz counts this scene among his favorites: "It says so much about what they went through in their prior life as student and teacher, and highlights why it's so funny, at least early on, that Walt and Jesse are stuck together." Egyptian illustrator Omar Samy paid homage to this episode in his digital painting *Breaking Bad Fanart*, which shows Jesse goofing off as Walt tinkers with a generator in an attempt to restart the RV. As artist Chris Sharples puts it, Walt and Jesse's partnership is one forged "from the best of a bad situation."

ABOVE and OPPOSITE: Armando Mesías | *The Cook* and *W.W.* | Oil, acrylics, spray paint, pencil, markers on paper and canvas | London, UK | 2014
www.armandomesias.com | armandomesias

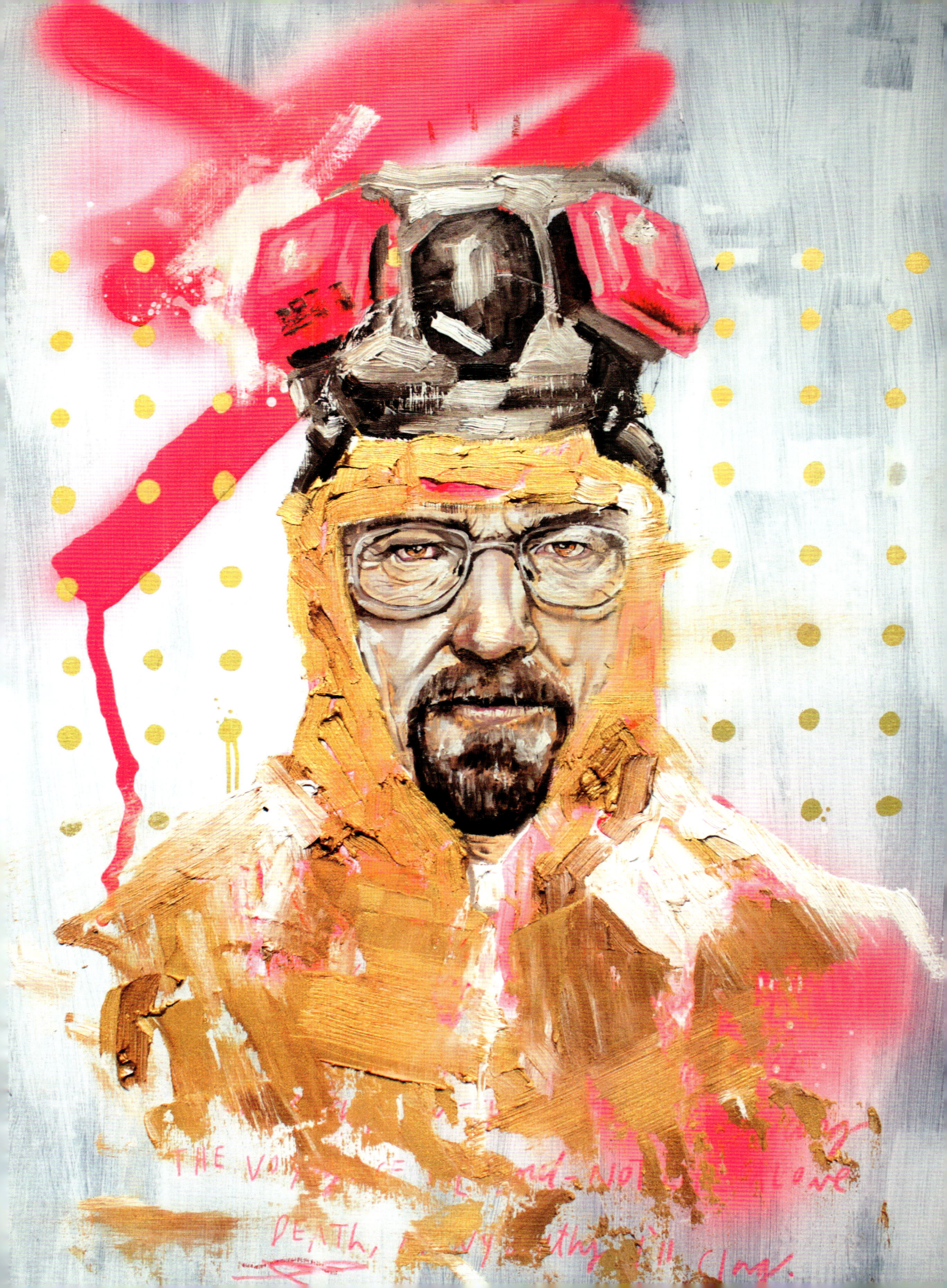

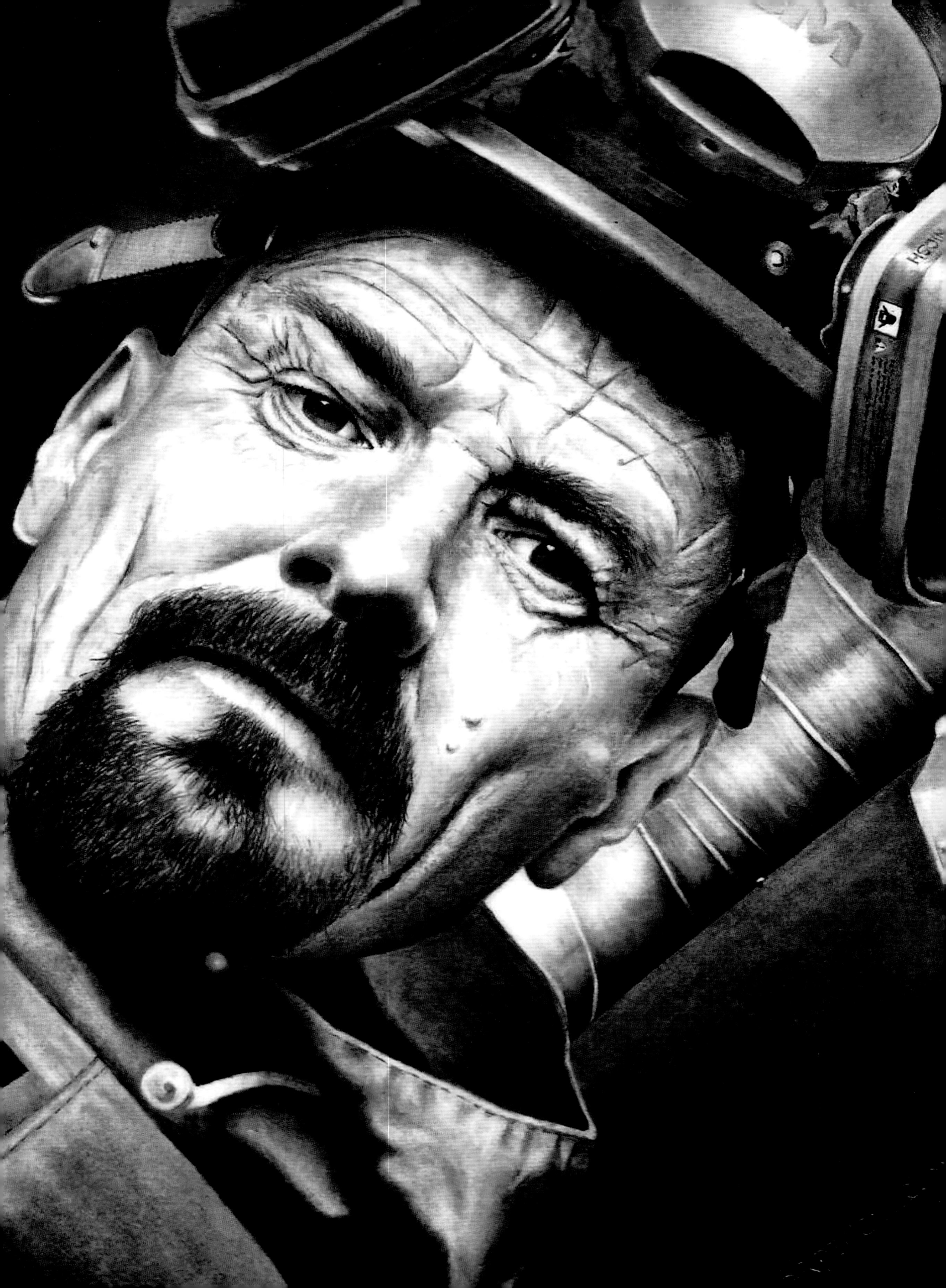

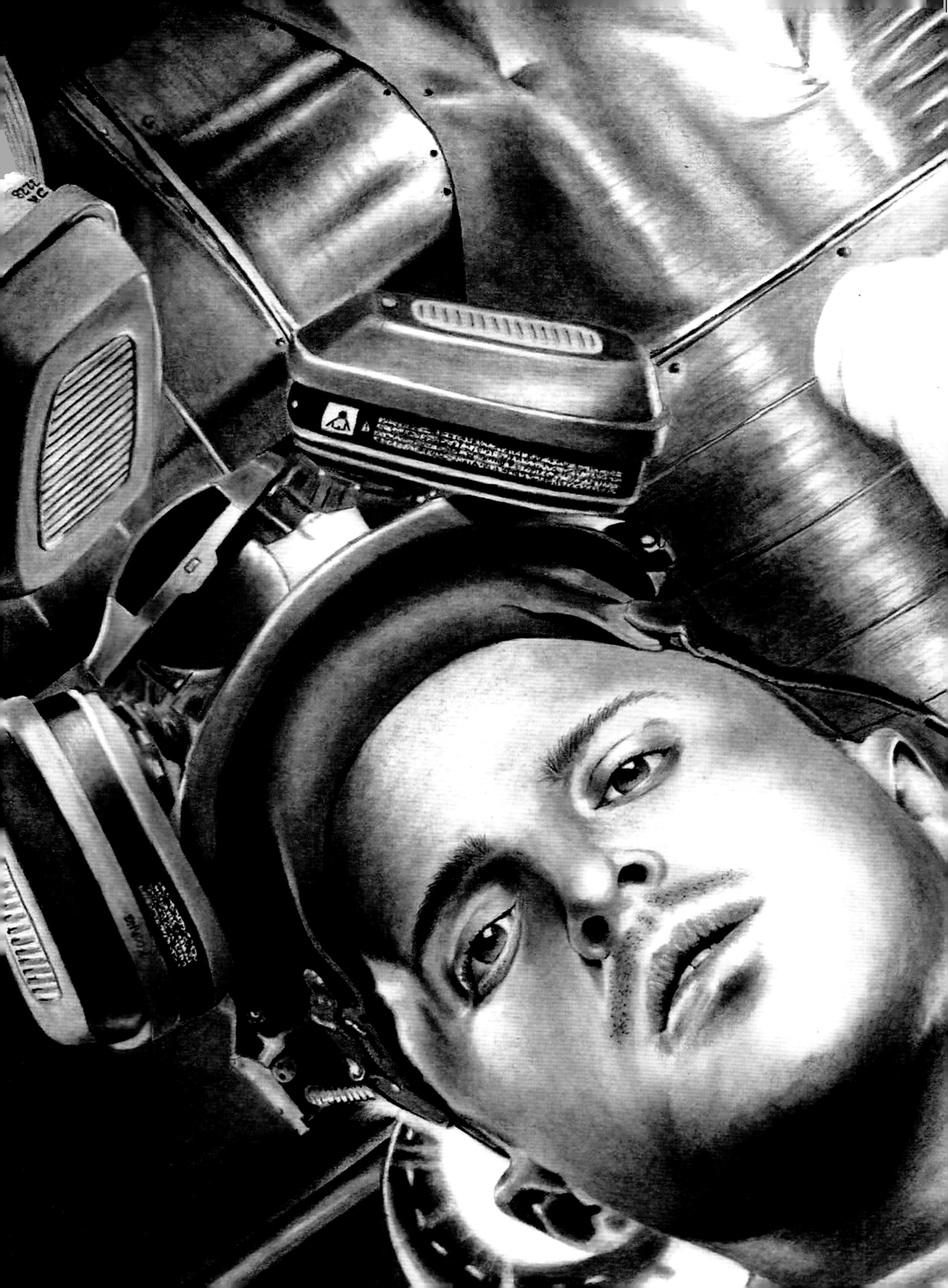

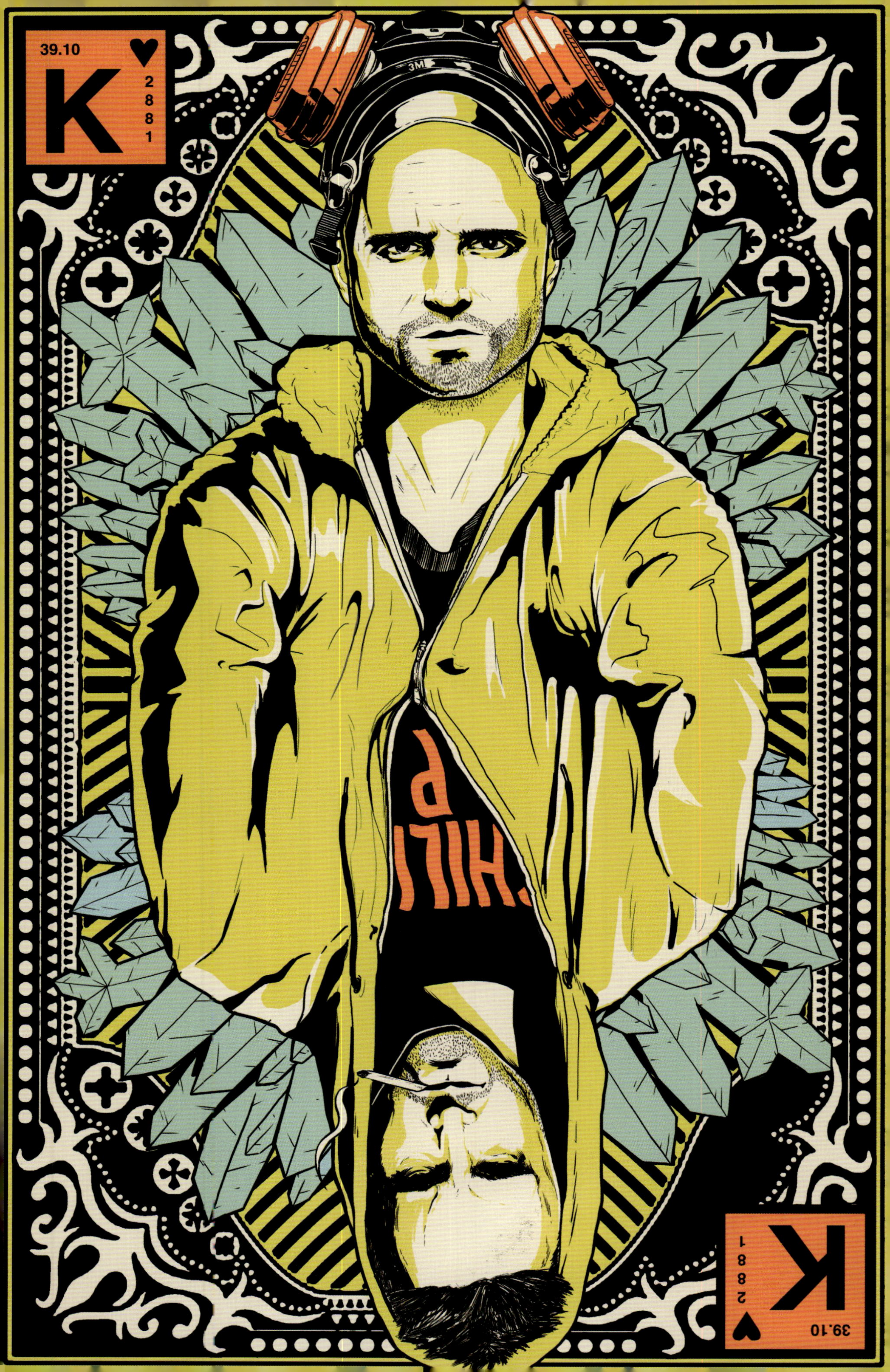
39.10
K
2
8
8
1
3M

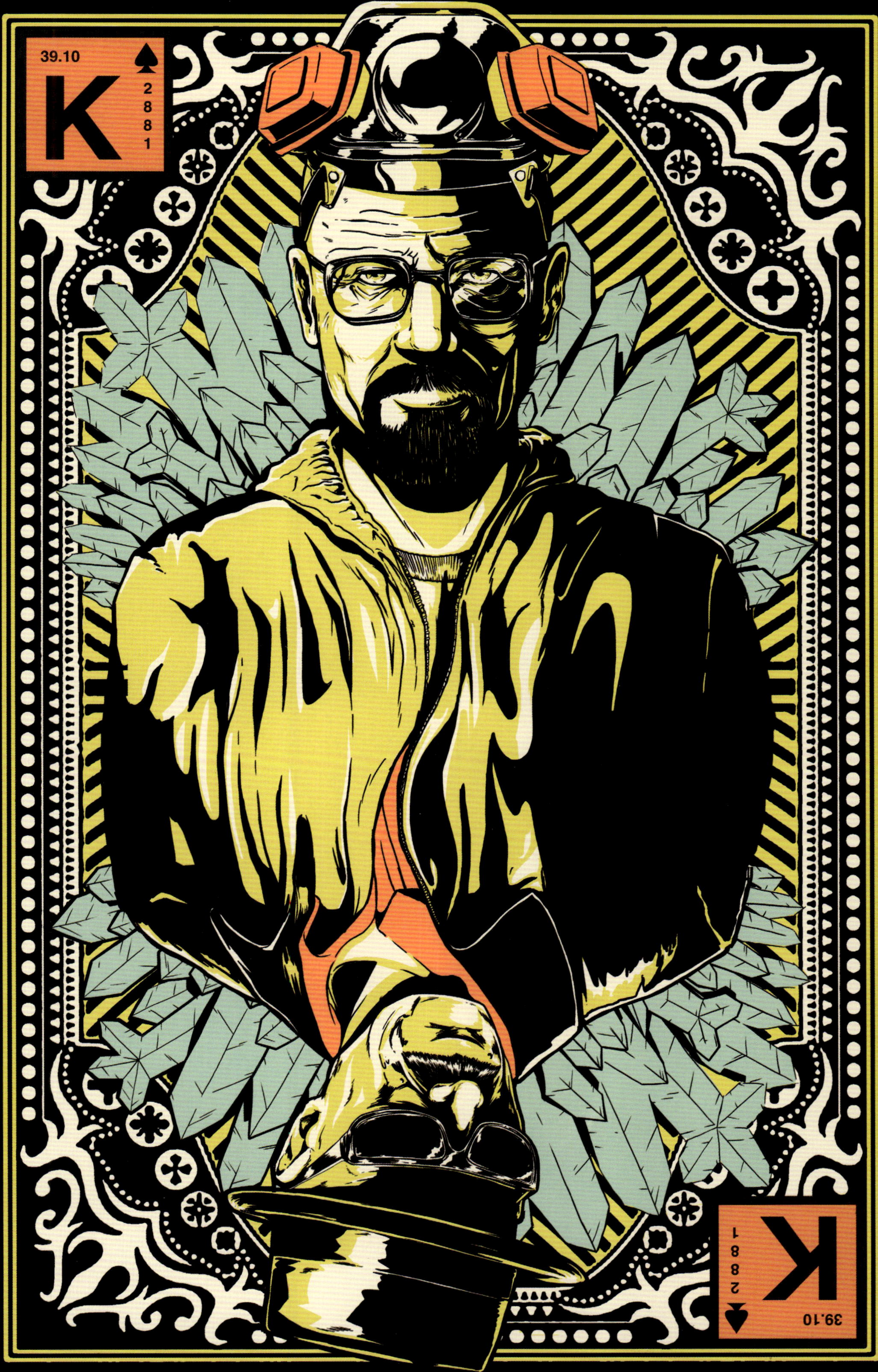
39.10
K
2
8
8
1
39.10
K
2
8
8
1

PAGES 44–45: Rick Fortson aka DrPencil | *Superlab* | Staedtler drawing pencils, Strathmore Bristol Smooth drawing stock | Chicago, Illinois, USA | 2010–2014 | www.DrPencil.com

PAGES 46–47: Jeff Ward | *King Jesse / King Walt* | Digital painting | Virginia Beach, Virginia, USA | 2014 | www.dxxdlines.com | dxxd_lines

OPPOSITE: Chris Ellinas | *Baby Blue* | Digital painting | Athens, Greece | 2017 | www.chrisellinas.com | chris_ellinas

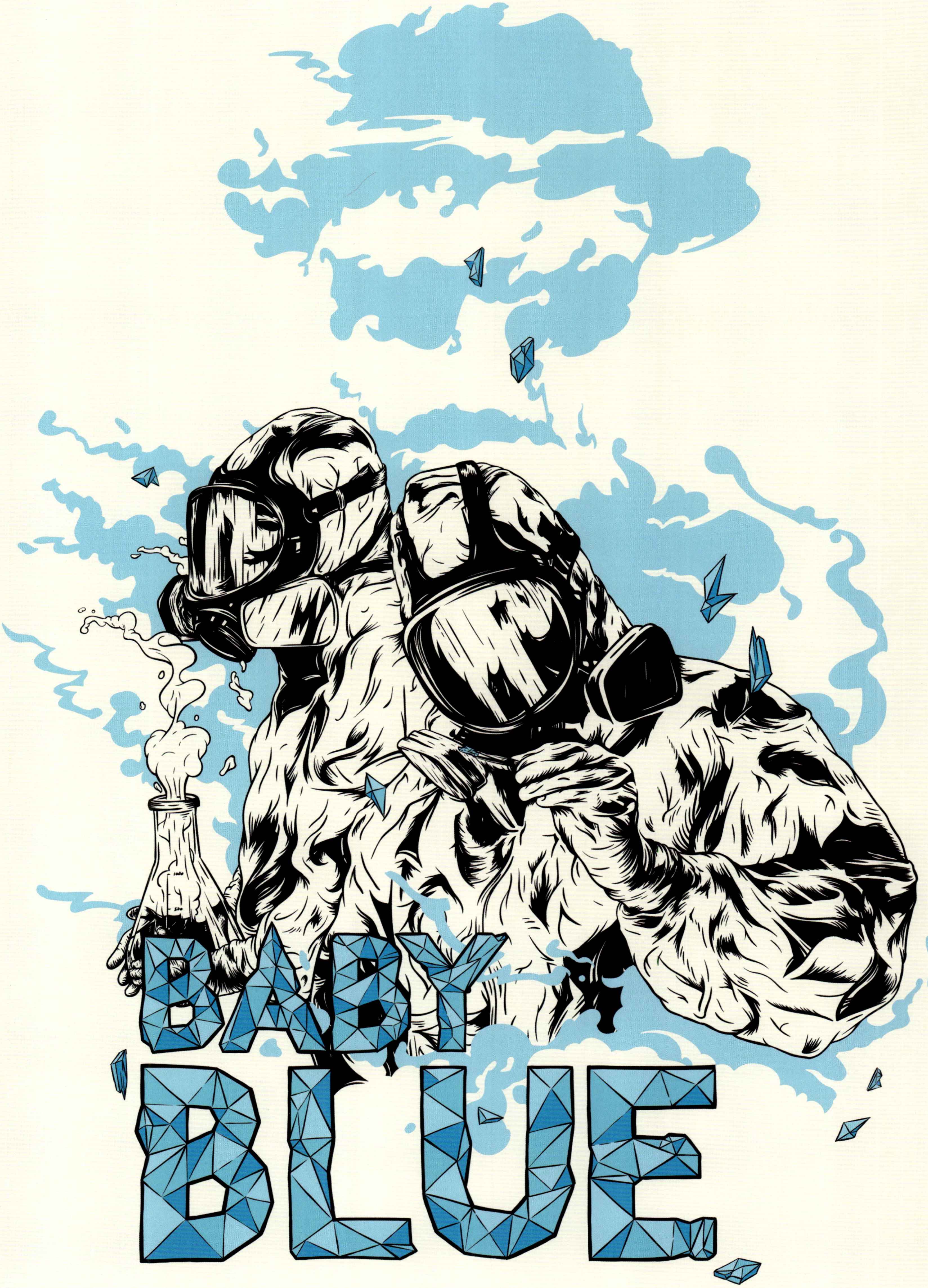
BABY
BLUE

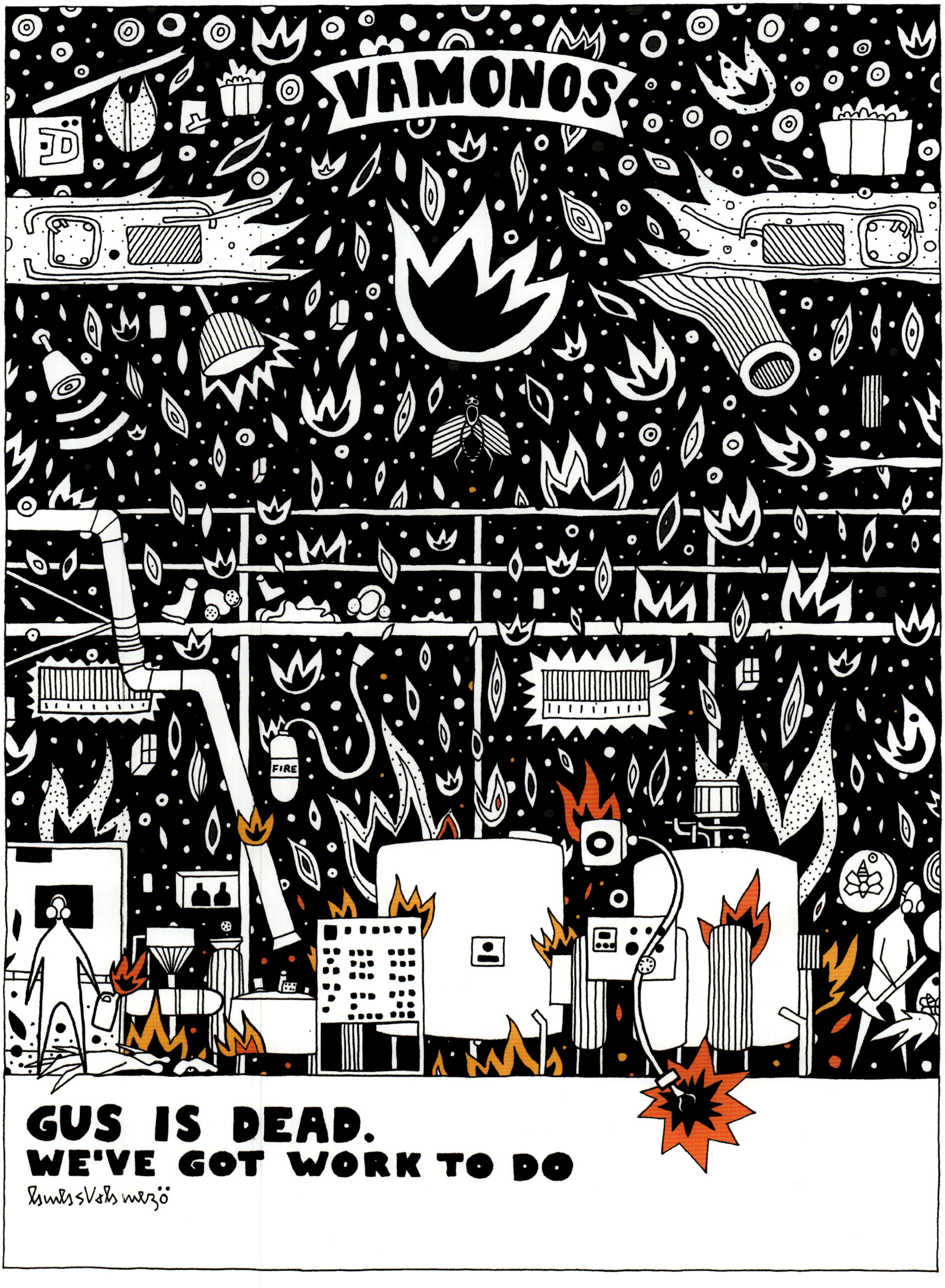
VÁMONOS
FIRE
GUS IS DEAD.
WE'VE GOT WORK TO DO

OPPOSITE: Carlos Valarezo | *The Destruction of the Superlab* | Ink and digital painting | Loja, Ecuador | 2019 | www.carlosvalarezoart.com

ABOVE: f.buffy | *Heisenberg and His Partner* | Digital painting | Ho Chi Minh City, Vietnam | 2018 | f.buffy

Chris Sharples | *Time to Cook* | Vector illustration | UK | 2015 | www.cksharples.com

Beth Evans | *We Have Good Chemistry* | Watercolors | Chicago, Illinois, USA | 2013 | bethdrawsthings

THESE PAGES: Sarath.V (patient zero art) | *Jesse Pinkman* | Digital painting | India | 2019 | patient_zero.art

PAGE 56: Carlos E. Valverde Yovera | *Heisenberg Typographic* | Digital art | Piura, Peru | 2017 | v4lverde_c
PAGE 57: Alan Maia | *I'm the Danger* | Digital illustration | Brazil | 2014 | alan.maia.prints

CIERRA LA BOCA 20936 DÉJAME 20936 MORIR EN PAZ
SI TU NO SABES QUIEN SOY
ENTONCES TALVEZ SERÍA MEJOR QUE ANDES CON CUIDADO
HOMBRE DEL CANCER SKYLER MARIE
YO SOY EL PELIGRO
PROFESOR CRISTALES
PINKMAN IMPERIO
WALTER
WHITE
HEISENBERG
METANFETAMINA
DESLIZANDOSE
CARGA MORTAL
CINCUENTA Y UNO
BRYAN CRANSTON
ESTO ES TODO
HE TERMINADO
NUEVO MEXICO
FELINA
QUE PROTEGE
QUE EL MIEDO
A COCINAR CRISTAL
SABEN EXACTAMENTE

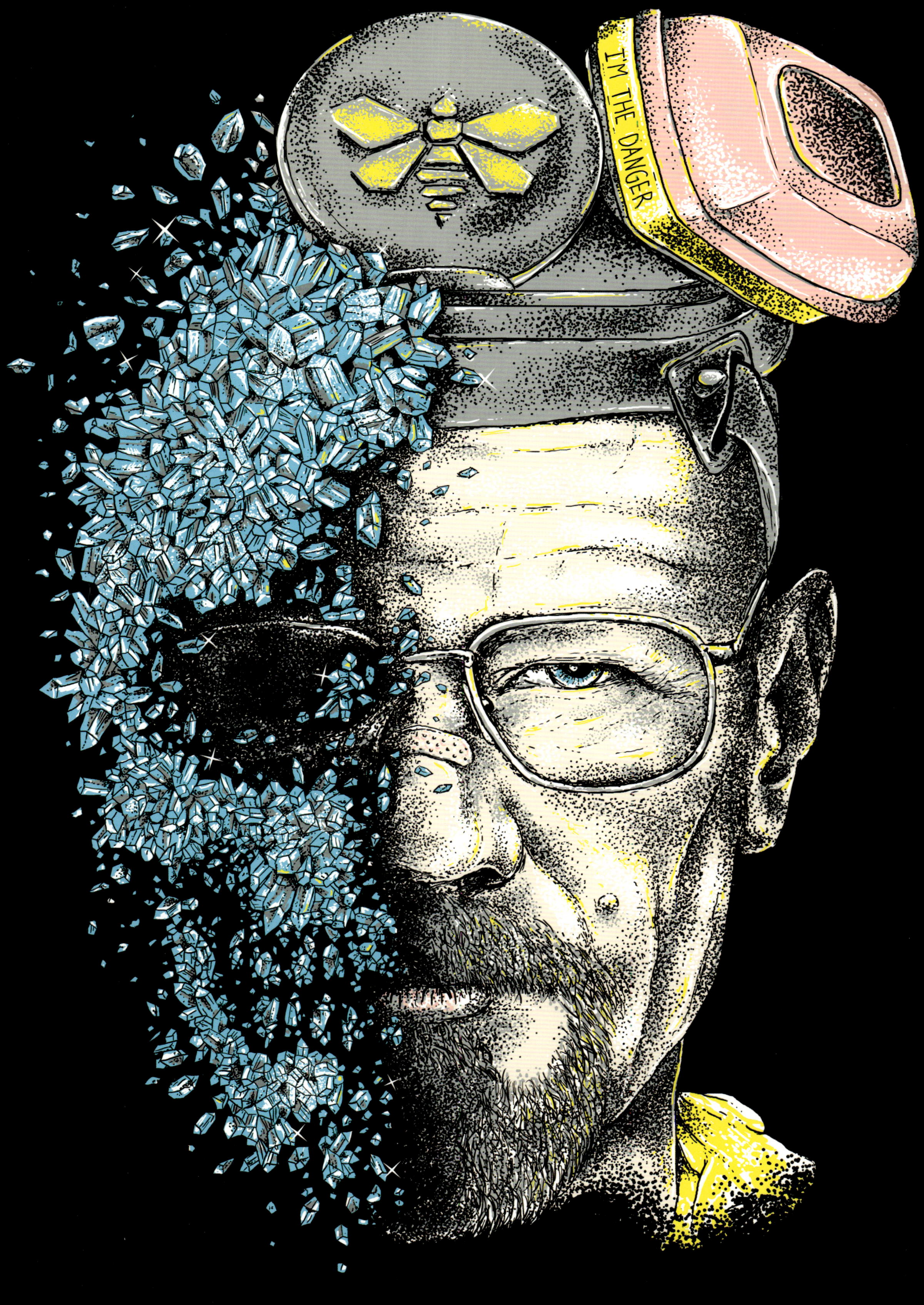
I'M THE DANGER

ABOVE: Jake Giddens | *In the Kitchen* | Digital painting | Sarasota, Florida, USA | 2013 | www.jakegiddens.com

OPPOSITE: Ceci N'Est Pas Francesca | *Breaking Bad – The Son of Heisenberg* | Crayons and echoline on Fabriano paper | Rome, Italy | 2019 | ceci_nest_pas_francesca

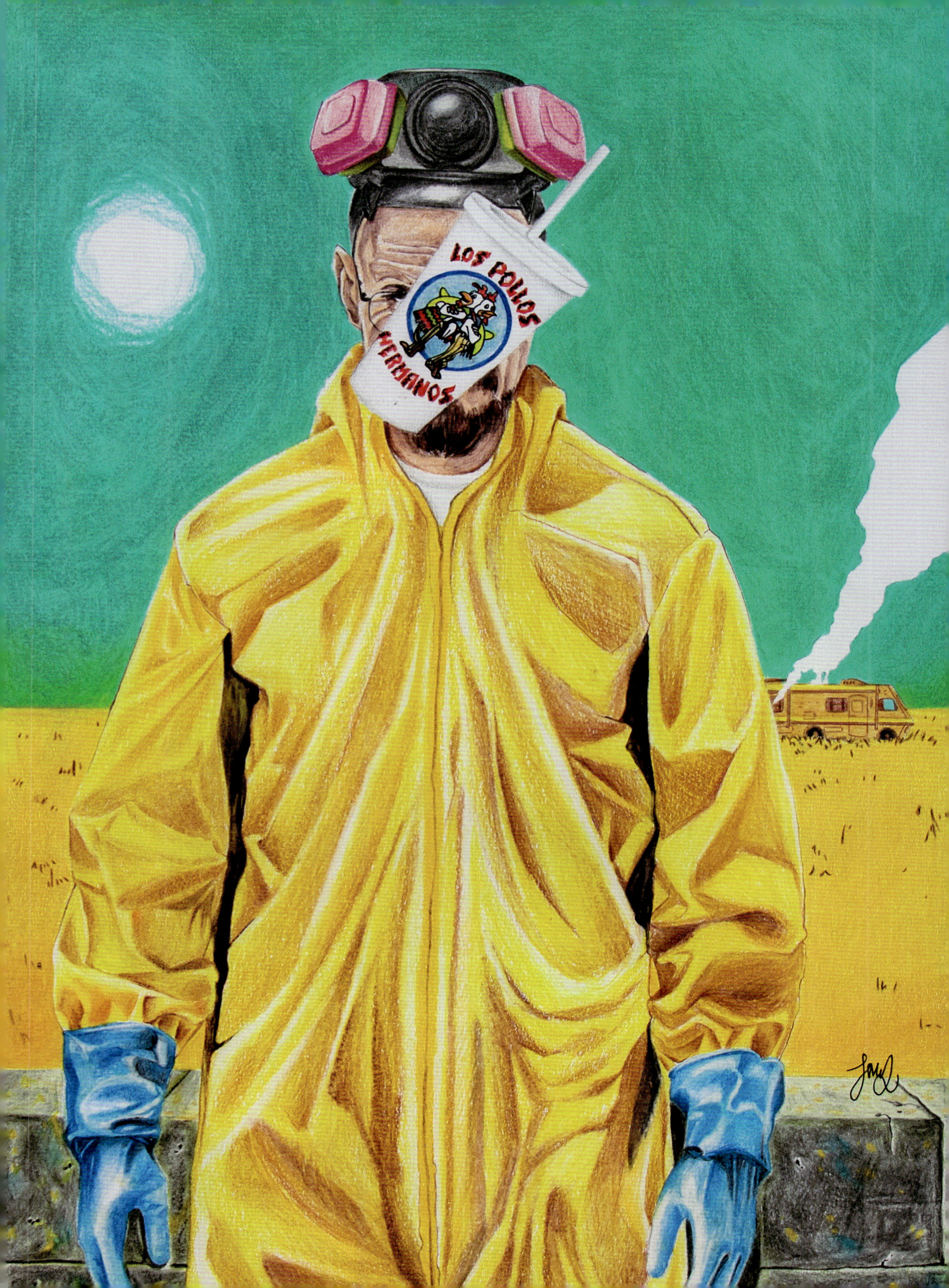
LOS POLLOS
HERMANOS

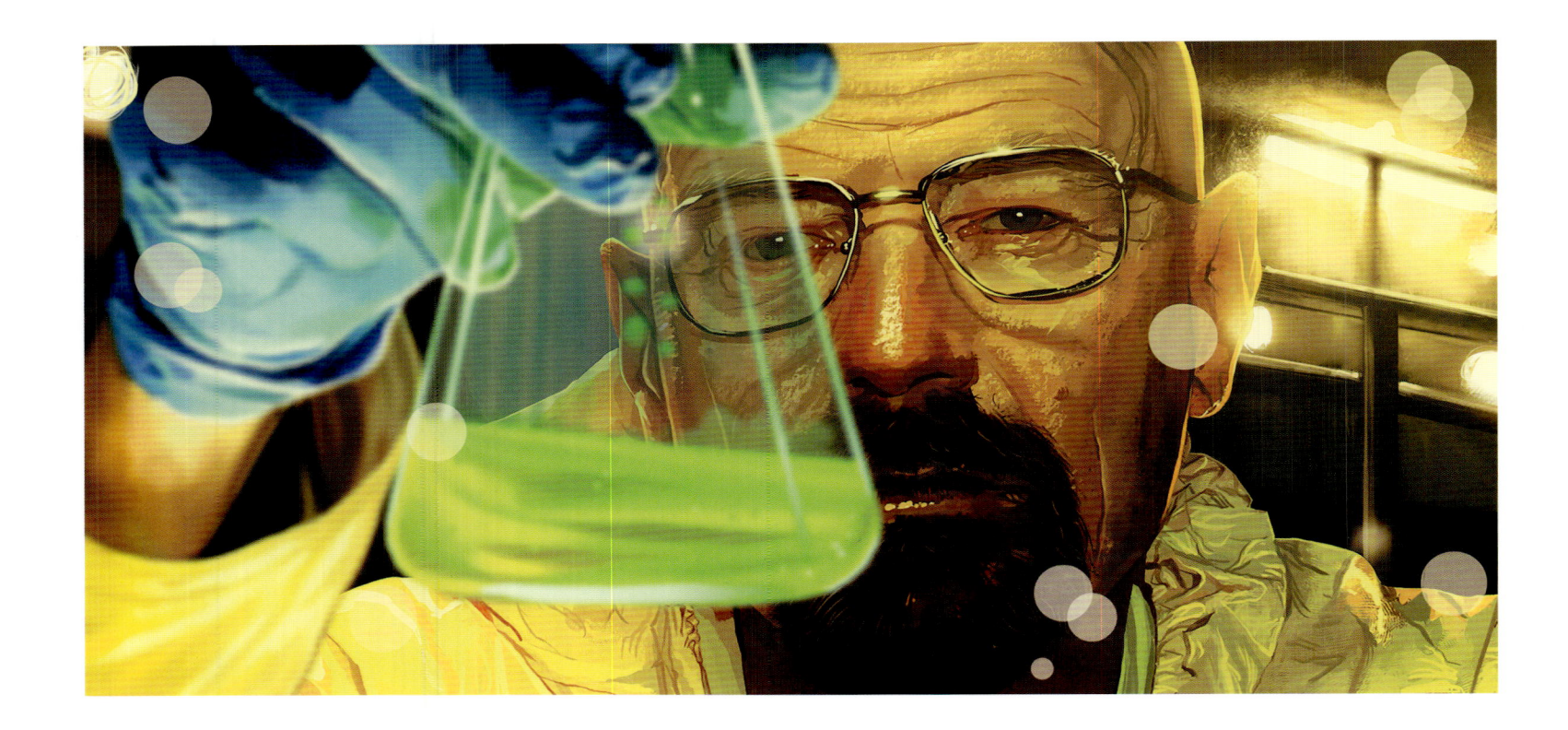

ABOVE: Miriam Migliazzi and Mart Klein | Digital painting | Berlin, Germany | 2013 | www.dainz.net
OPPOSITE: David Redon aka Ads Libitum | *Pulp Breaking Bad* | Photomontage | Paris, France | 2016 | adslibitum

BREAKING BAD

15¢ MARCH

PULP BOOK

by Vince Gilligan

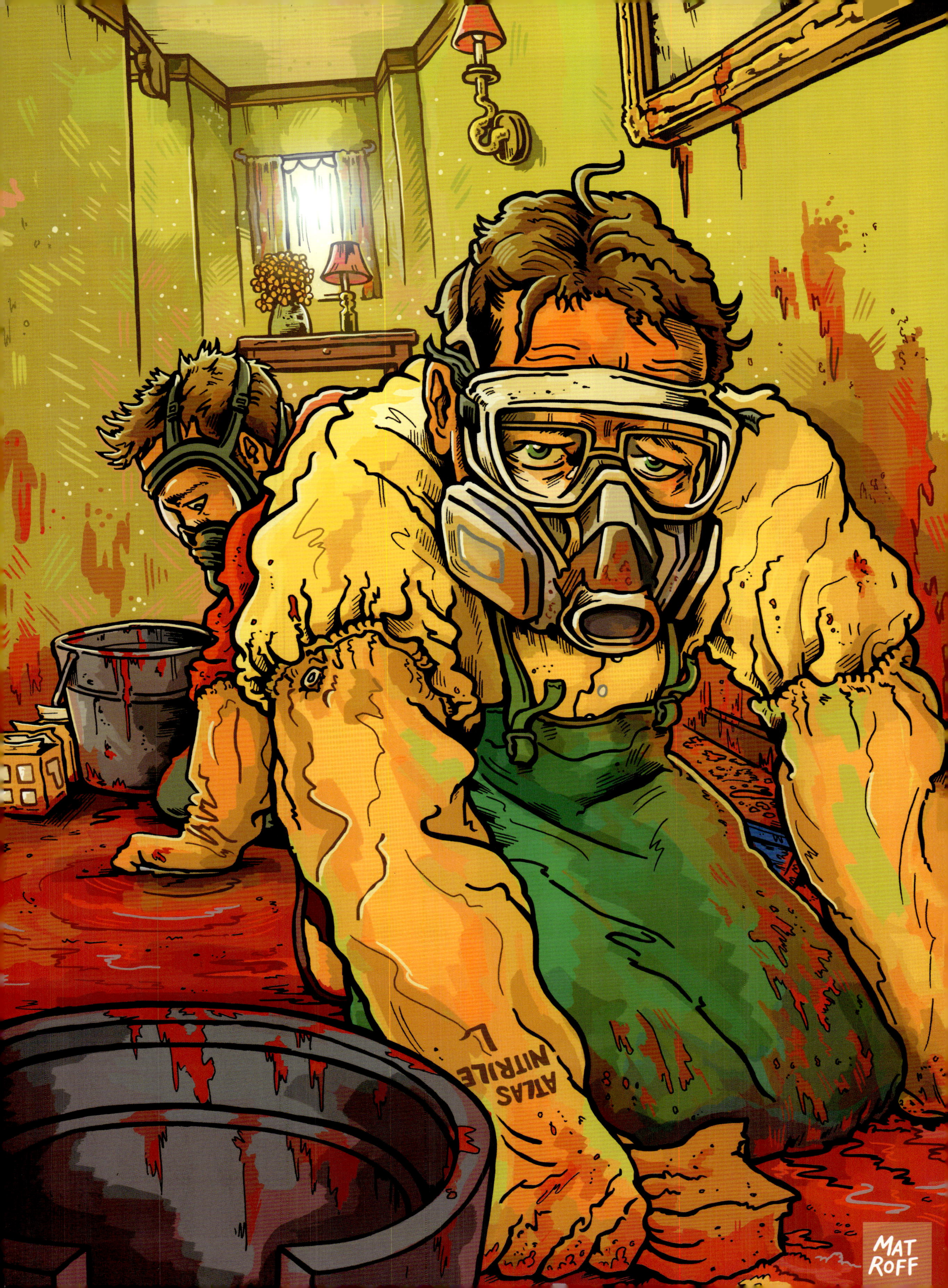
ATLAS NITRILE
L
MAT ROFF

OPPOSITE: Mat Roff | *Acid Will Do the Job* | Pencil and digital painting | UK | 2015 | www.matroff.co.uk | ⓘ matroff

ABOVE: Petter Schölander | *Study of Change* | Vector graphics | Sweden | 2015 | www.petterscholander.com

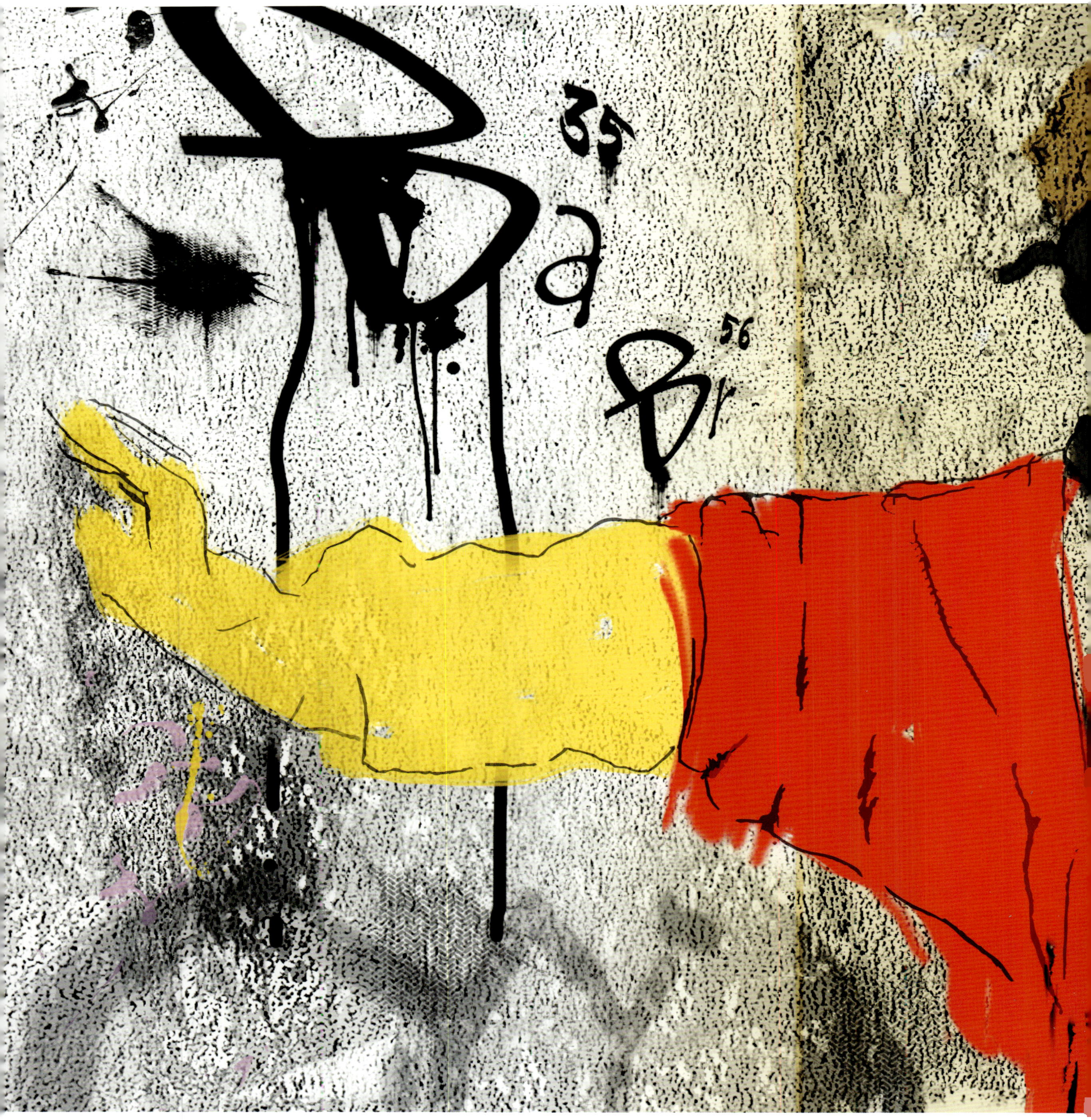

THESE PAGES: Scott Ortner | *Jesse* | Digital painting | Los Angeles, California, USA | 2008 | www.sccttortner.com

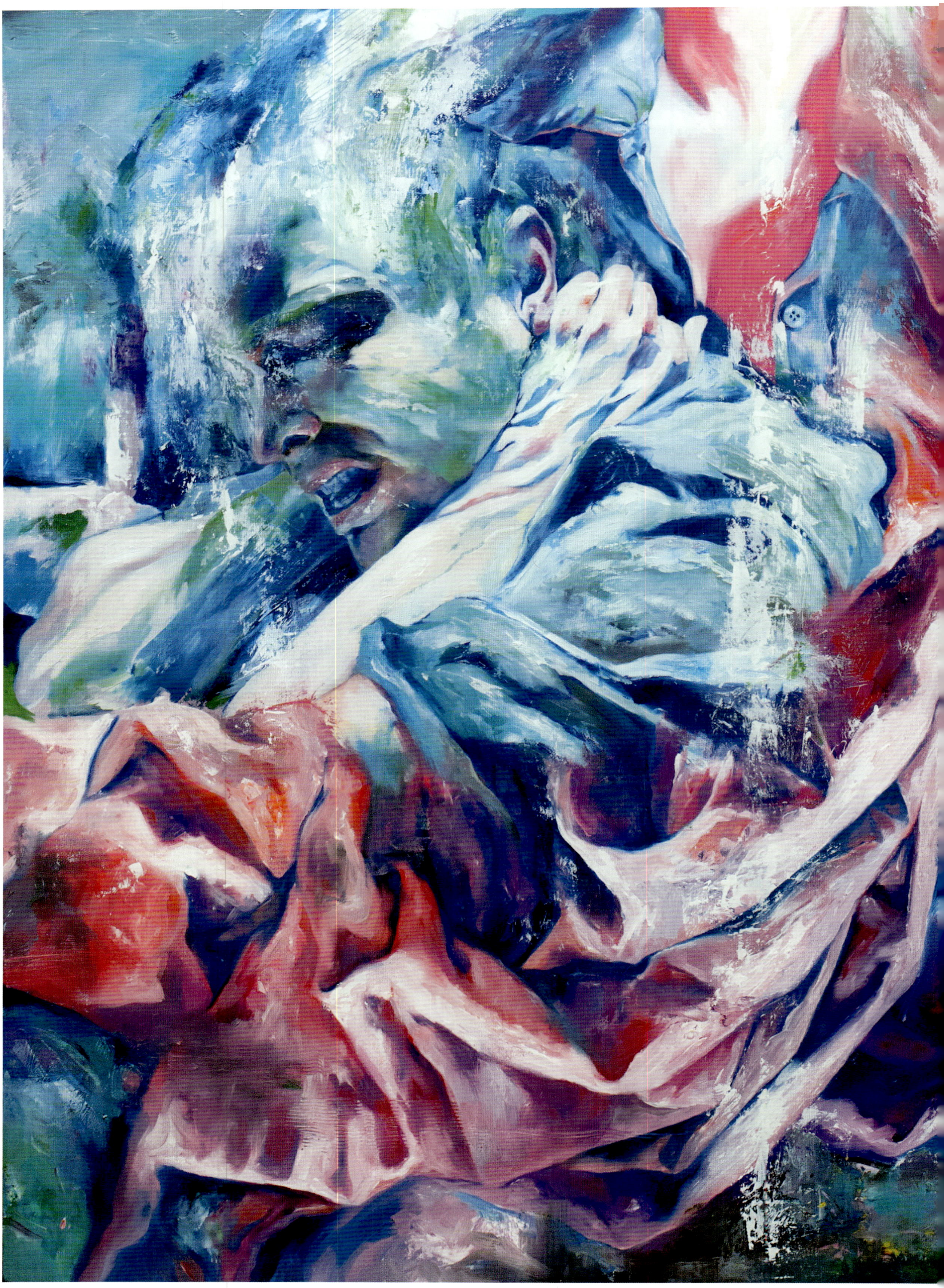

OPPOSITE: Isobel Francisco | *Cocoon (Detail)* | Oil on canvas | Philippines | 2015 | www.stainedpaper.me

THESE PAGES: Yang Kwang Tatt | *My Baby Blue Series: Jesse* | Digital painting (Photoshop) | Kuala Lumpur, Malaysia | 2020 | stevenyangkt

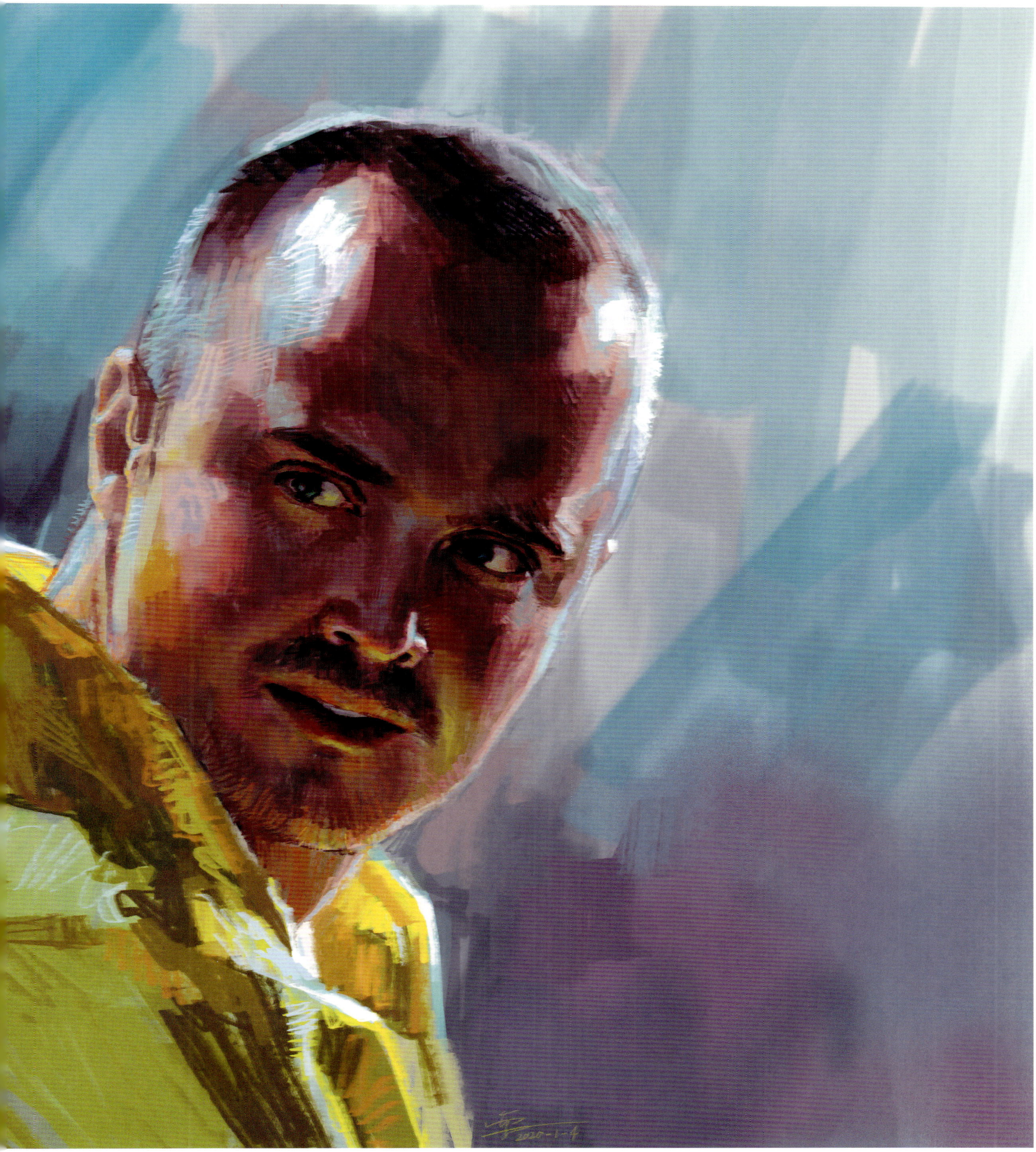
2020-1-4

No Half Measures
CAP*N BLOWFISH
FEAT.
CAP*N COOK
2015

Jesse

Cap'n Blowfish

OPPOSITE TOP: Nancy Vanadia | *No Half Measures* | Ink and graphite pencil | 2015
OPPOSITE BOTTOM LEFT: Nancy Vanadia | *Jesse at Work* | Ballpoint pen | 2014
OPPOSITE BOTTOM RIGHT: Nancy Vanadia | *Cap'n Blowfish* | Colored pencil, spray paint, and graphite pencil | 20˜3
ABOVE: Nancy Vanadia | *JPi* | Acrylic point pen, felt pen, fineliner pen, and graphite pencil | Marseille, France | 2020 | capn.nanz

Br 35
Ba 56

OPPOSITE: Crow Lee Segawa | *Face Off* | Digital painting | Brisbane, Australia | 2014 | 🐦 crowlees

ABOVE: Cait Chock | *Yeah, Science!* | Pen and paint | Los Angeles, California, USA | 2019 | www.caitchock.com | 📷 caitchock | 📷 imadisastercartoon

74

OPPOSITE and ABOVE: Nora Adame | *Jesse* and *Heisenberg* | Repurposed clothing tags over Foamular | Cholula, Puebla, Mexico | 2014 | www.noraadame.com | noraadame

I MET A TRAVELLER FROM AN ANTIQUE LAND...

OPPOSITE: Reducto1 | *Ozymandias* | Digital painting | Hong Kong | 2014 | ⓘ reducto1

ABOVE: Stuart Herrington | *Breaking Bad* | Digital illustration | Sheffield, UK | 2019 | www.sjhillustration.co.uk | ⓘ sjhillustration

THESE PAGES: Plastic Cell | *Breaking Bad Sculptures* | Hand-painted sculptures | Orange County, California, USA | 2012 | www.plasticcell.com | 🅞 Plasticcell

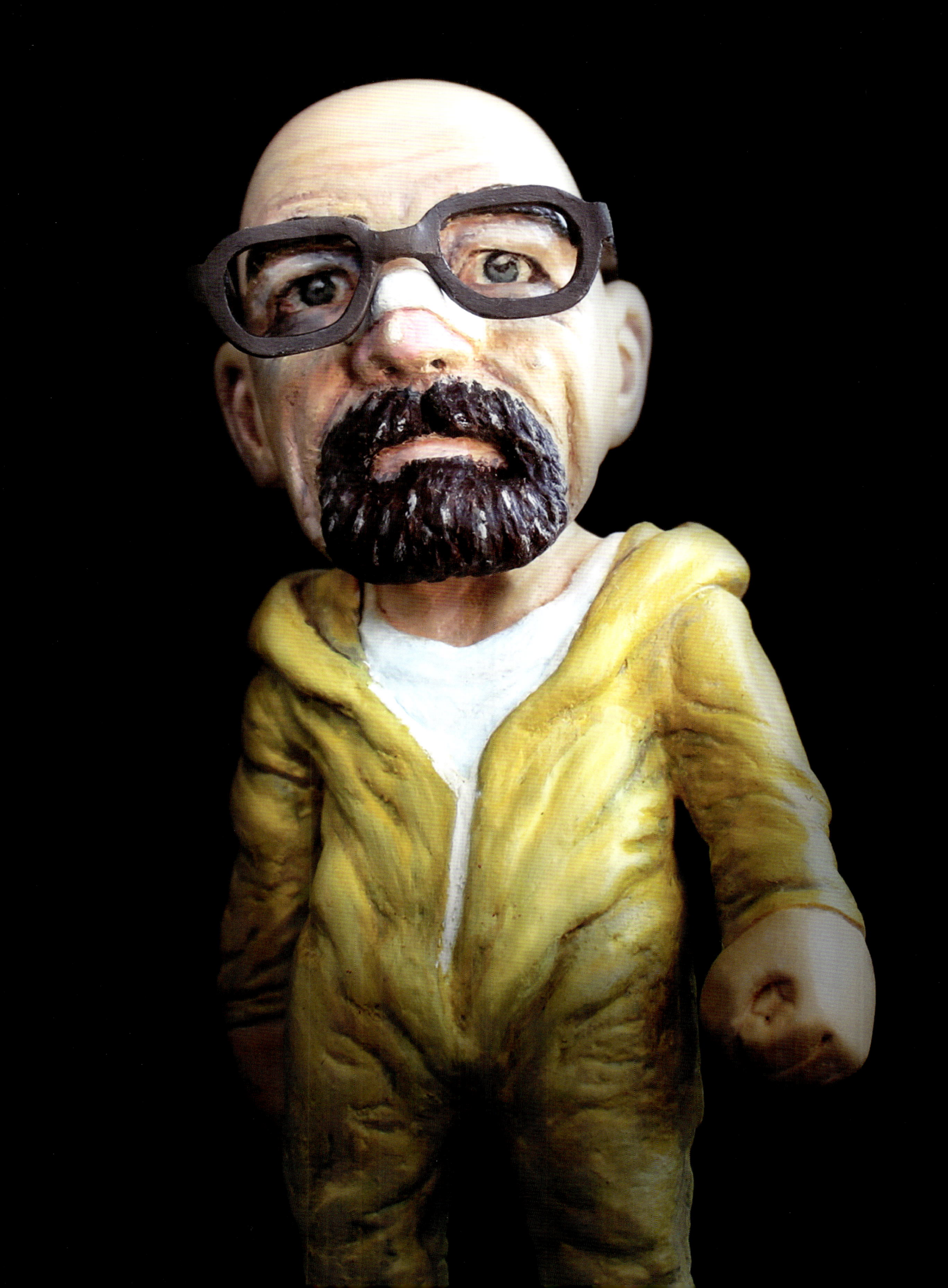

ABOVE: Nico Di Mattia | *Rusty Walt & Jesse* | Watercolor | 2017
OPPOSITE: Nico Di Mattia | *Rusty Heisenberg* | Digital | Córdoba, Argentina | 2019 | 📷 🐦 nicodimattia

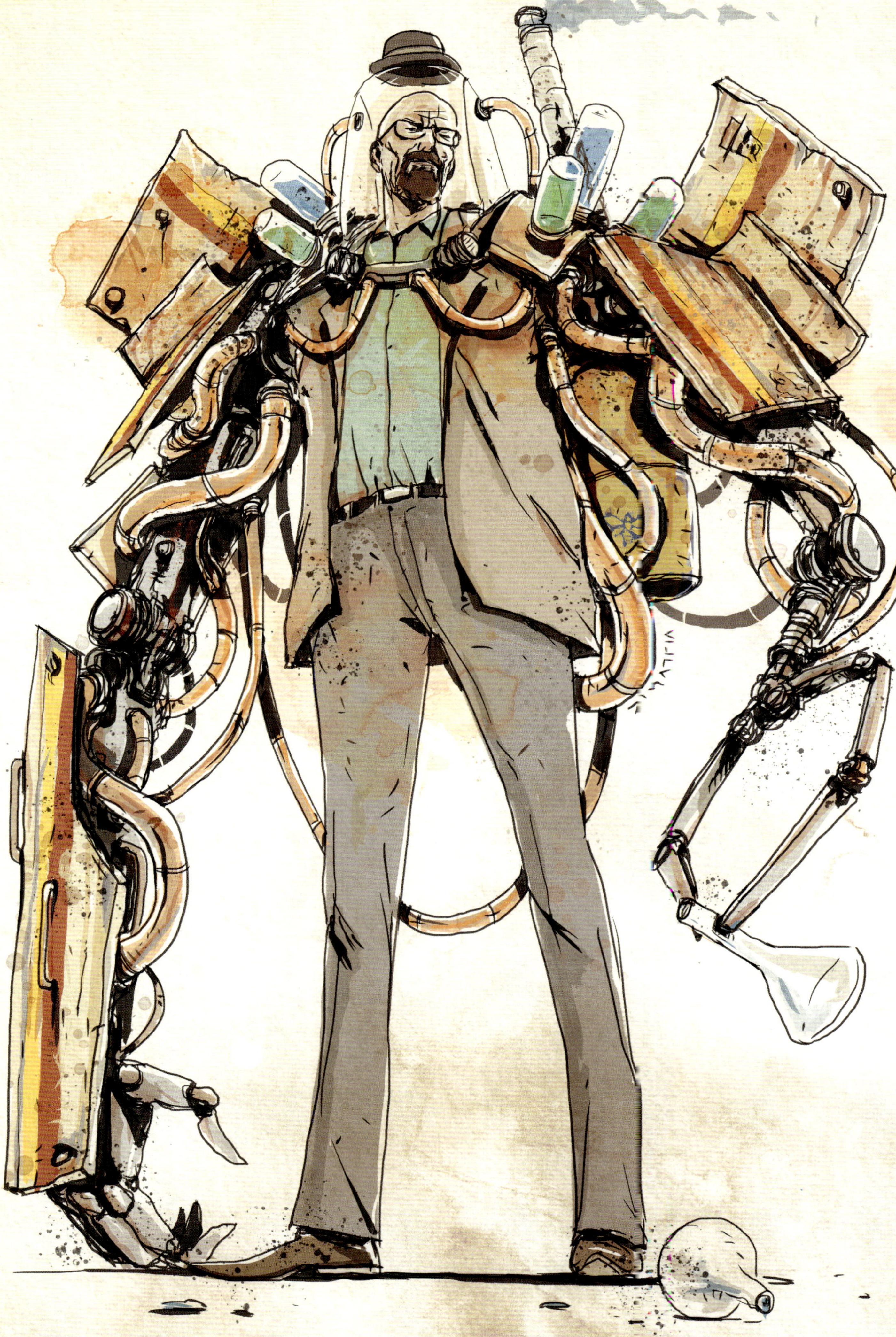

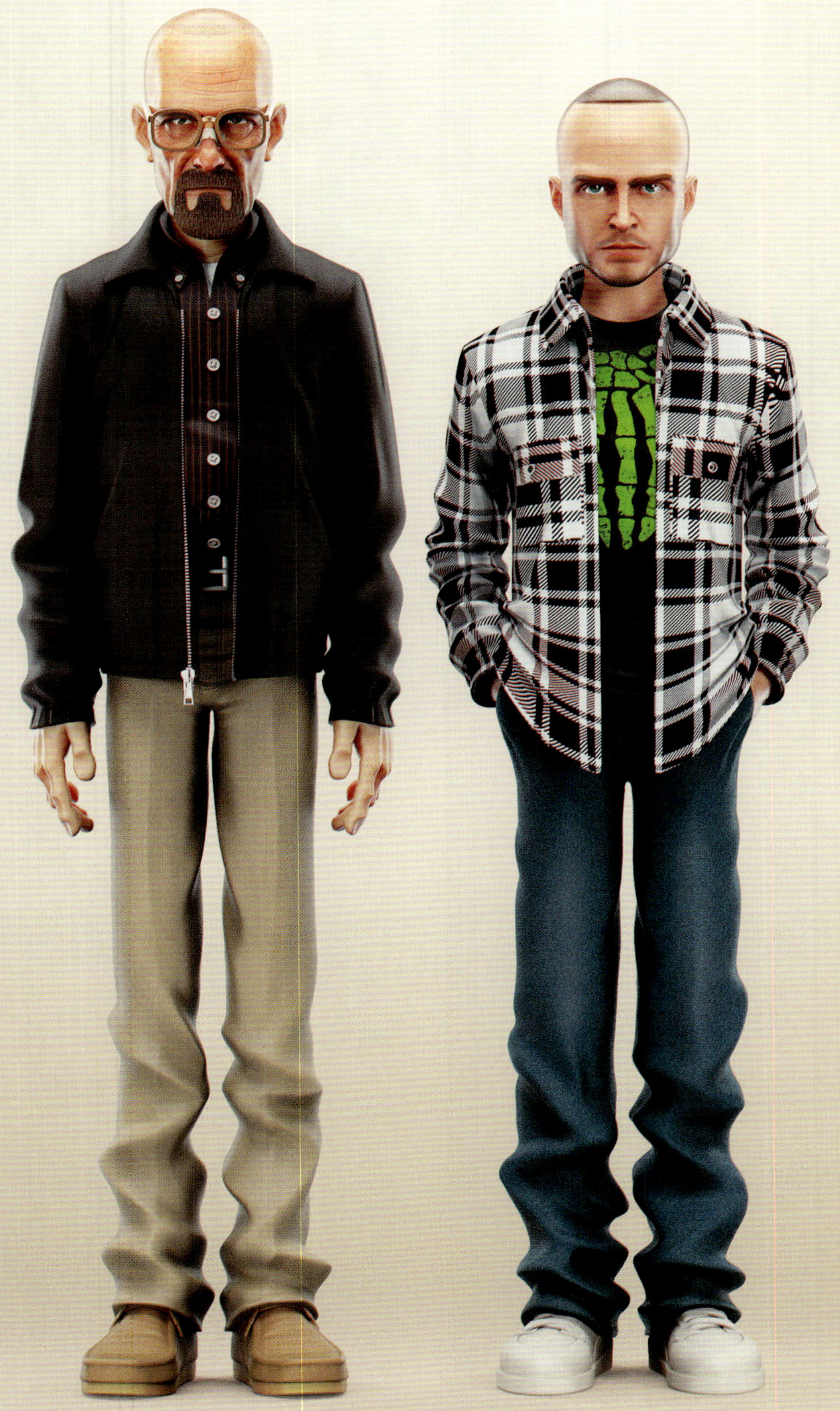

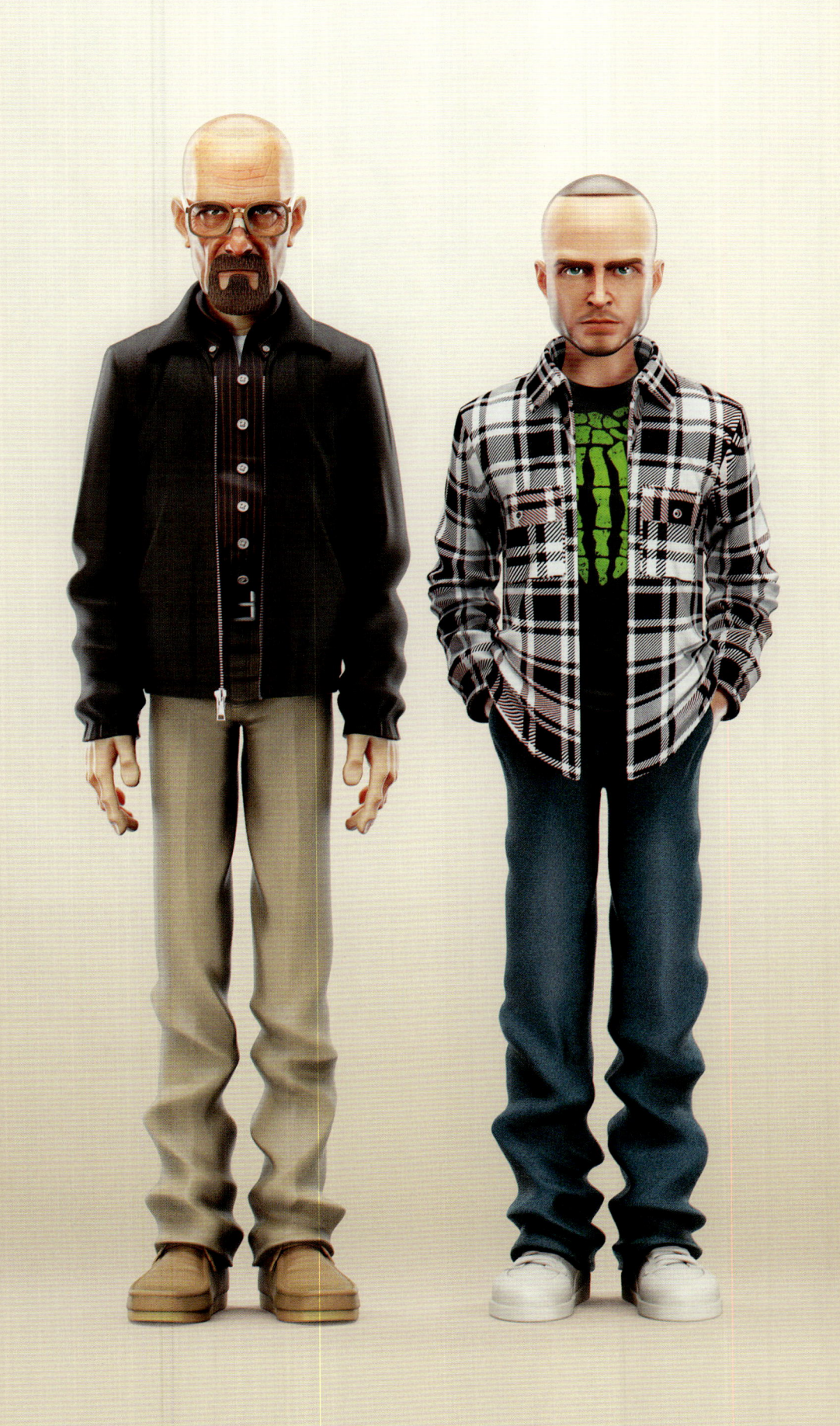

OPPOSITE: Iancarlo "Conqui" Reyes | *Breaking Bad Toys* | 3D digital sculpts | Carolina, Puerto Rico, USA | 2019 | www.iancarlosreyes.carbonmade.com

ABOVE: Glucka Pixels | *BB Voxels* | 3D computer graphic | Ramat Gan, Israel | 2018 | glucka_pixels

THESE PAGES: Alberto Reyes Francos | *Breaking Bad Portraits* | Digital painting | Terrassa, Spain | 2017 | www.albertoreyesfrancos.com

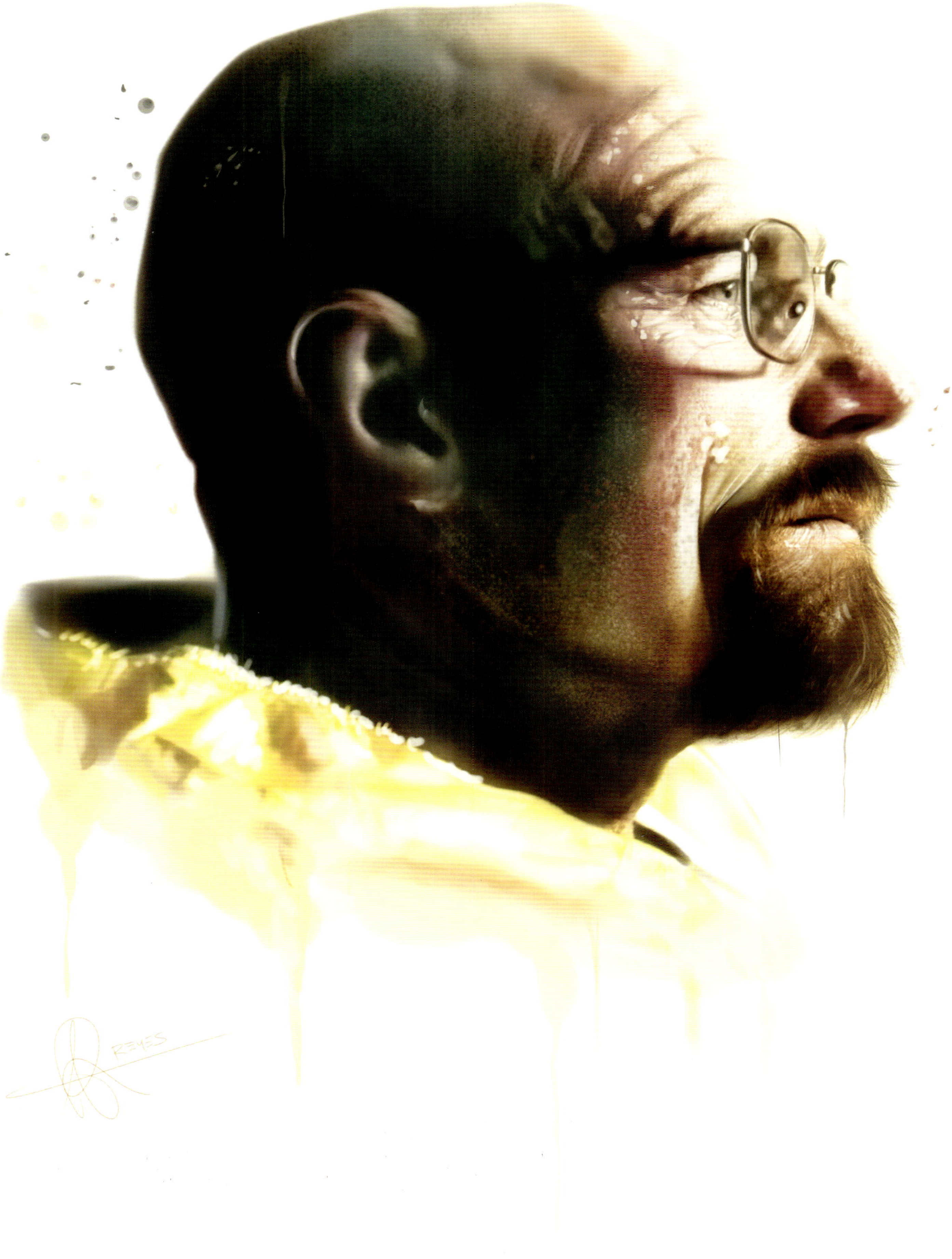

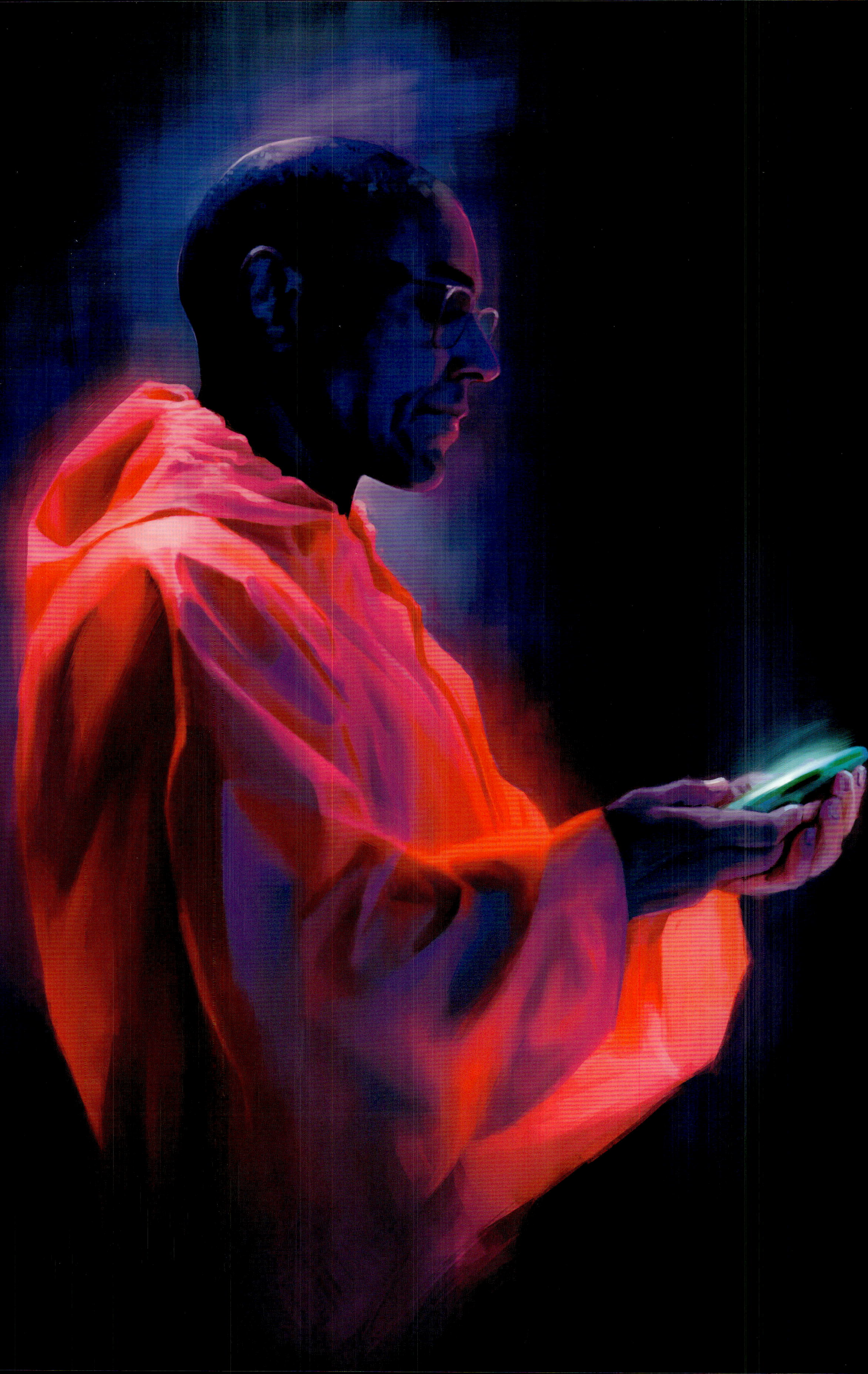

THESE PAGES (Clockwise from opposite page): Xenia Shatova | *Talion Law, Dirty Blue, Smoke and Embers, The Prodigal Daughter, Smolder*
Digital painting | Yekaterinburg, Russia | 2014–2015 | shatova_k

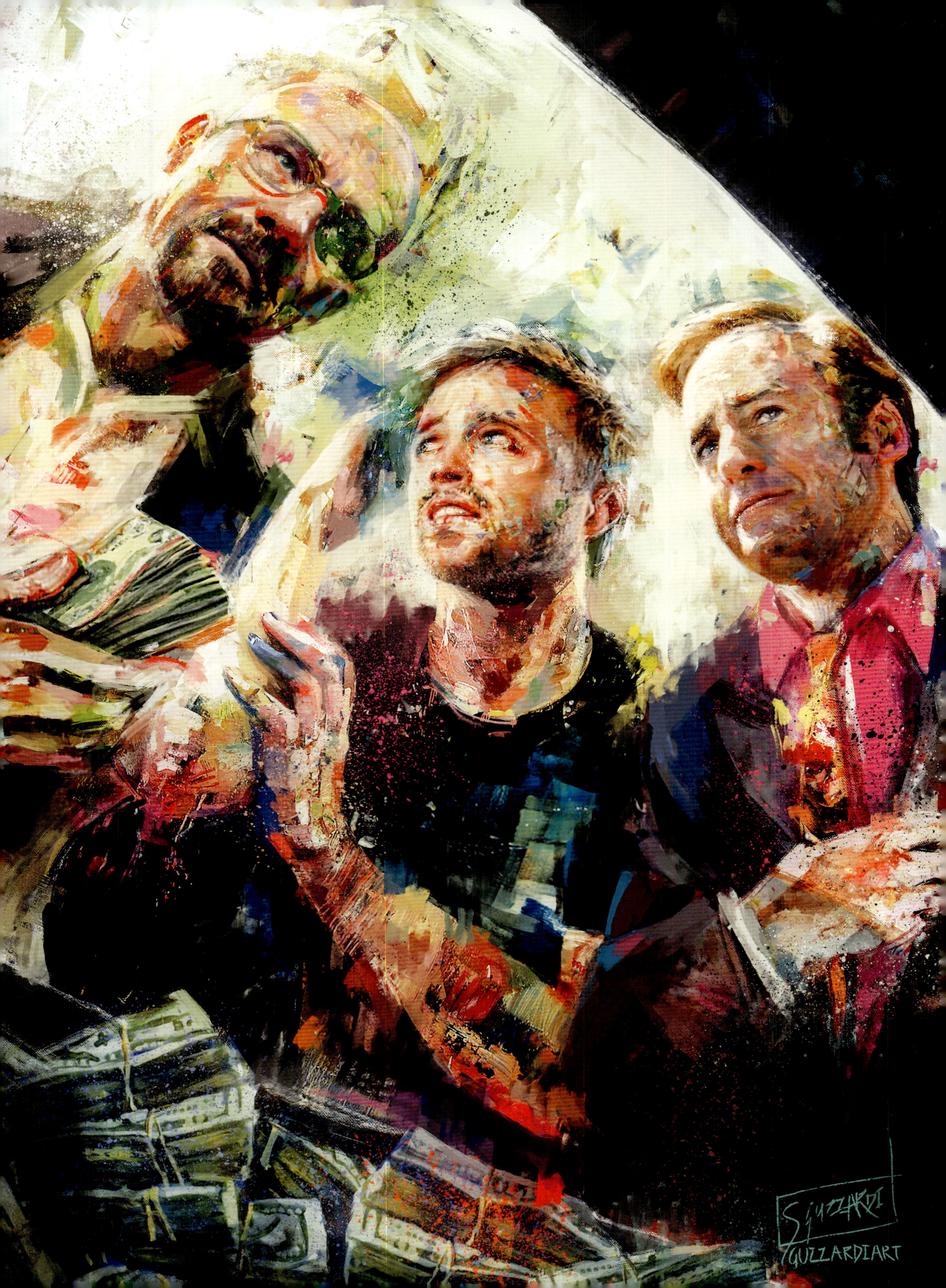
GUZZARDIART

chapter 3

The emPire Business

Heisenberg didn't settle for half measures. When offered a chance to leave the meth business altogether for five million dollars, his answer was firm: Why sell out in the low millions when he could rule an empire worth billions? Walter White's egotistical pursuit of power, aided by a colorful cast of associates led by smooth-talking attorney Saul Goodman, not only took the lives of innocent victims but also cost him the thing he loved most.

FOR THE FAMILY

Walt began cooking meth in order to make enough money—$737,000 to be exact—to ensure that his wife and children would be taken care of after his passing. As the stakes grew higher, however, the intoxicating thrill of being Heisenberg began to obscure the best interests of his family. Argentine artist Pablo Guaymas identifies the murder of Walt's brother-in-law Hank Schrader at the hands of Walt's criminal associates as Walt's "point of no return, when he ultimately destroys everyone around him." Guaymasi's *We Are Family!* reimagines this moment from the Season 5 episode "Ozymandias" as a comic book cover, with an unyielding Hank in the foreground, moments before his execution. Behind him stand Walt's wife, Skyler, and son, Walter Jr., looking on in horror. To Guaymasi, "this is the real defining moment when Walt loses his family and we as viewers lost all hope in him."

While Hank remains oblivious until shortly before his death that his elusive white whale is right under his nose, Skyler must shoulder the burden of keeping Walt's double life secret from not just Hank, but from her teenage son and her increasingly concerned sister, Marie. In her piece entitled *Shut Up*, Canada-based Nikki White captures Skyler's meltdown in the Season 5 episode "Hazard Pay," in which Skyler repeatedly screams "Shut up!" as Marie confronts her about her smoking habit. White reflects: "It was a culmination, or boiling point, if you will, of someone finally breaking down."

OPPOSITE: Shenae Guzzardi | *Cash in the Trunk* | Digital painting | Australia | 2015 | www.guzzardiart.com | GuzzardiArt

Marie's fierce loyalty to her sister is perhaps rivaled only by her penchant for the color purple. Vanessa Harmel, a digital artist based in Frankfurt, Germany, used Copic markers to create a portrait of Marie against a vivid purple backdrop. She conceptualizes Marie as "actively staying in between" the two poles of "calm and righteousness" and "risk and crime," attributing the color blue to the former and red to the latter, which together form Marie's signature color, purple. Costume designer Jennifer Bryan, who joined the show in its fifth season, took pleasure in focusing on "the variances of the color purple from the palest of lilacs to the blackest of aubergines."

Marie, for all her quirks, was a far less polarizing character to the audience than Skyler. "I want to believe that the fans who hated Skyler were a small minority. The hatred that was aimed at her was sobering and a little strange—clearly the character hit a tender spot for some fans," says *Breaking Bad* writer Peter Gould. The backlash divided viewers into two camps: those who understood Skyler to be protecting her family as best she could, and those who saw her as an antagonist standing in Walt's way, trying to keep him from the very family he was working so hard to support. Los Angeles–based Pana Stamos falls into the former category: "I think you're bound to see a glimpse of your mother or even yourself when you look at Skyler. She wasn't perfect, but she did what she could." Her digital painting *Protect This Family* features a knife-wielding Skyler ferociously defending her children against Walt after realizing that he was complicit in Hank's murder.

Walter Jr.'s resentment toward his mother for ostracizing his father only worsened Skyler's paper-thin emotional state. Walter Jr., as played by RJ Mitte, is "the son through whom we see . . . the gentle, innocent, and decent side of Walter White," Costa Rican illustrator Daniesca observes. Her piece *Breakfast King* portrays Walter Jr. in his familiar spot at the breakfast table. Mitte graciously accepts his anointment as breakfast king: "Breakfast is the most important meal of the day, so it's a title I wear with pride."

SAUL GOODMAN & ASSOCIATES

The deterioration of Walt's personal life did not stop him from his relentless pursuit of money and power. Without Saul Goodman's expertise in all things illegal, Walt could not have navigated his way from small-time meth cook to feared drug lord. Australian illustrator Shenae Guzzardi views Saul as the "connecting thread between Walt and Jesse, the mediator of their disagreements," who at the same time is fighting a battle with his own moral compass. In her piece *Cash in the Trunk*, Guzzardi used bold brush strokes to depict Saul, Walt, and Jesse huddled over a trunk full of money, as seen from a low-angle perspective inside the trunk. In recognition of Saul's integral role in Walt's operation, Barcelona-based Romanian illustrator ICSD used a high-contrast digital painting technique to draw Saul mid–eureka moment in his piece *I Can Make It Legal!* Italian paper artist Elisabetta Quaraniello had her own eureka moment when rewatching one of Saul's television commercials, inspiring her to create a three-dimensional portrait of the master self-promoter with his index finger pointed out in classic salesman mode.

Saul's Rolodex of criminal clients generated a string of ill-fated partnerships for Walt and Jesse, culminating in their disastrous alliance with Jack Welker and his gang of white supremacists. Toronto-based illustrator Ashley Floréal took on the challenge of drawing her least favorite character, Jack's nephew Todd Alquist. Her piece *Chamomile, Soy Milk, Stevia, Delusion* shows Todd cradling Madrigal executive Lydia Rodarte-Quayle's lipstick-stained coffee mug, a waft of steam in the image of her red mouth rising like a speech bubble toward his chest. Floréal considers Todd's misinterpretation of this professional working relationship an example of his "disturbing creepiness," a trait that is evident in his imprisonment of Jesse and his matter-of-fact shooting of a child, Drew Sharp, who witnessed Walt and Jesse's train heist in the Season 5 episode "Dead Freight."

Even as Walt and Jesse found themselves in progressively deeper trouble, Saul soldiered on with flair. After all, he is a consummate showman. In assembling Saul's wardrobe, Jennifer Bryan was guided by his fondness for calculated risks—"the brashness of his suits, the bravado of his ties, the eccentricity of his socks and those color-soaked shirts." "I had to take my design sensibilities and unlearn whatever I knew about 'good taste,'" she quips. "Saul Goodman is already a cartoon," comments Venezuelan illustrator Ed Vill, who drew inspiration for his cartoon-style piece *It's All Good, Man!* from midcentury commercial illustrations and advertisements. Vill paints Saul with a devious expression, as if he's formulating his next scam. Peter Gould, writer of the Season 2 *Breaking Bad* episode "Better Call Saul" and co-creator of the eponymous spinoff series, remarks: "Saul was always going to be Walt's opposite—he's a peacock! He wants your attention; everything he wears, everything he does says: *look at me!*"

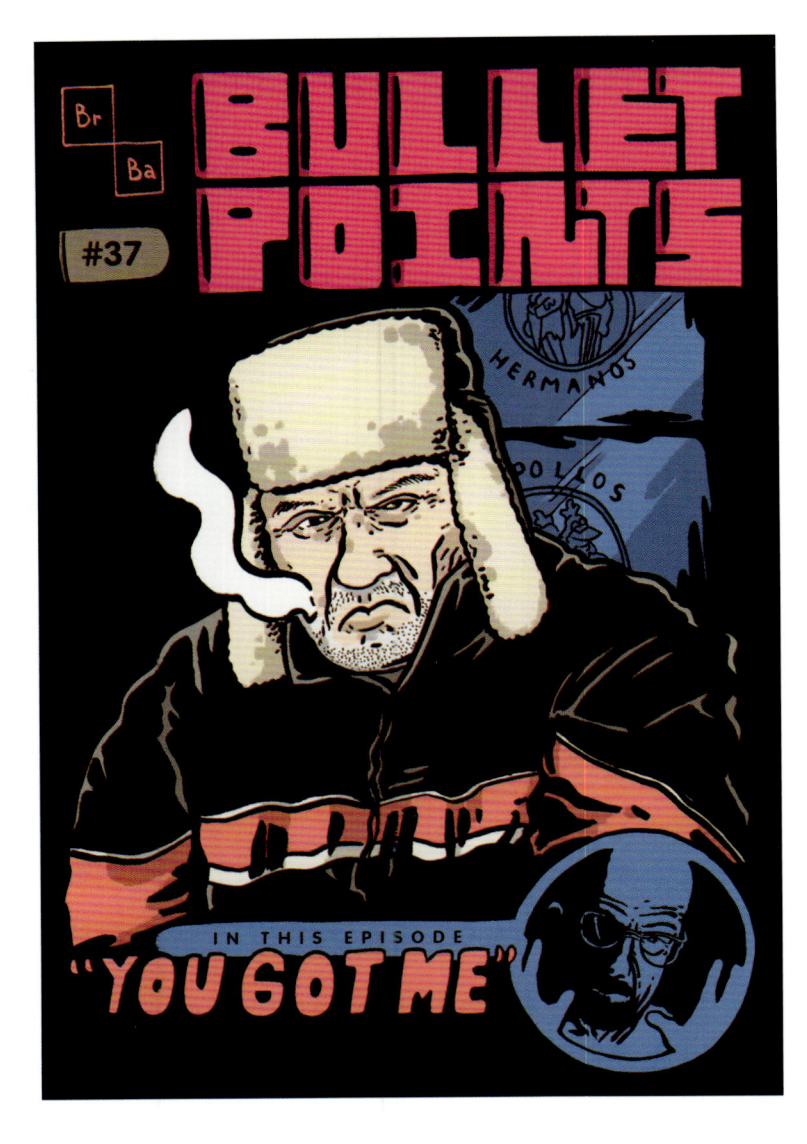

THIS PAGE and OPPOSITE: Pablo Guaymasi | *Bullet Points #37, Peekaboo,* and *We Are Family!*
Brush and ink drawing with digital painting | Córdoba, Argentina | 2015 | pg.comix

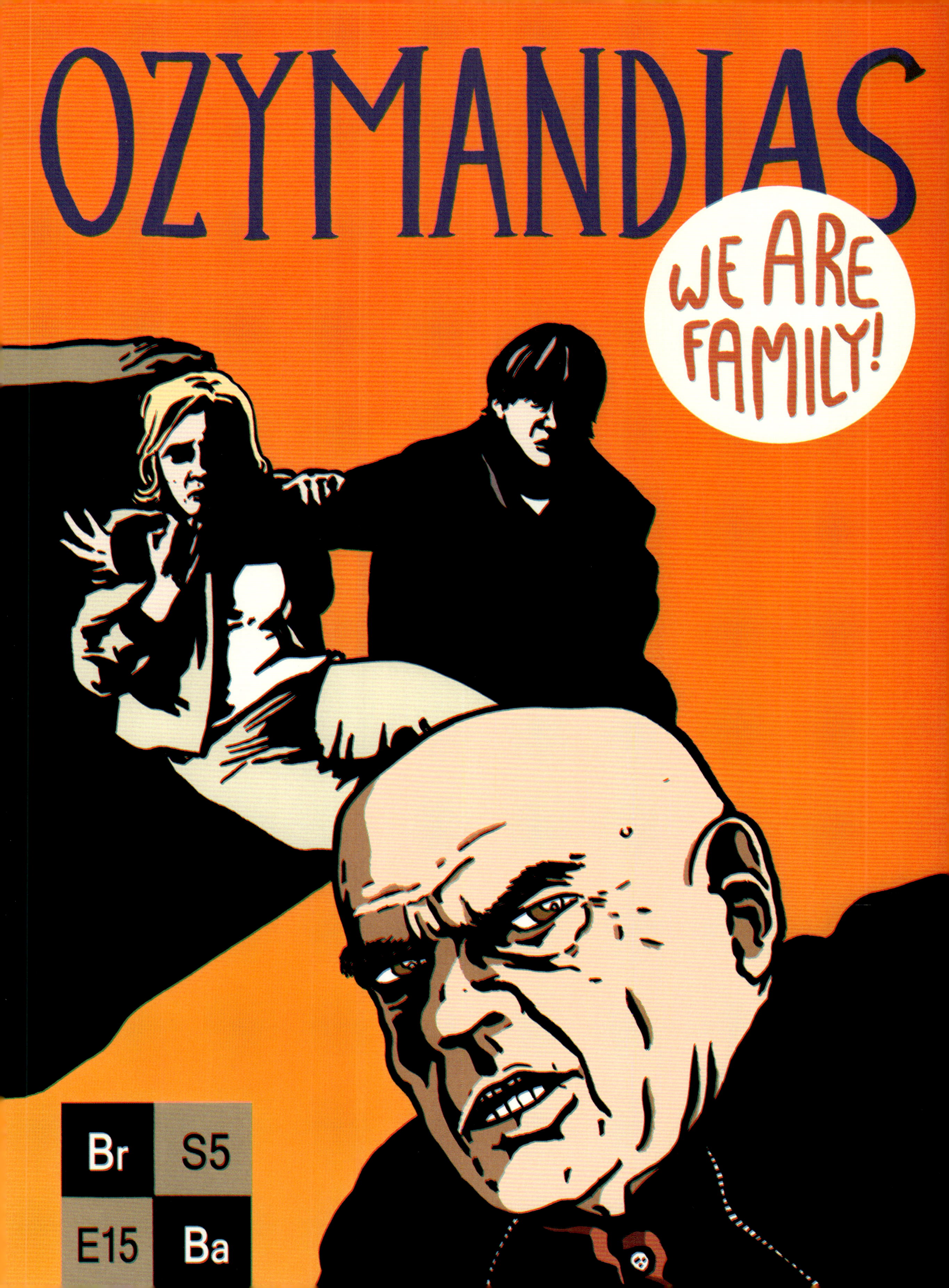
OZYMANDIAS
WE ARE FAMILY!
Br
S5
E15
Ba

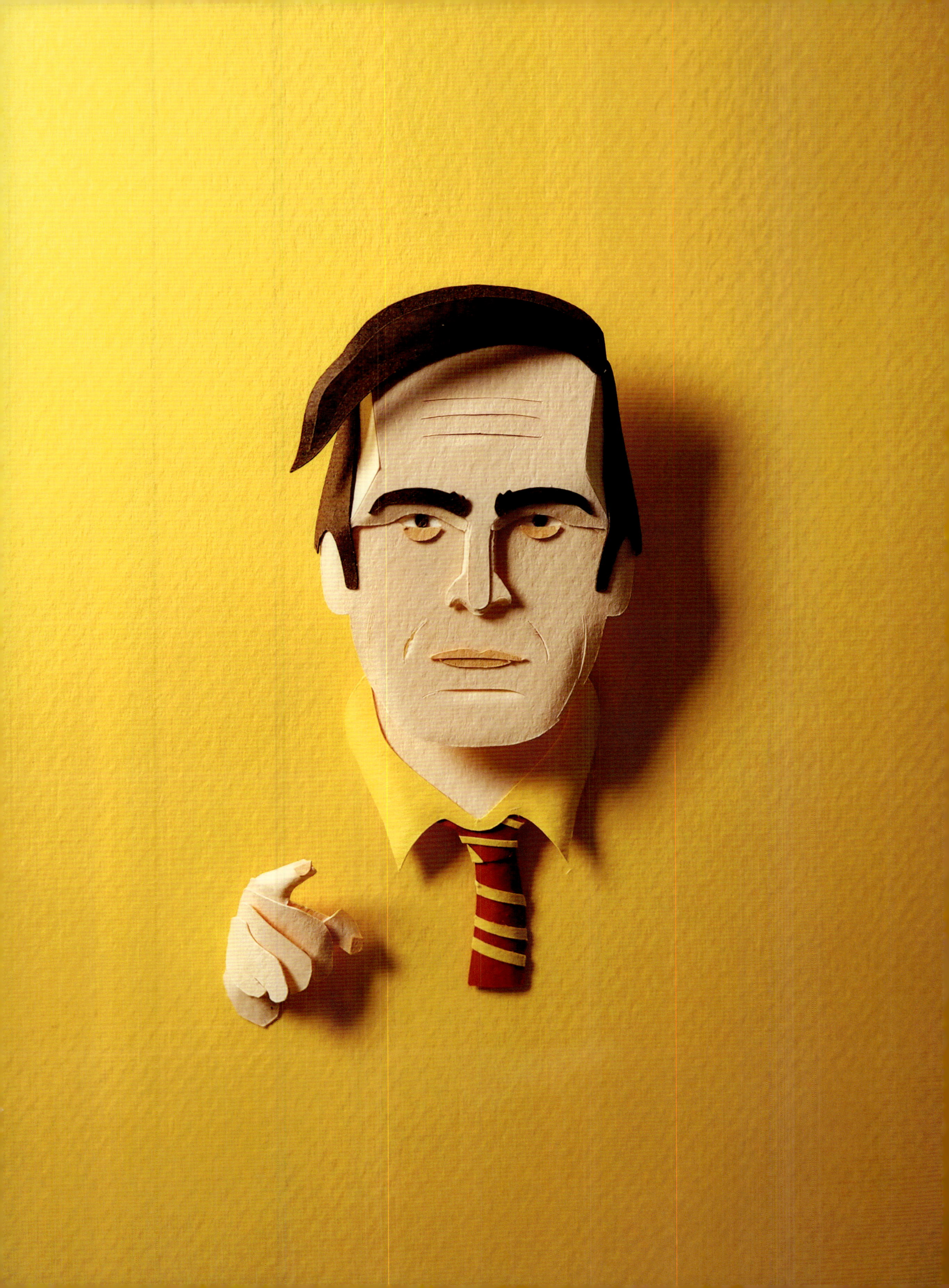

OPPOSITE: Elisabetta Quaraniello | *Kiritori Better Call Saul* | Paper | Rome, Italy | 2019 | www.kiritori.it

ABOVE: Gabe Lanza | *Drew Sharp* | Gouache and acrylic on wood panel in antique wood | Chicago, Illinois, USA | 2014 | www.gabelanza.com | robotlover

96

ABOVE: Crystal Curtis | *Lydia* | Digital art | Alabama, USA | 2013 | www.crystalcurtisart.com

OPPOSITE: Ashley Floréal | *Chamomile, Soy Milk, Stevia, Delusion* | Digital painting | Toronto, Canada | 2014 | www.ashleyfloreal.com | ashleyfloreal

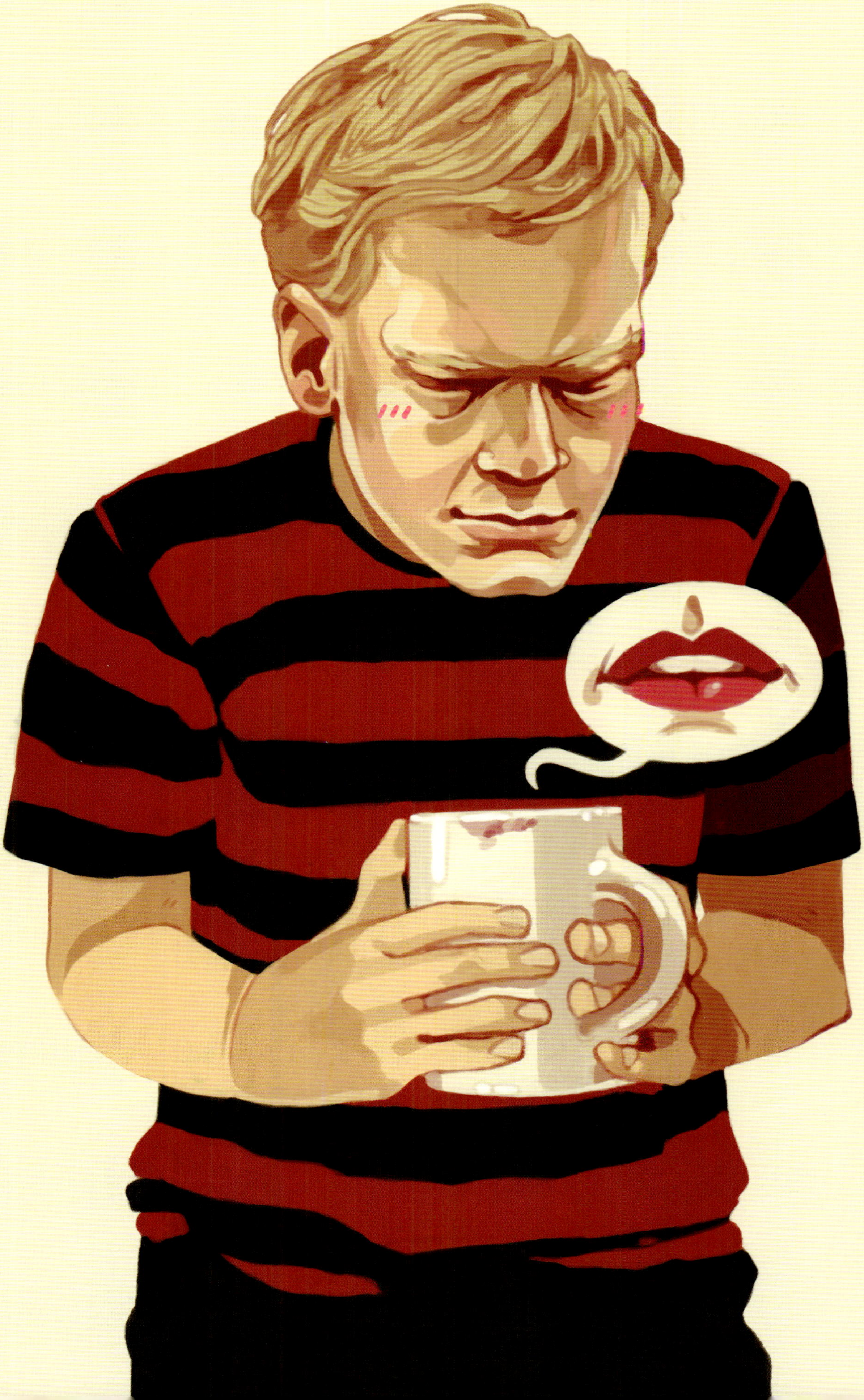

All Hail the
Breakfast King
#cutthebull
STOP
Bullying
NO
BULLYING
#cuttheBull
Two Scoops!
Raisin
Bran
Crunch
DANI
ESCA

OPPOSITE: Daniesca (Daniela Espinoza Castro) | *Breakfast King* | Digital painting | Costa Rica | 2016 | daniesca.art | art.daniesca

ABOVE: Jimmy Rogers | *Huell Awaits* | Digital painting | Birmingham, UK | 2015 | www.booyeah.co.uk

PAGE 100: Marcello Restaldi | *Cheer Up, Beautiful People* | Digital painting | Turin, Italy | 2018 | marcellorestaldi_art

PAGE 101: Josh Filhol | *Skyler White* | Digital illustration | England, UK | 2018 | jf_illustration

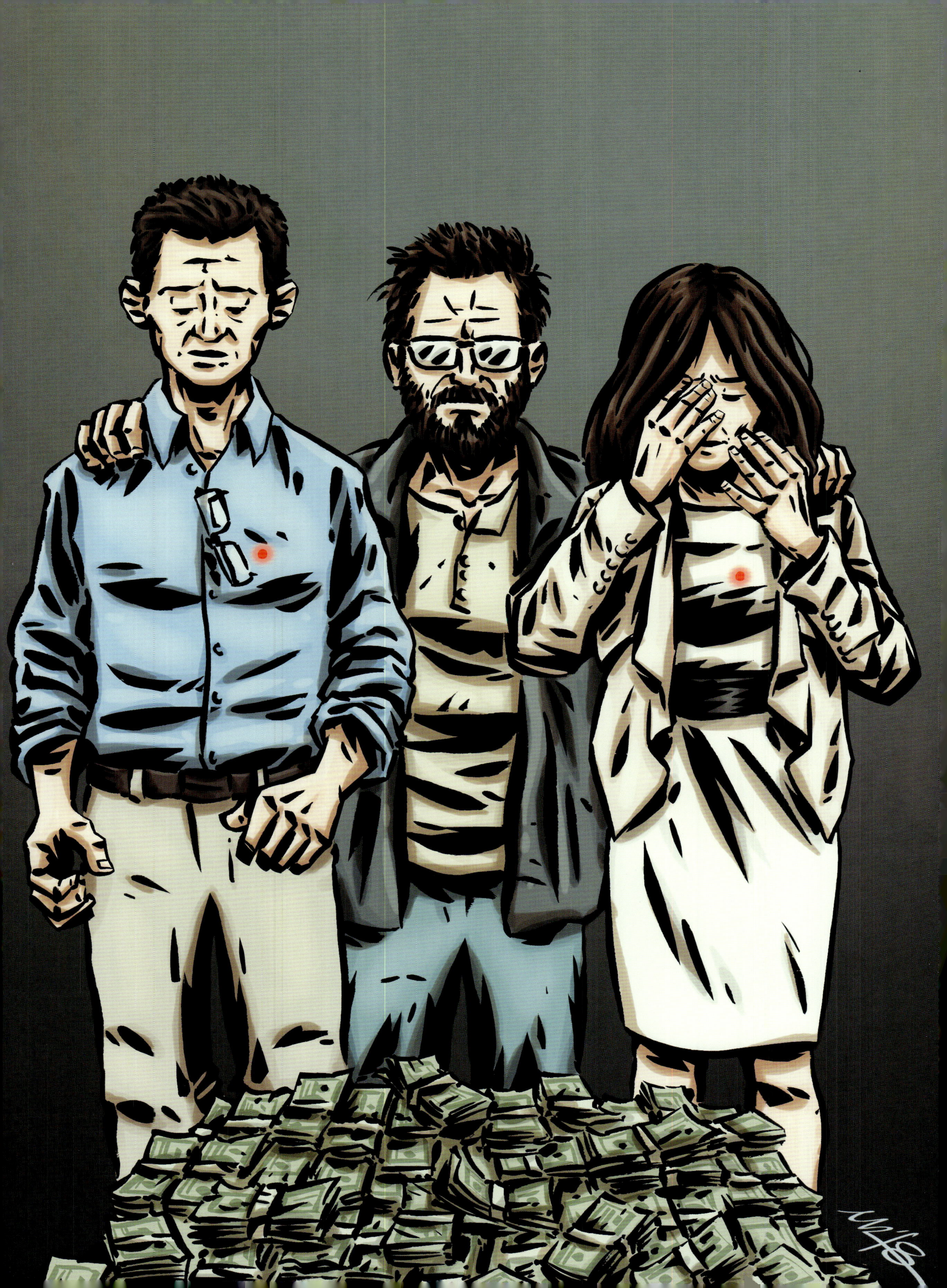

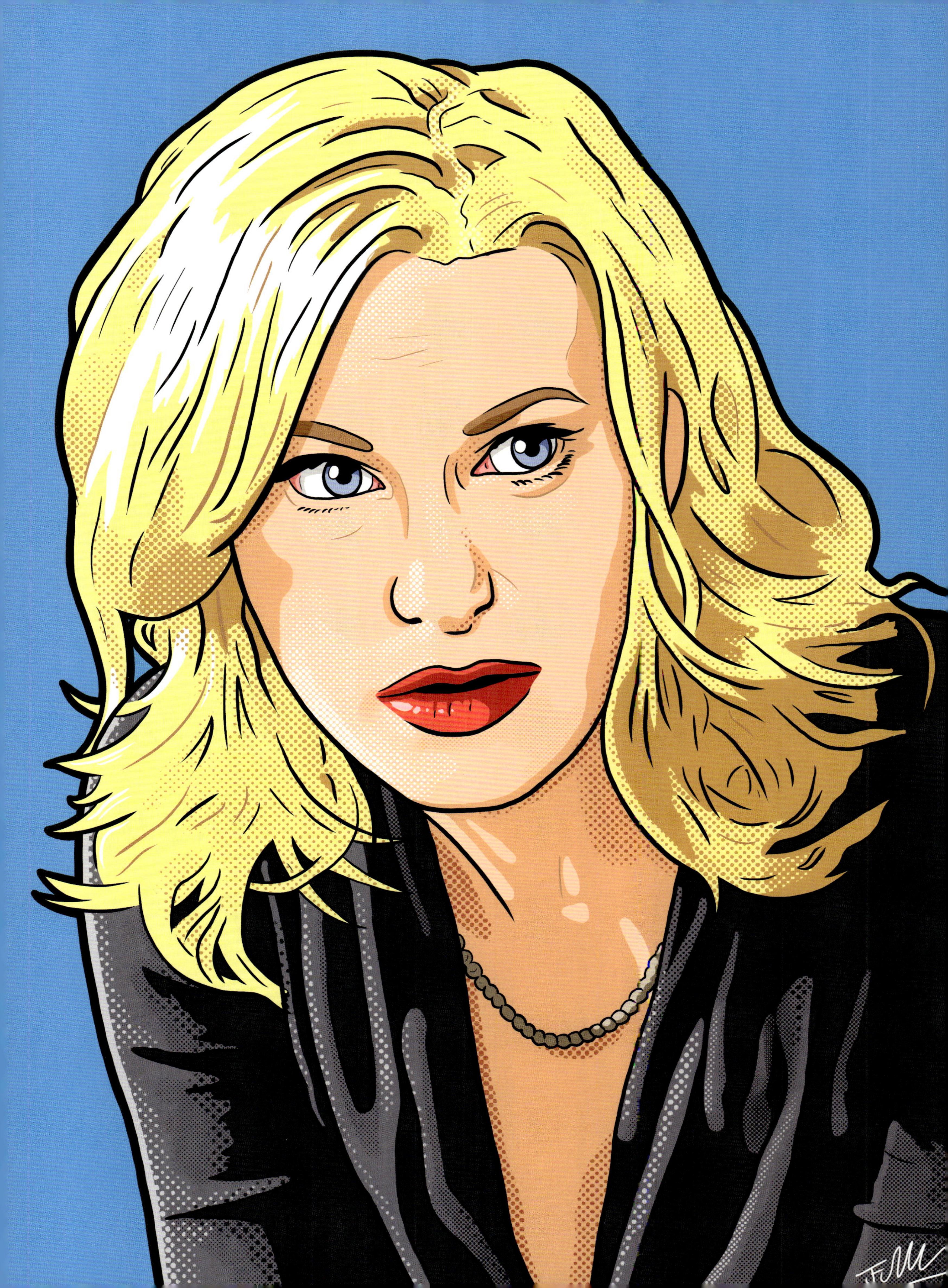

THESE PAGES: Rafael Barletta | *Breaking Bad Minimal Characters* | Digital illustration | Santa Cruz do Sul, Brazil | 2015 | barlettarafael | barletta

WALTER WHITE

Br Ba

104

Mika Bacani | *I Heart Wendy* | Digital illustration | Manila, Philippines | 2012/2020 | junemonsters

Brittany Busch | *Ain't No Skank* | Colored pencil | Amarillo, Texas, USA | 2017 | www.brittanybusch.com

ABOVE: Lisa Brawn | *Pinkman, Heisenberg, Schrader* | Painted woodcut blocks | Calgary, Canada | 2016 | www.lisabrawn.com

OPPOSITE TOP: Andrea Bochicchio | *Better Call Saul* | Digital painting | Potenza, Italy | 2019 | andreabochicchio_

OPPOSITE BOTTOM: Ed Vill | *It's All Good, Man!* | Digital painting (Procreate) | Mexico City, Mexico | 2019 | www.edvill.com | edvill

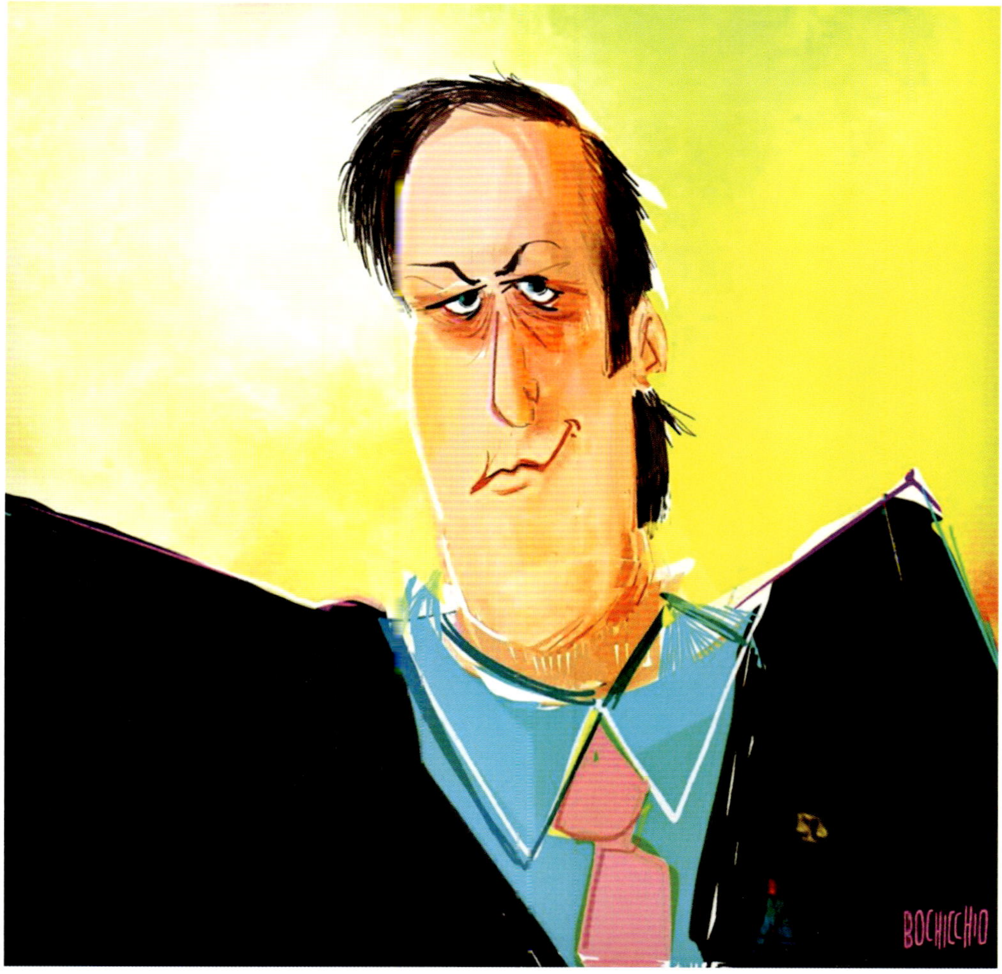
BOCHICCHIO

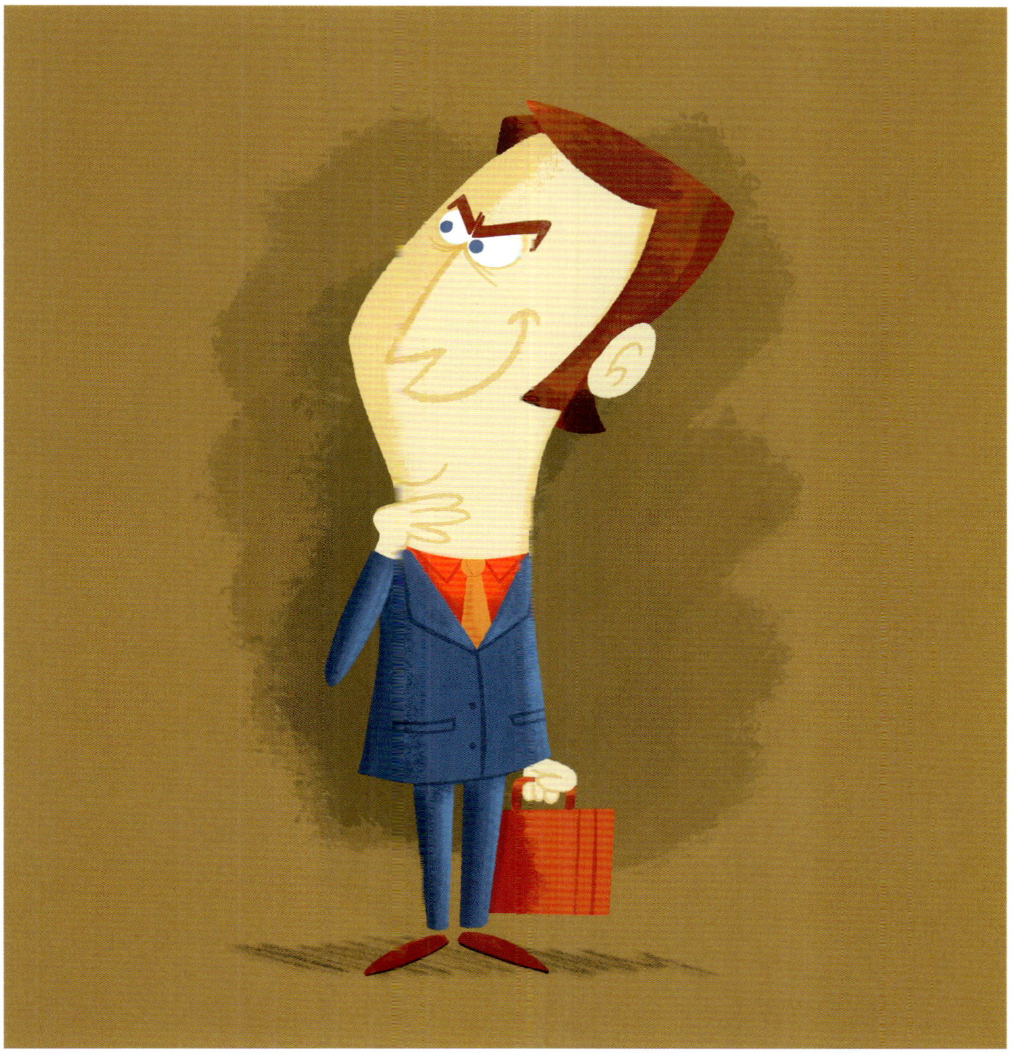

ABOVE: ICSD | *I Can Make It Legal!* | Digital painting | Bucharest, Romania | 2018 | icsd

OPPOSITE: Mariko Kumano | *Apology Girl / Gomenne Girl* | Watercolor, pencil | Tokyo, Japan | 2016 | marikokumanoart | kumano-mariko | marikumano

ごめんね
ガール

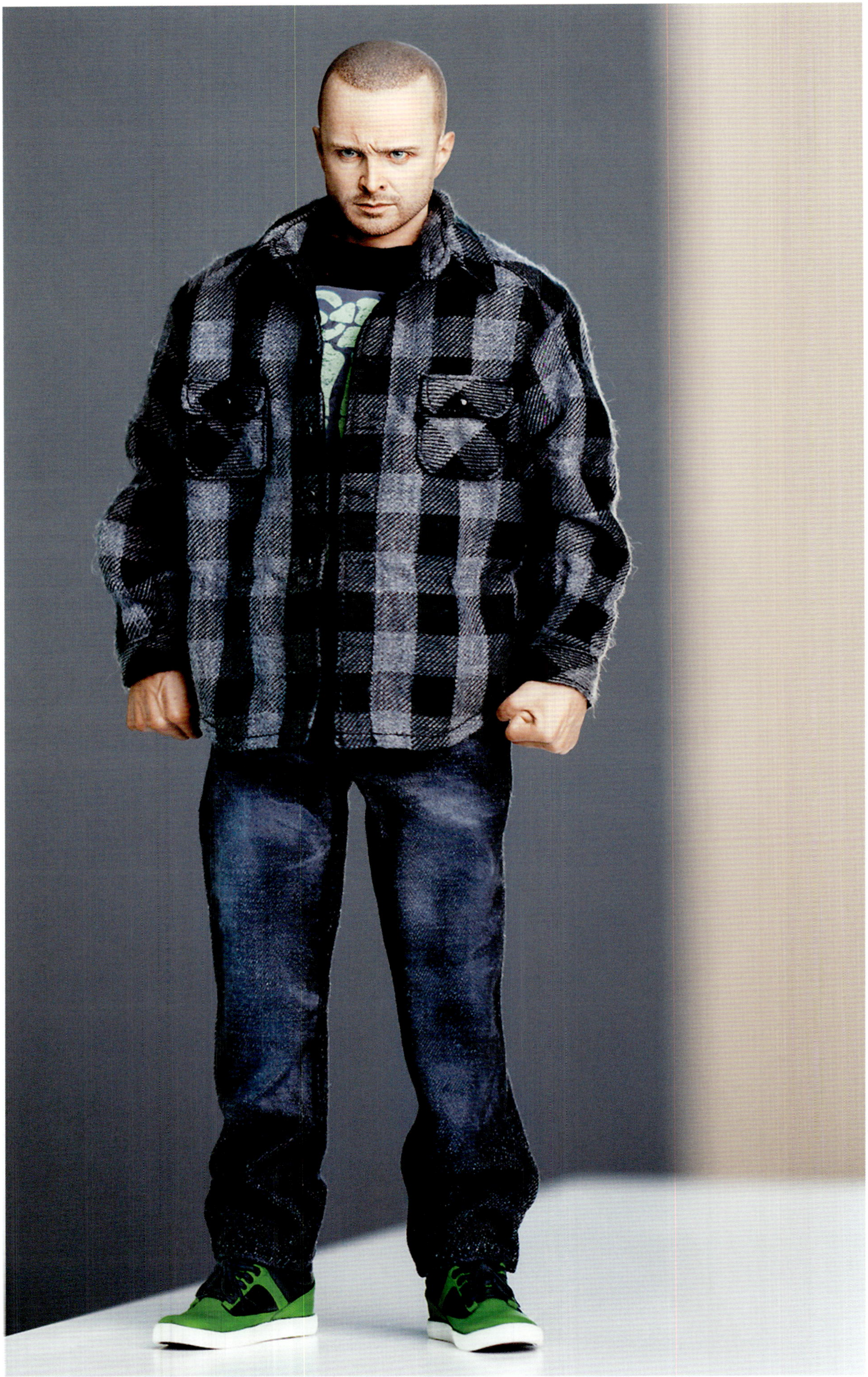

OPPOSITE: Hosam Al-Ghamdi and artists: Trevor Grove, Yelim Choi, Wonder Doll Tailor, 陳日炘 (RC) | *Yeah Bi**h!* | Custom 1/6 scale figure
USA, South Korea, Hong Kong, Taiwan, Saudi Arabia | 2017–2018 | hos1m

ABOVE: Hosam Al-Ghamdi and artists: Rainman, Toribox, Kato, Trevor Grove, SilentSurfer, Full Metal Customs | *My Baby Blue* | Custom 1/6 scale one-off figure
South Korea, Hong Kong, USA, Philippines, Saudi Arabia | 2016–2018 | hos1m

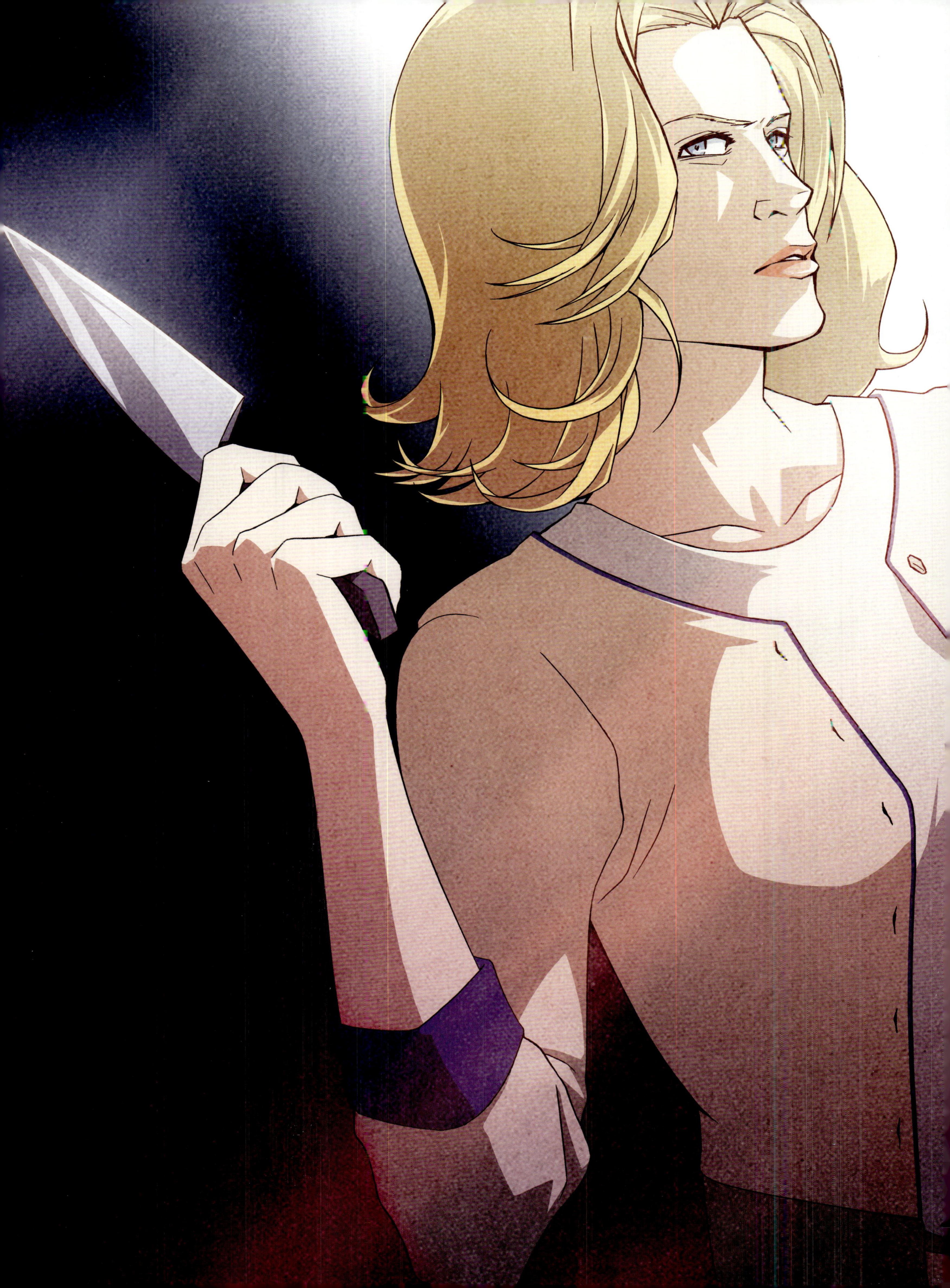

OPPOSITE and ABOVE: Pana Stamos | *Protect This Family* and *Ten of Swords* | Digital | Los Angeles, California, USA | 2014 | www.panastamos.com

OPPCSITE: Pauli Díaz | *Jane Margolis* | Pencil on Bristol paper | Santiago, Chile | 2015 | ⌾ paulidiaz

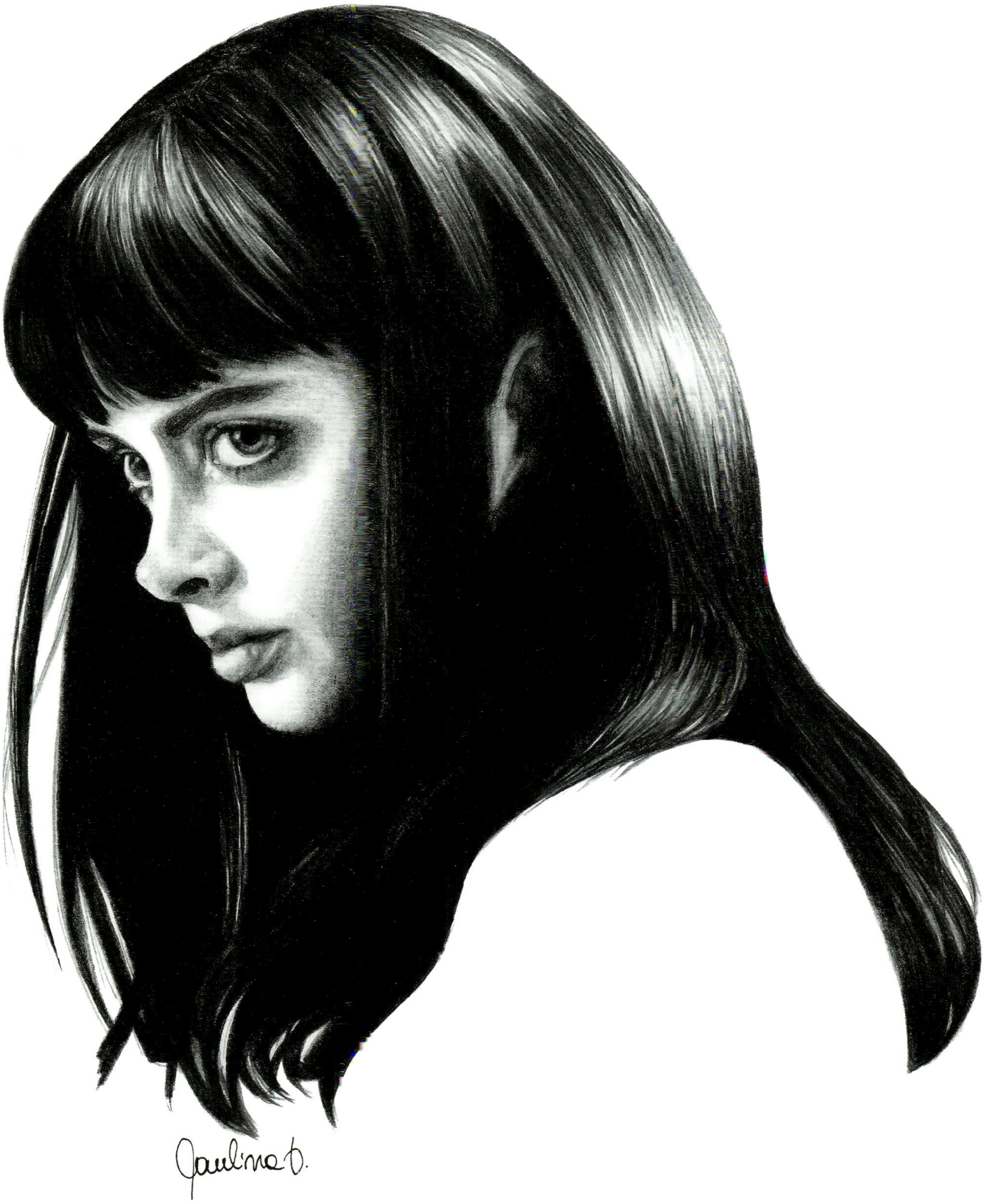

THESE PAGES: Yán Senninha Dŏng | *Have a Good Rest of Your Life, Kid* | Digital painting | Boston, Massachusetts, USA | 2017 | yansenna

117

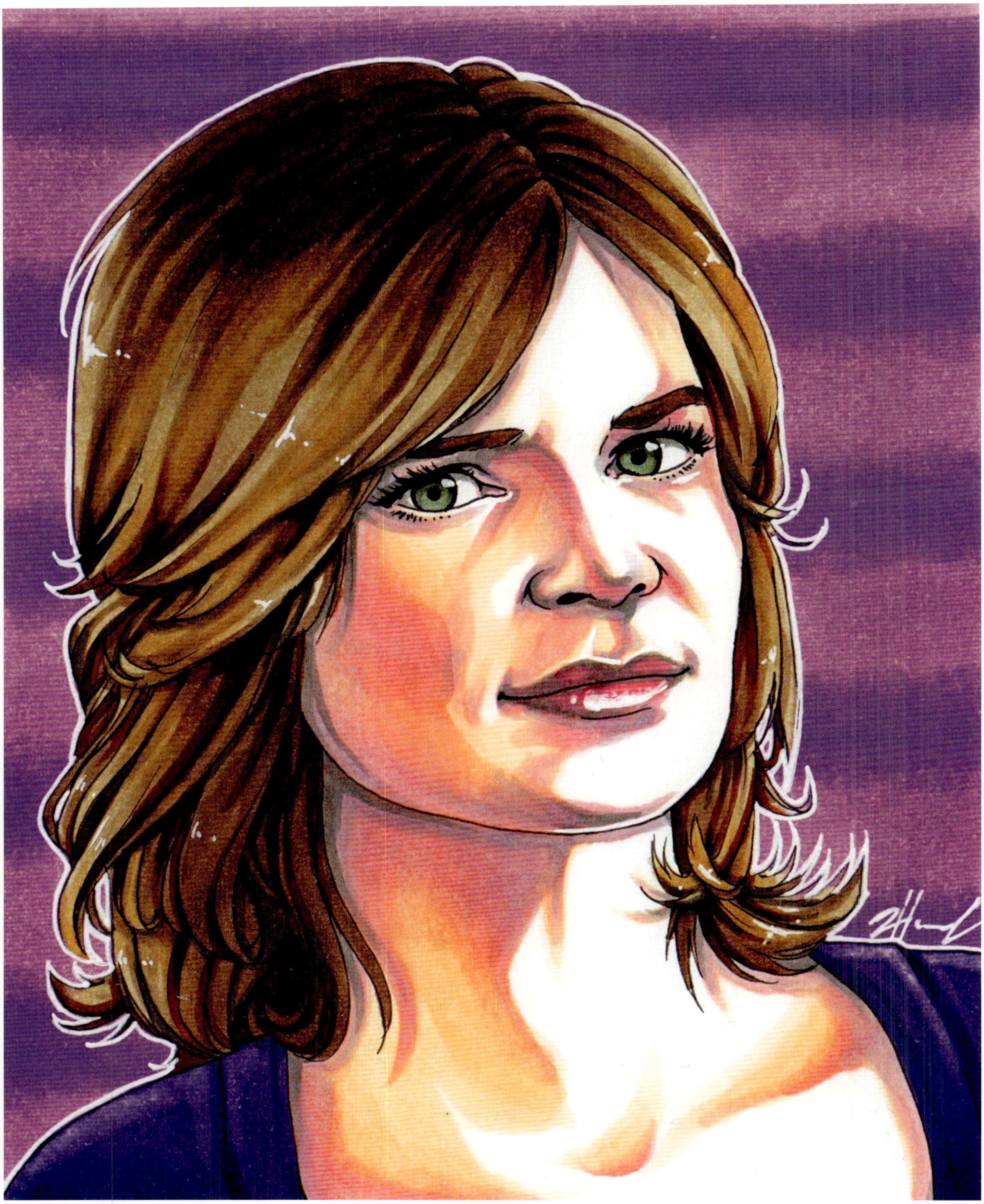

OPPOSITE: Vanessa Harmel | *Marie Schrader* | Black and white pens, Copic markers | Frankfurt, Germany | 2015 | nessasan

ABOVE: auguzzz | *This Way to Saving* | Digital painting | Thailand | 2019 | auguzzz
OPPOSITE: Nicki White | *SHUT UP* | Digital illustration | Toronto, Canada | 2013 | www.nikki-white.com | whitenikki

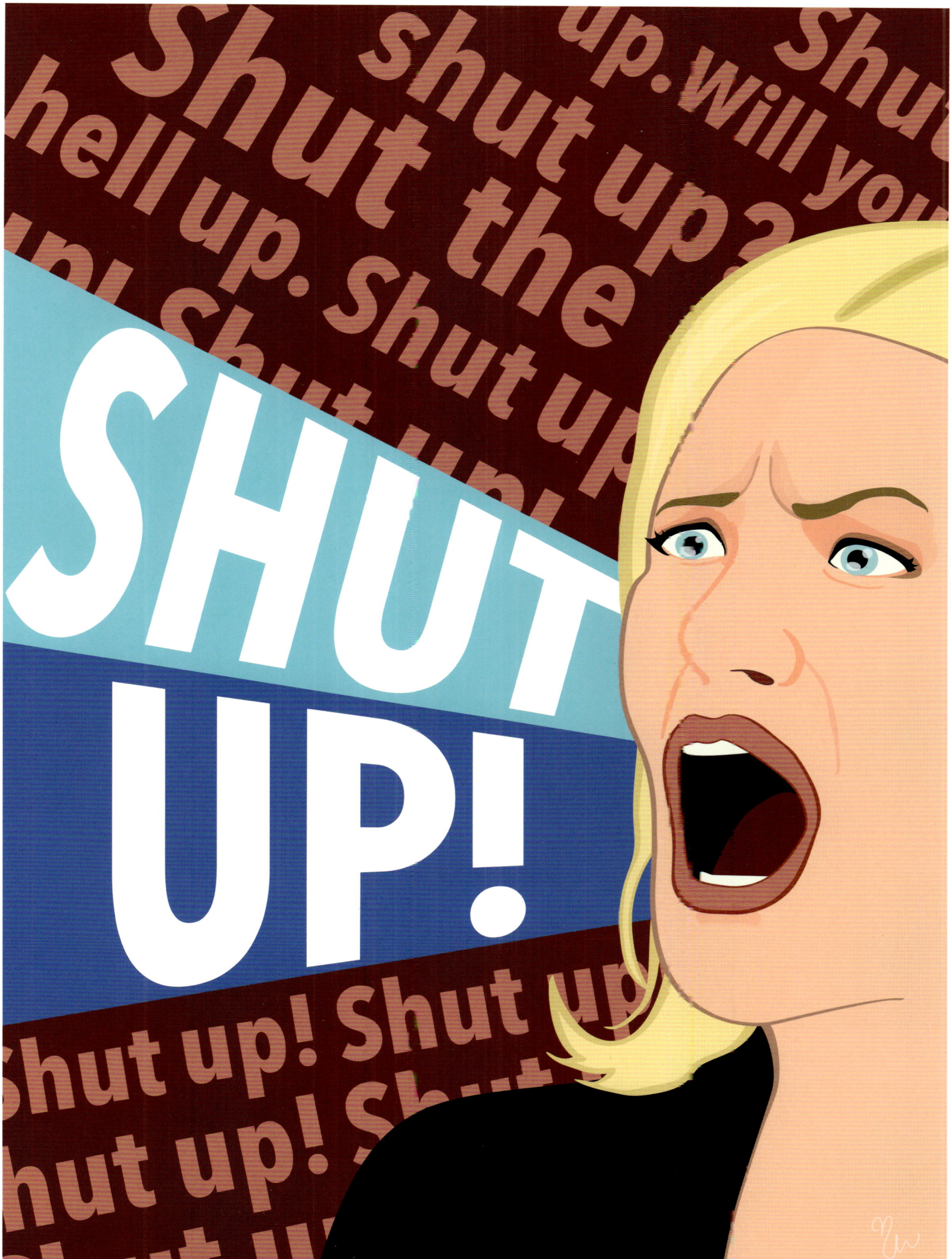
SHUT UP!
Shut up! Shut up
Shut up?
Shut the hell up.
Will you

THESE PAGES: Steve White | *Breaking Bad Pez Dispensers* | Pez, acrylic paint | Albuquerque, New Mexico, USA | stevewhitefolkart@gmail.com | steve.white.18294053

123

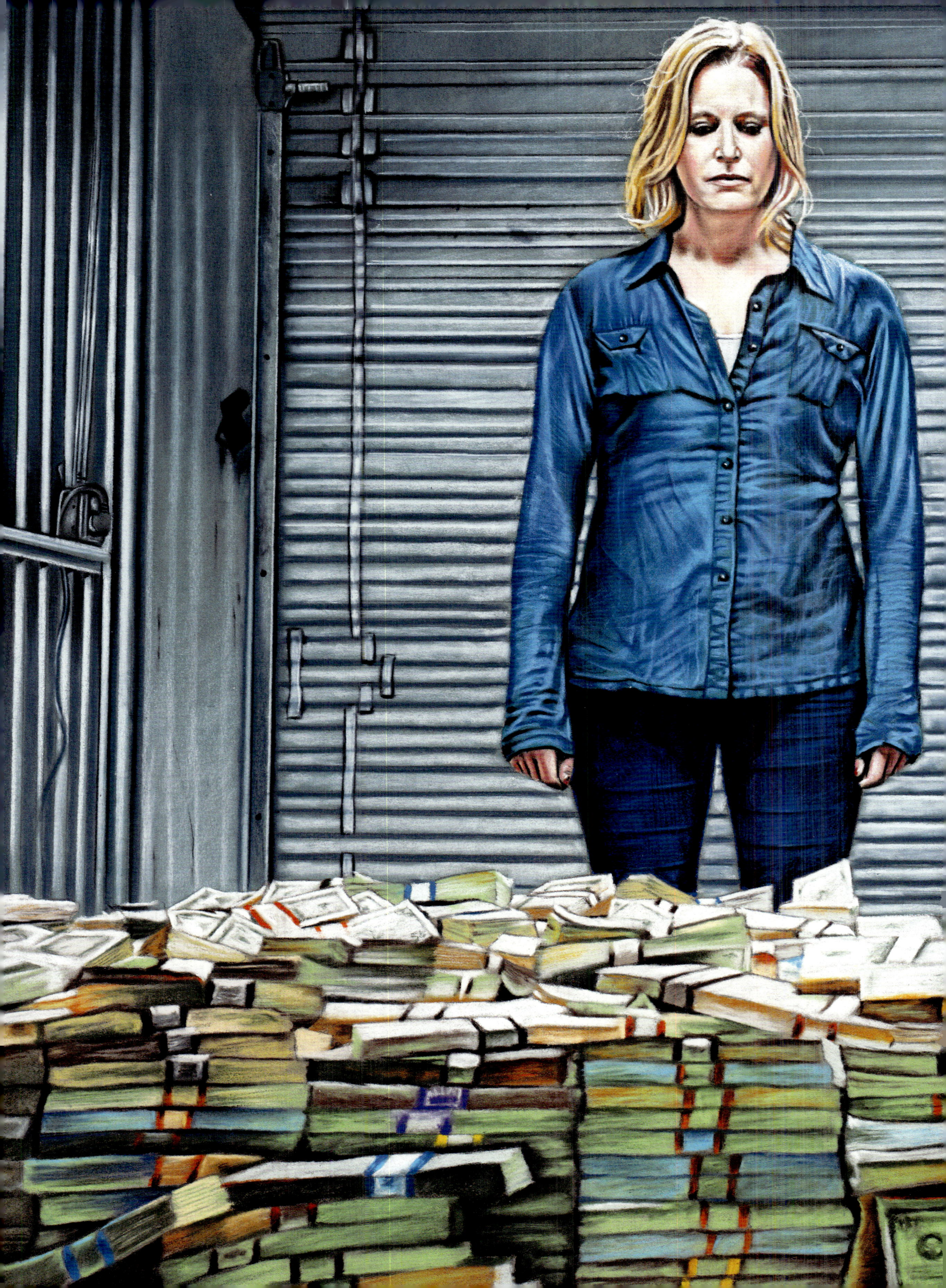

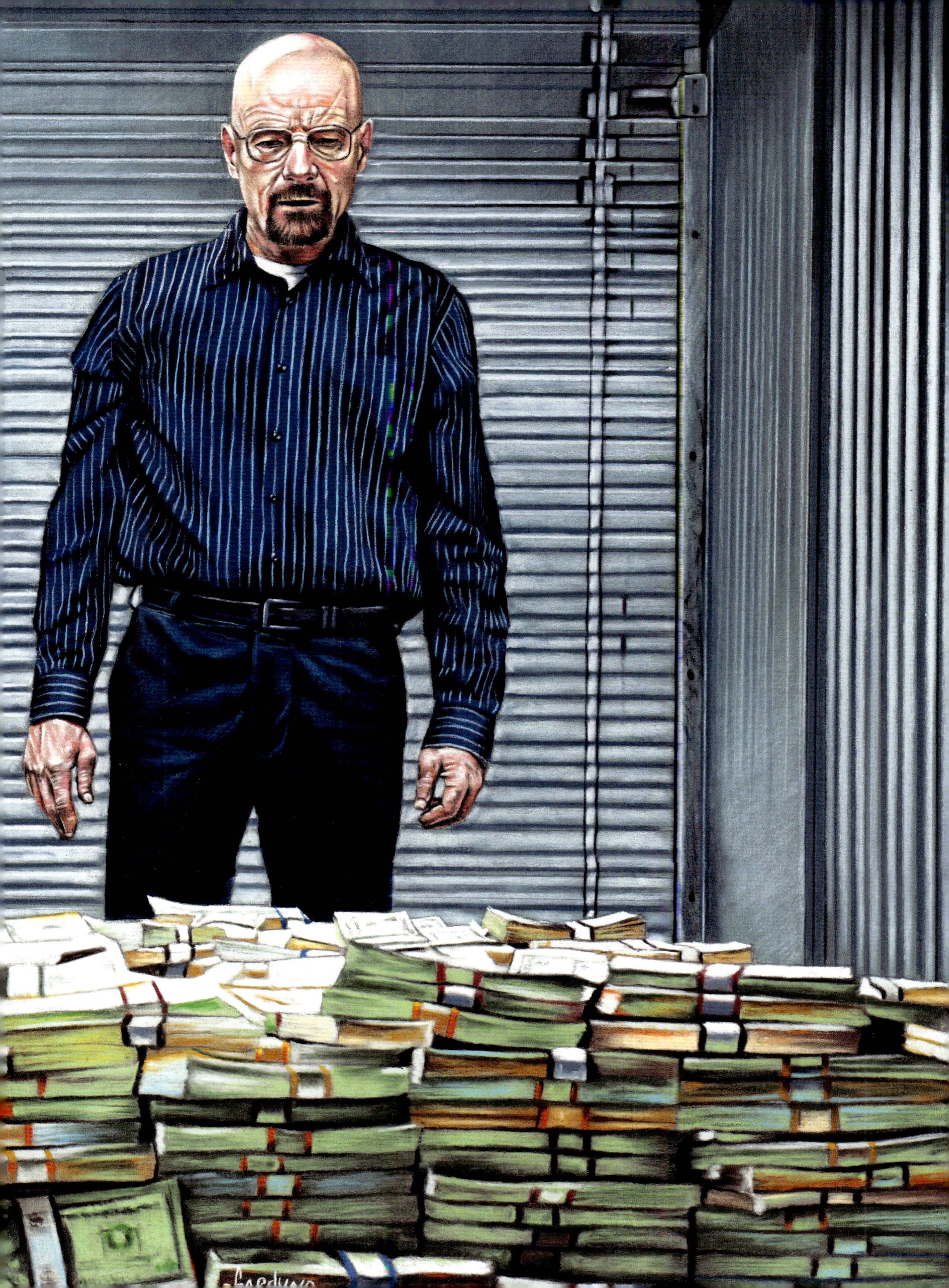

PAGES 124–125: Victor Garduno | *Overwhelmed* | Colored pastel pencils | Las Vegas, Nevada, USA | 2018 | ⌾ artofgarduno

ABOVE and OPPOSITE: Eric Guan | *Breaking Bad Poster* and *Man on Fire* | Digital painting | USA | 2013 | ⌾ Eman27

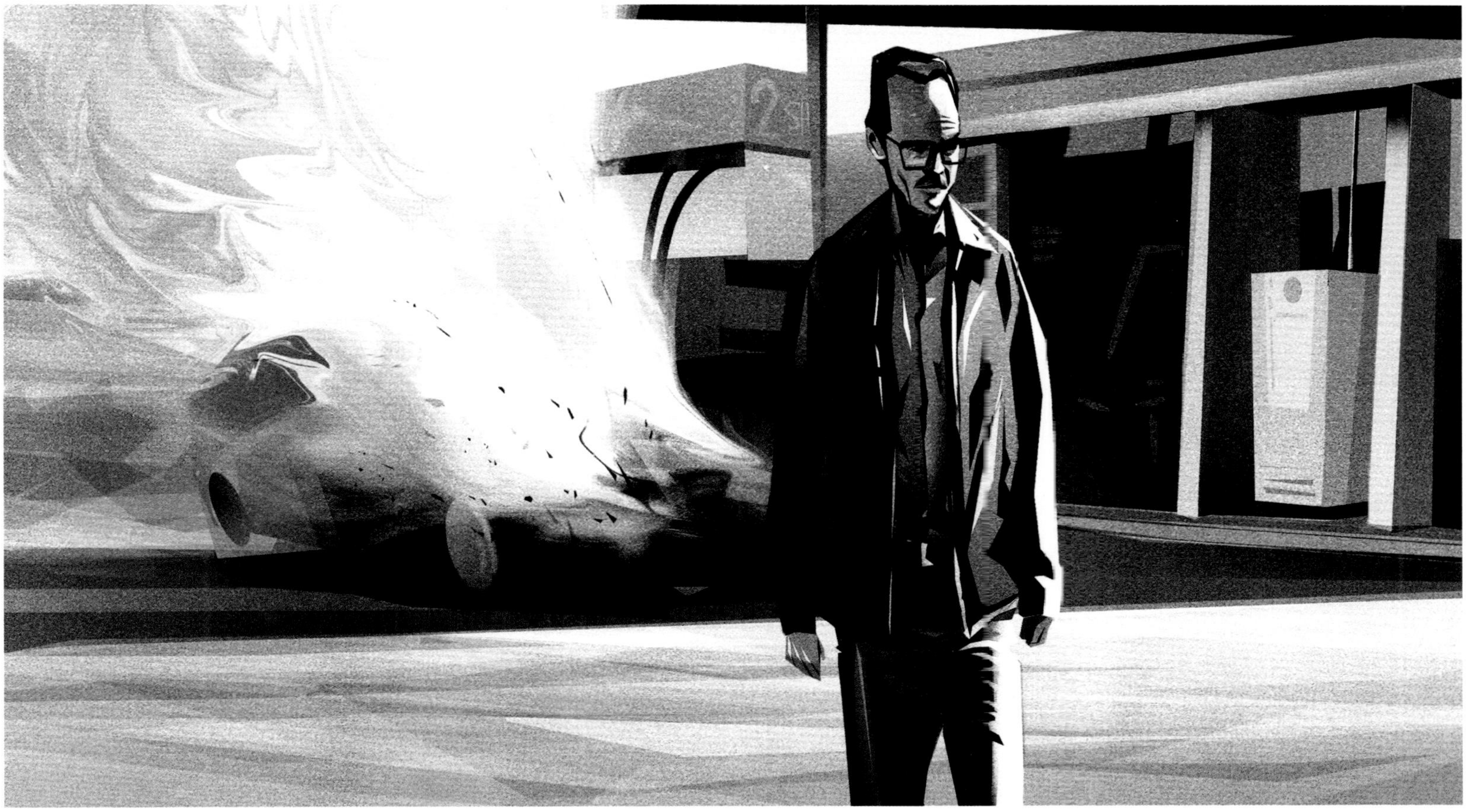

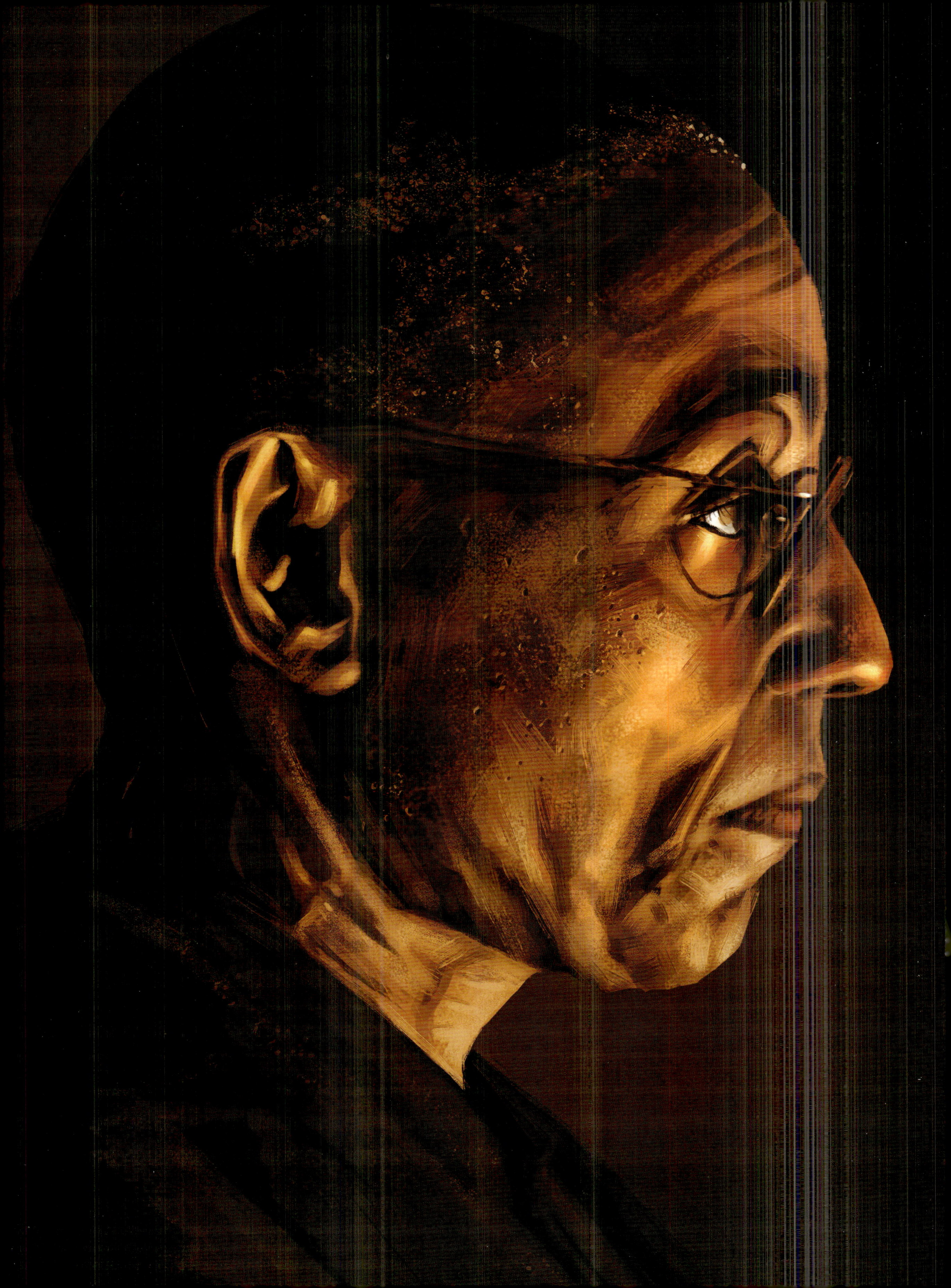

chapter 4

saNgre Por sangRe

They say heroes are only as good as their villains. Walter White certainly found a worthy adversary—and erstwhile ally—in Gustavo Fring. Proprietor of fast-food franchise Los Pollos Hermanos by day and drug lord by night, Gus entangled Walt in a dangerous criminal web populated by cold-blooded Mexican cartel players, including Hector Salamanca, the patriarch of the most feared family in the region, and his formidable nephews. The bloodshed that ensued, exacerbated by Fring's own insatiable need for revenge, made for many unforgettable *Breaking Bad* moments.

THE CHICKEN MAN

Daniel and Luis Moncada, who portray the stone-faced Salamanca twins, both cite Gustavo Fring as their favorite villain (other than their own characters, of course). "Gus is a chameleon—he can be charismatic, charming, polite," Daniel Moncada notes. "However, behind that mask of benevolence, he is dark, ruthless . . . a sophisticated intellectual gangster."

Utah-based illustrator Anna Tillett paid tribute to "the Chicken Man, [her] absolute favorite TV bad guy of all time," by painting Gus as a caricature whose head is a supersized Los Pollos Hermanos cup, atop his signature manager's uniform. This piece, entitled *Is Everything to Your Satisfaction?*, combines anthropomorphic food and objects with pop culture references, recurring motifs in Tillett's art. Gus's restaurant proprietor persona and his drug lord persona are, in Tillett's words, "hilariously juxtaposed," and she sought to capture the comedic side of Gus's dual identity in her work.

Toronto-based cartoonist Faez Alidoosti finds Fring's duality fascinating. Although Gus is a perfect gentleman on the surface, "deep inside, he is like a snake—vigilant, fast, and cruel." Alidoosti created ink-and-watercolor caricatures of both Gus and his fixer, Mike Ehrmantraut, entitled *I Hide in Plain Sight* and *Let Me Die in Peace*, respectively. "Seeing two smart professionals like Gus and Mike working together" is, for Alidoosti, "quite satisfying." Chicago-based Mike Noren, who goes by the moniker Gummy Arts, used colored pencils to draw the two men, among others, in the style of classic baseball cards. For Noren, an avid

OPPOSITE: Fan Chen | *Gustavo* | Digital painting | Shanghai, China | 2017 | Be fancher

card collector, it was "a way of placing familiar faces in a different light."

A man of few words, Mike Ehrmantraut is steadfastly loyal to his boss. "Gus is such a powerhouse, you'd expect cronies to cower in his presence," muses *Breaking Bad* script coordinator Jenn Carroll. "But Mike's not like that. Actor Jonathan Banks carries himself with so much gravitas that the character feels loyal, but never subservient." New Jersey–based artist Skullboy, who painted multiple characters from the show on hand-carved, recycled skateboard decks, depicts Mike in his fur aviator hat, an image from the opening scene of the Season 4 episode "Bullet Points." Skullboy admires how Mike "operates with precision" and the way he "prefers to know the odds, has years of experience to work with, and is able to improvise if needed." He observes that "Gus values all these traits, yet isn't afraid to push the limits of Mike's loyalty as he wages a personal war against the cartel."

Gus does not always reward loyalty, however. Perhaps the best example of this is his bone-chilling murder of trusted colleague Victor in "Box Cutter," the episode that kicks off Season 4. Canadian portrait artist Joel Snell recalls experiencing pure shock when he watched Gus holding Victor's limp body upright, blood spurting from his slain associate's neck: "In that moment, I was put in the exact same place as Walt and Jesse. I almost didn't want to watch because the scene felt so real." In his pieces *Acceptable* and *Knocked*, Snell drew graphite-charcoal portraits of Gus and Walt, respectively. He based his drawings on stills from the show, paying attention to the smallest of details, down to the fine hairs and pores on their faces, while altering certain aspects of Walt's shirt and Gus's tie ever so slightly to impart a personal touch.

Shanghai-based Fan Chen took a similar approach in his arresting portraits of Gus and his archnemesis, Hector Salamanca, the man responsible for brutally executing Gus's partner Max Arciniega in the Season 4 episode "Hermanos." Chen drew inspiration from stills that cast Gus and Hector in a moody, orange glow evocative of the chiaroscuro lighting inside Casa Tranquila, the nursing home where the two men meet their eventual demise.

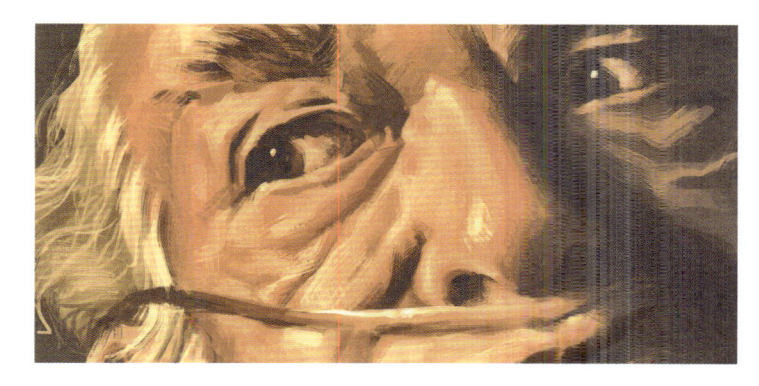

FACE OFF

Hector Salamanca commits the ultimate act of revenge against Gus Fring in the Season 4 episode "Face Off." Sydney-based Bruno Mota took special care in his digital illustration *Ding!* to capture Hector's snarling, almost feral expression as he taunts Gus, right before triggering the deadly explosion that would claim both their lives. Gus's subsequent exit from Hector's bomb-blasted room, fastidiously straightening his tie while the camera slowly tracks to reveal a hollow eye socket and exposed bone, inspired Racknar Teyssier's comic-book-style piece *Ding, Ding, Ding!* Teyssier, a digital artist based in Tijuana, Mexico, ranks the scene as his favorite of the series and appreciates the fact that "even in this situation, [Gus] tries to calmly step out of the room and fix his tie, right before dying."

Special effects coordinator Werner Hahnlein reflects: "Gus's death scene was one of those rare wonderful moments when practical effects, makeup effects, and computer-generated effects all came together to create a visually seamless sequence of events that stunned audiences." Hahnlein considers it one of the highlights of his career. Producer Diane Mercer, head of *Breaking Bad*'s postproduction department, adds: "Vince always saw it as one shot. We blew the door in one take, then blended it seamlessly with a second take of Gus walking out, straightening his tie, and collapsing."

Florida-based sculptor Rocco Tartamella was on the edge of his seat during this sequence, which he felt was heightened by the initial "smugness of Gus versus the anger and patience of Hector." Tartamella used Castilene, a wax-based sculpting material, to craft a lifelike bust of Hector as well as multiple busts of Gus, including one that showcases his gruesome injuries. He applauds the performances of actors Giancarlo Esposito and Mark Margolis, who play Gus and Hector, respectively, remarking that "you can just feel the opposition and hatred they had for each other." Boston-based Rich Pellegrino, whose acrylic and gouache painting *Breaking Gus* depicts a stoic, zombified Gus adjusting his tie, was "blown away, pardon the pun, by how Giancarlo Esposito captured a sense of dignified grace and pride in his last moment as king drug lord . . . Total cool factor dialed up to eleven." Esposito himself paid particular attention to his tone and movements in those final seconds: "I wanted it to be completely believable in every way."

ABOVE and OPPOSITE: Faez Alidoosti | *I Hide in Plain Sight* and *Let Me Die in Peace* | Watercolor and ink on paper | Toronto, Canada | 2018 | www.alfazedsudc…

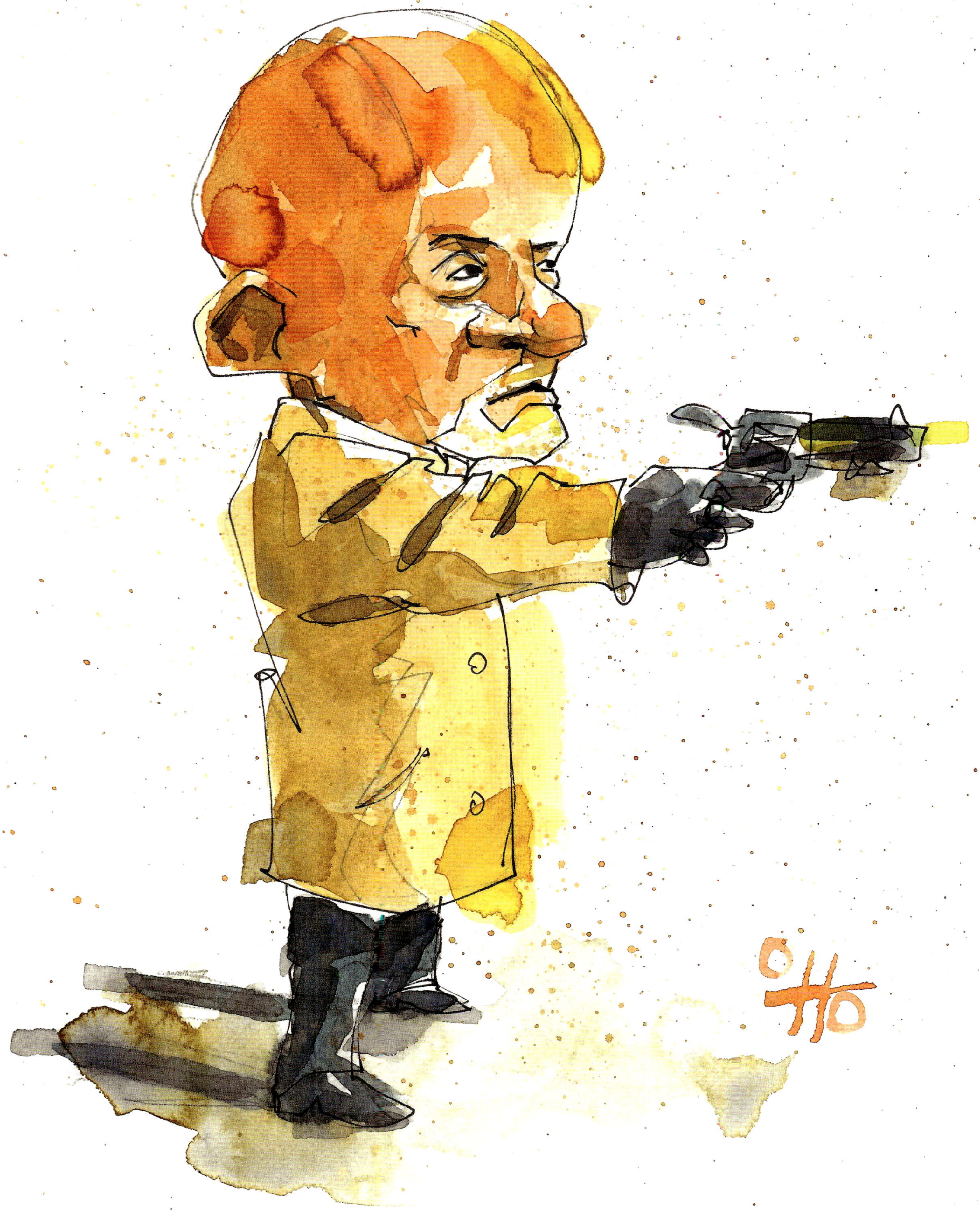

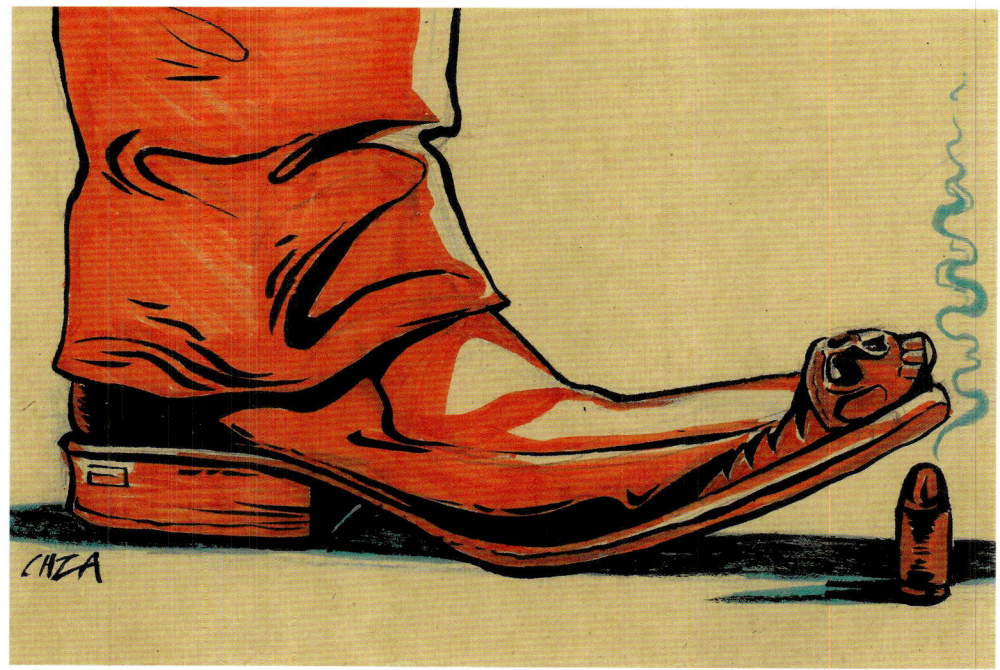

TOP: Marta Stawska "Smodyl" | *Tucan Salamanca* | Markers and fineliners | Poznań, Poland | 2019 | smodyl

ABOVE: Chad Stanhope | *Road to Hank* | Pen and ink | Fairfield, California, USA | 2016 | www.chadstanhope.com

OPPOSITE: Vinasz | *Tortuga* | Handmade drawing, ink and digital painting | São Paulo, Brazil | 2014 | vinasz_ilustrador | vinasz.arte

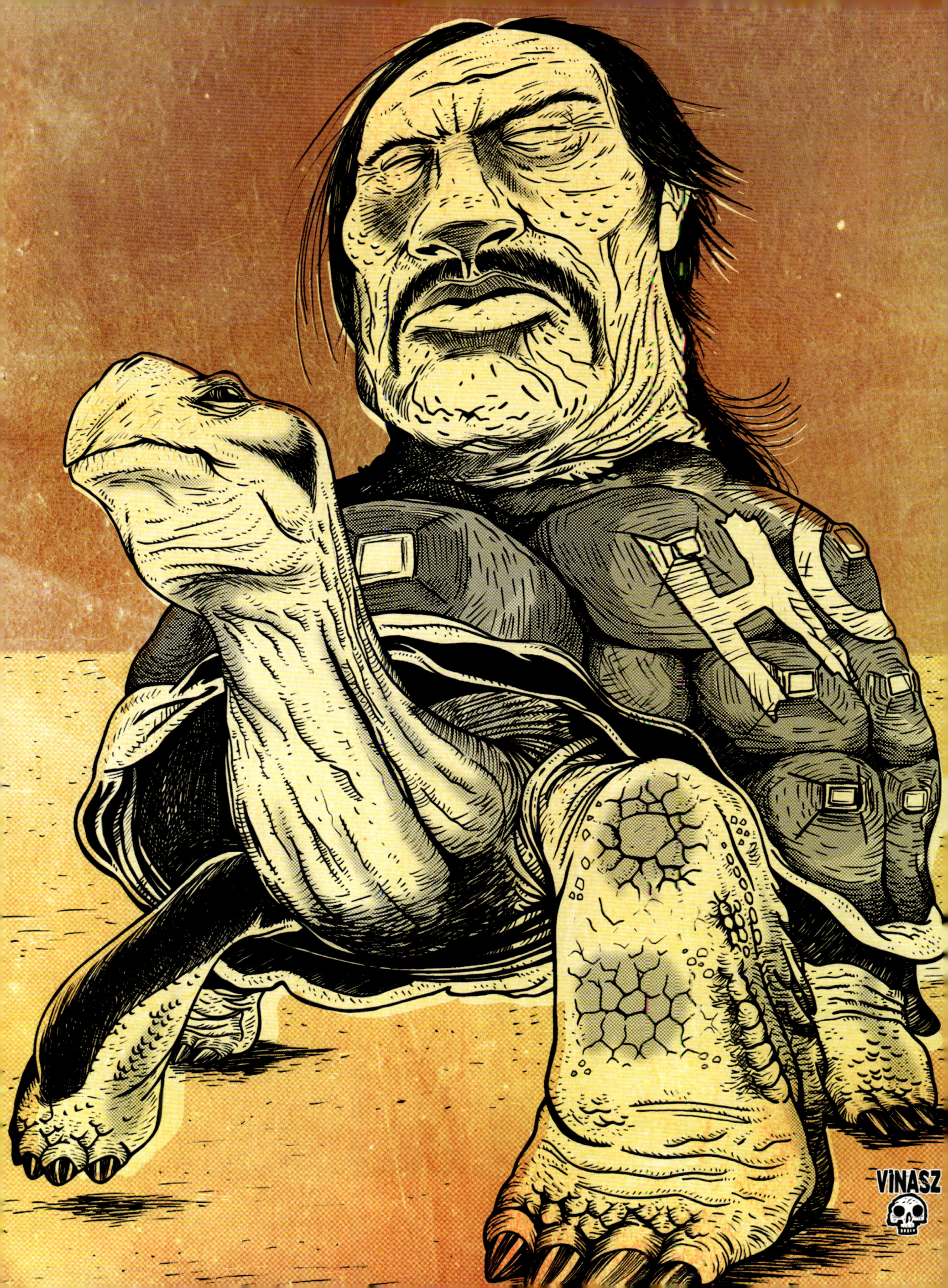
VINASZ

ABOVE and OPPOSITE: Joel Snell | *Walter White, "Knocked"* and *Gus Fring, "Acceptable"* | Graphite-charcoal pencil | Alberta, Canada | 2018–2019 | 🅾 🇫 Cegresdraws

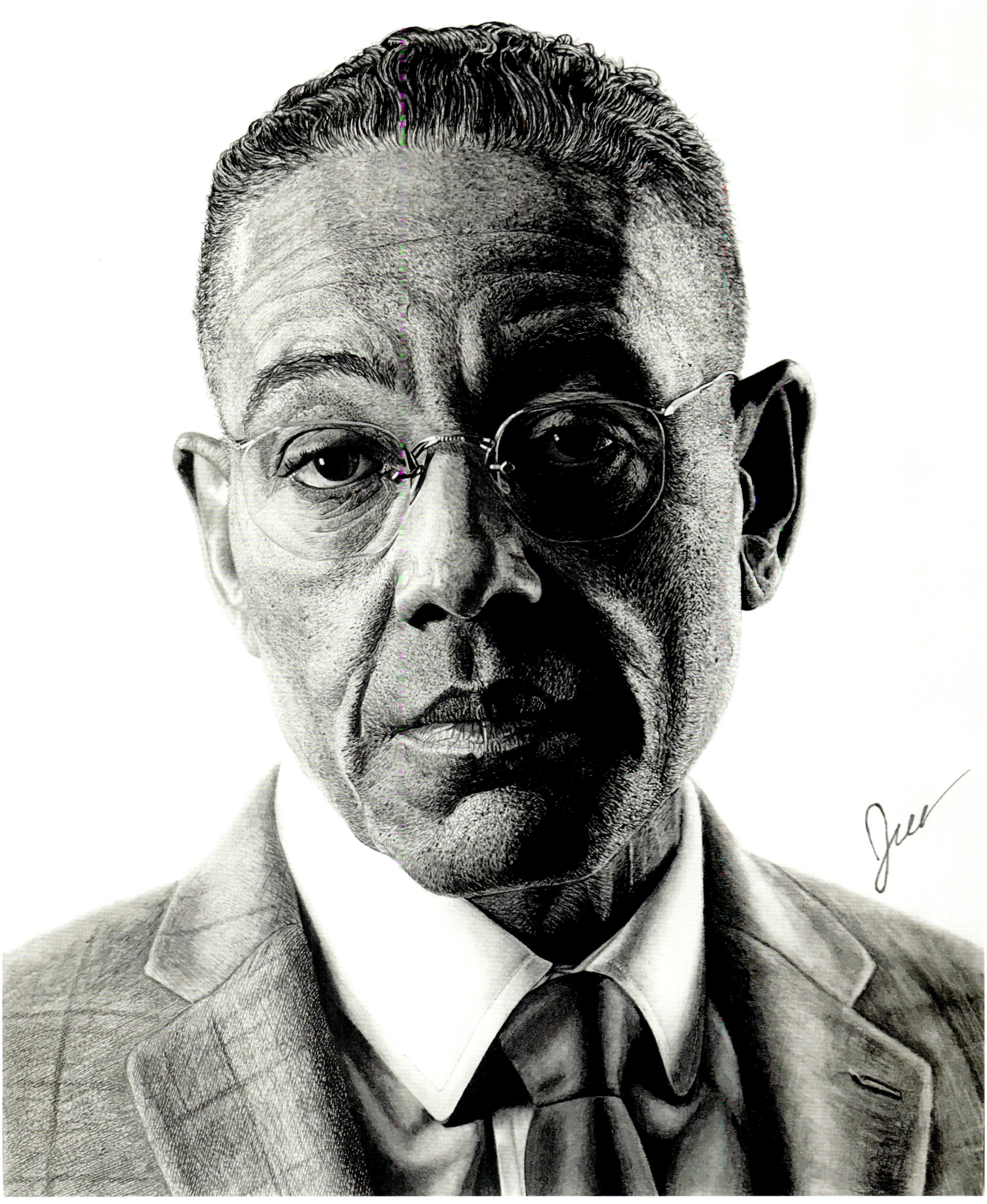

ABOVE and OPPOSITE: Rich Pellegrino | *Breaking Gus* and *Heisenberg* | Acrylic on panel | Boston, Massachusetts, USA | 2014 | www.richpellegrino.com | rich_pellegrino_art

139

ABOVE: Racknar Teyssier | *Ding, Ding, Ding!* | Digital | Tijuana, Mexico | 2015 | 🅞 artbyrtm

OPPOSITE: Chad Manzo | *Scientific Meth Head* | Digital illustration (Adobe Illustrator) | Cebu City, Philippines | 2013 | www.chadmanzo.com | 🅞 chadmanzo

PLAYER 01 ♥♥♥   HI-SCORE 999999

1UP

OPPOSITE: Fan Chen | *Salamanca* | Digital painting | Shanghai, China | 2017 | Bē fanchen

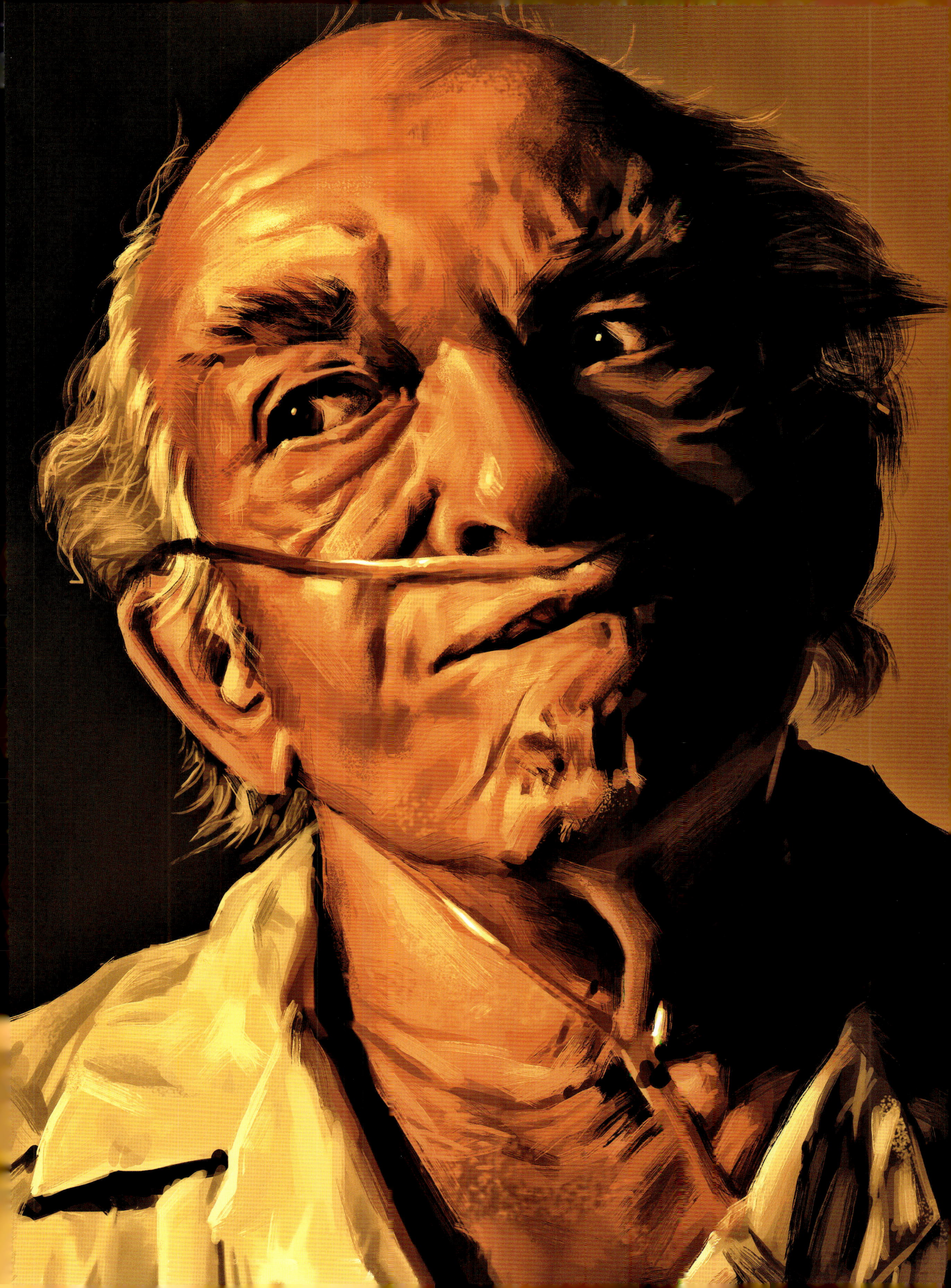

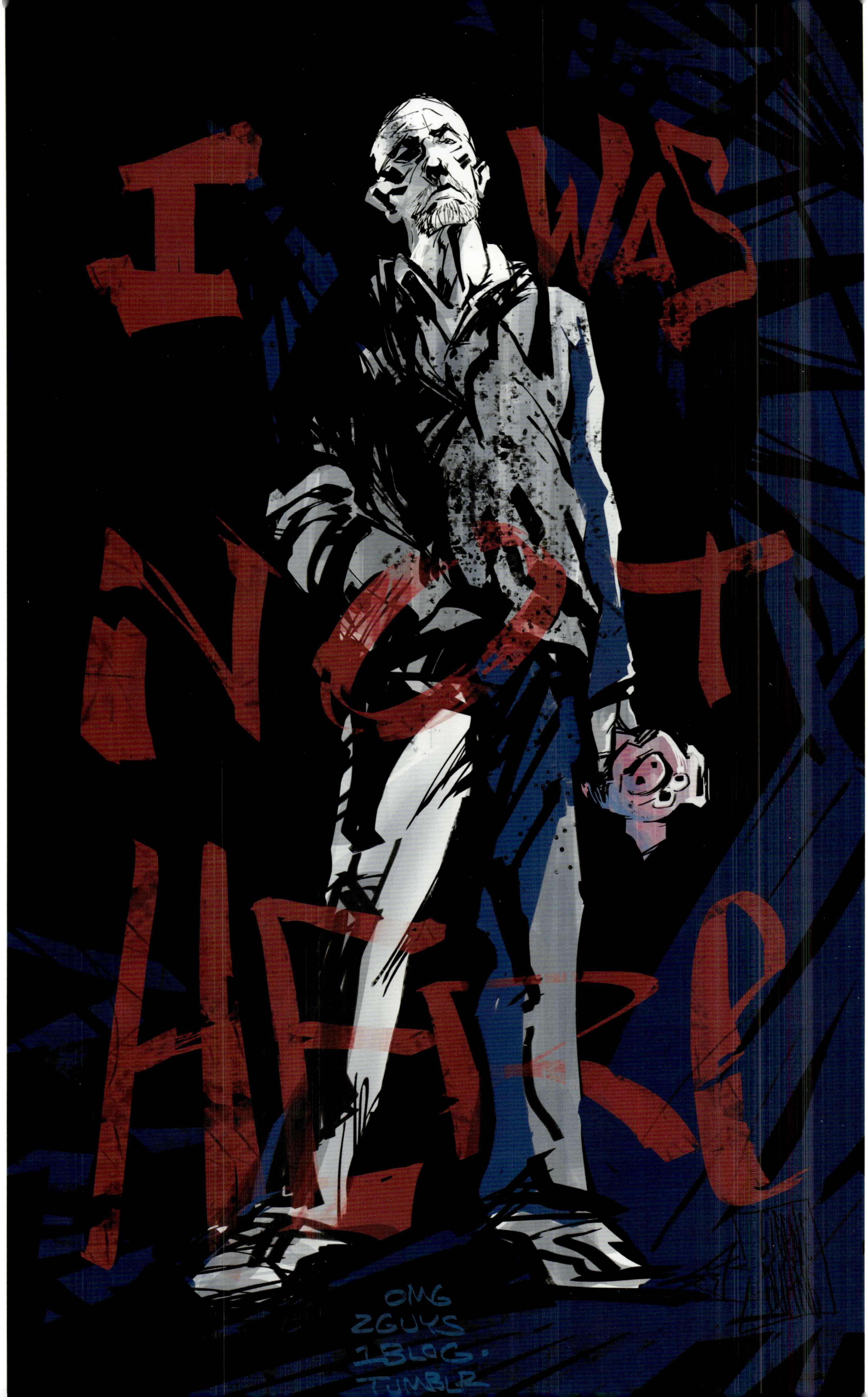
I WAS
NOT
HERE
OMG
2GUYS
1BLOG.
TUMBLR

OPPOSITE: Eugene Huang | *Ehrmantraut* | Digital painting | Los Angeles, California, USA | 2013 | www.thedukeoflies.com | ⓘ the_duke_of_flies
ABOVE: Kate Walsh | *"You're Never Too Old for Balloons"* | Digital illustration | Brighton, Massachusetts, USA | 2012 | 🐦 katelwal

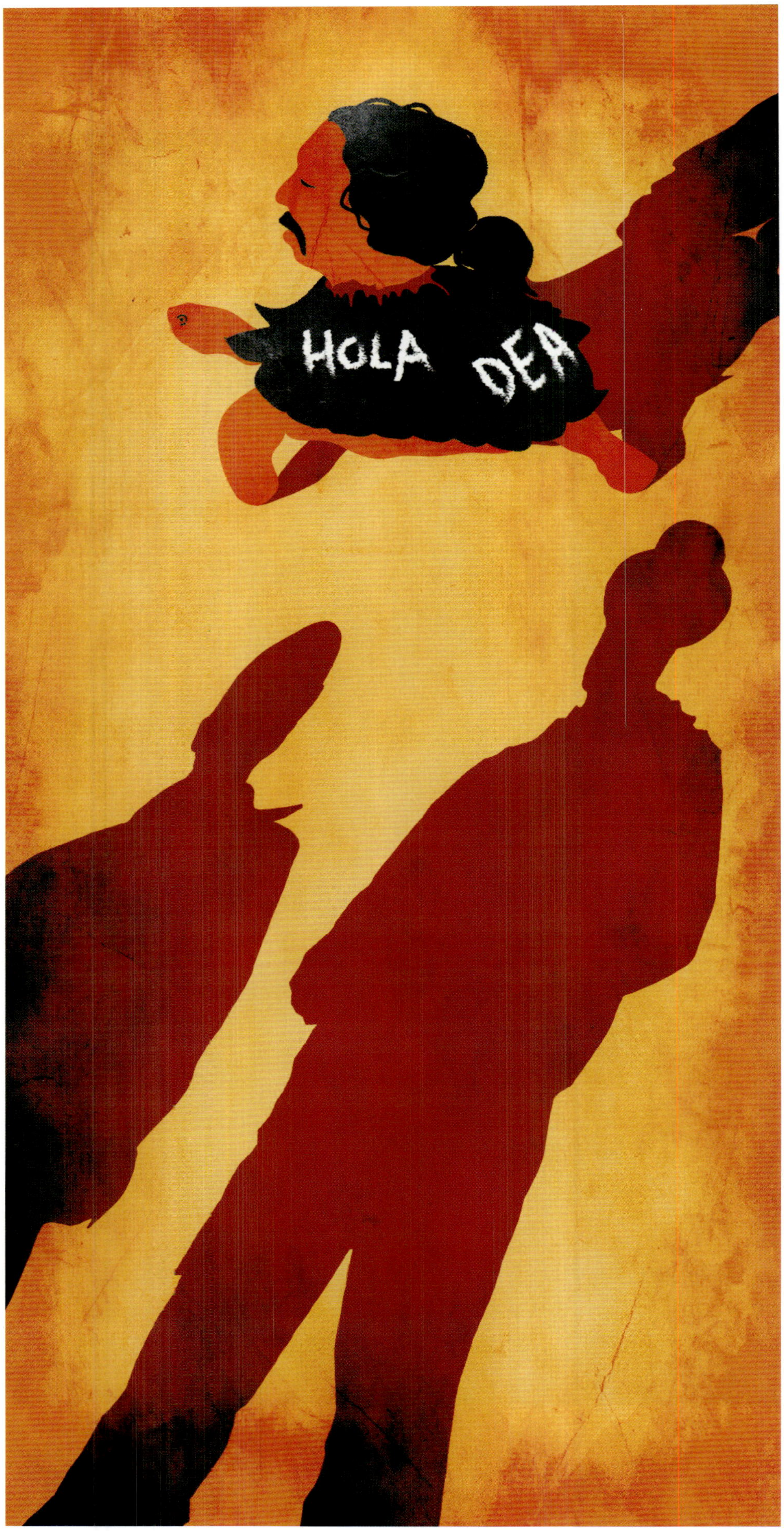
HOLA DEA

OPPOSITE: Marcos Arévalo | *Hola DEA* | Digital art | Madrid, Spain | 2017 | www.marcosarevalo.com

ABOVE: Studio Switchum | *Tortuga* | Acrylic paint on resin cast, 1/6 scale | Wichita, Kansas, USA | 2013–2015

ABOVE and OPPOSITE (Clockwise from top): Mike Noren / Gummy Arts | *Hola DEA, Gustavo Fring Baseball Card, Walter White Baseball Card, Mike Ehrmantraut Baseball Card, Hector Salamanca Baseball Card* | Colored pencil on cardstock | Chicago, Illinois, USA | 2018–2020 | gummyarts

LOS POLLOS HERMANOS
PROPRIETOR
GUSTAVO FRING

Br Ba
ALL STAR ROOKIE
WALTER WHITE

HECTOR
SALAMANCA

MIKE
EHRMANTRAUT
Br Ba

150

OPPOSITE and ABOVE: Skullboy | *Ehrmantraut* and *Tortuga* | Acrylic paint and marker on repurposed skateboard | 2020

PAGES 152–153: Skullboy | *Crystal Ship* | Acrylic paint and marker on repurposed skateboard | Highland Park, New Jersey, USA | 2020 | 🌀 skullboybrand

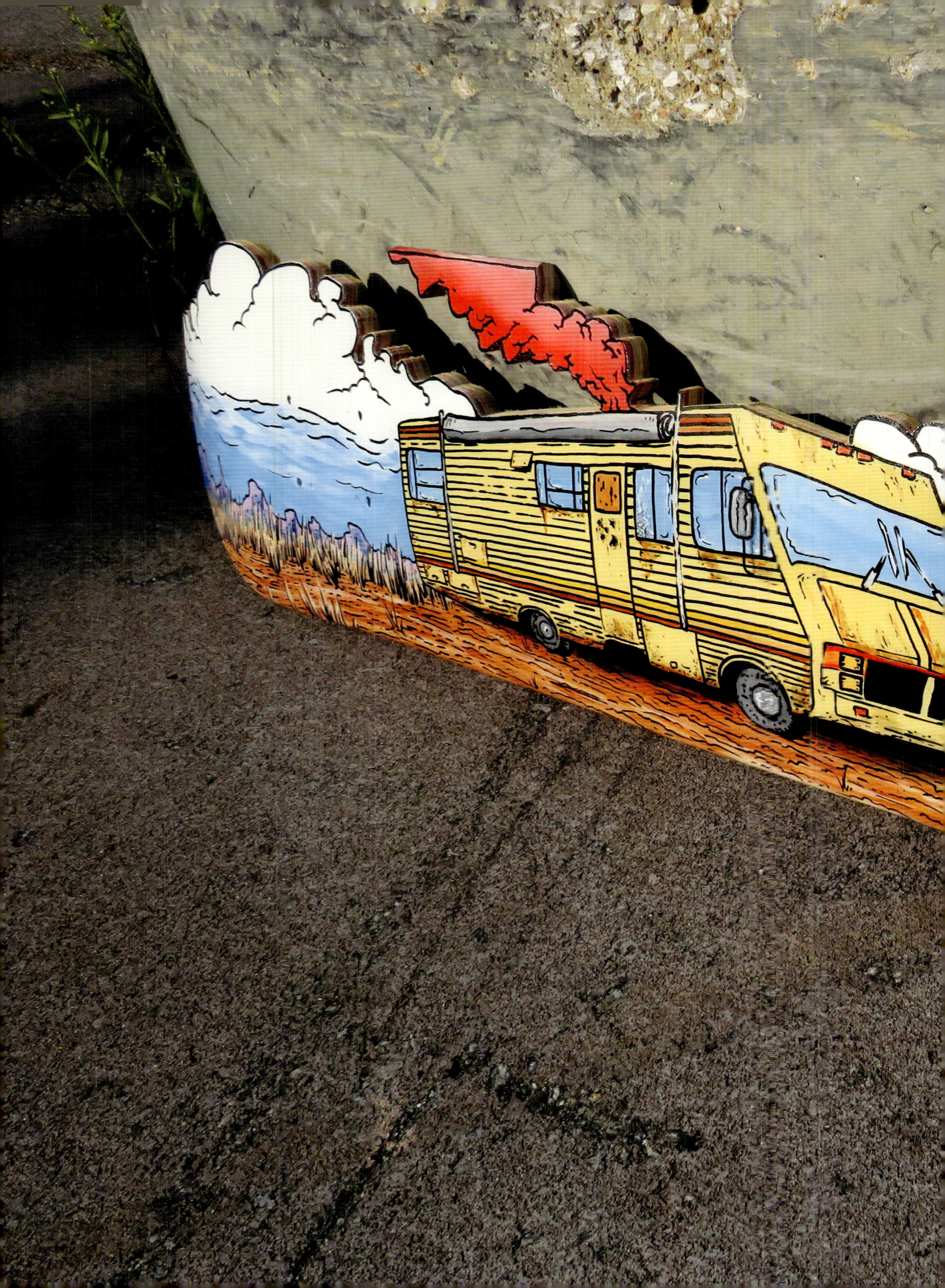

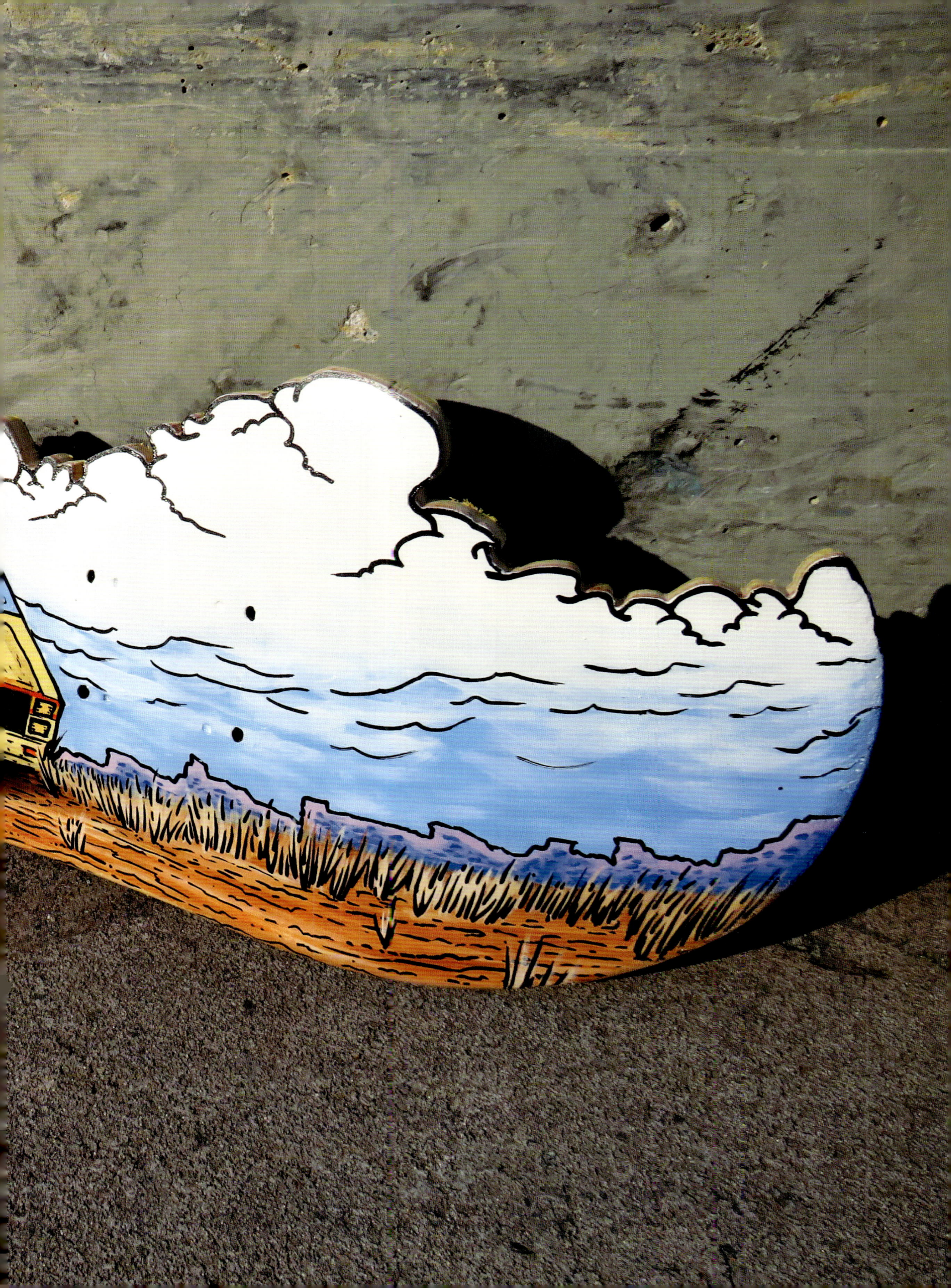

ABOVE: Bruno Mota | *Ding!* | Digital illustration | São Paulo, Brazil | 2016 | ⌾ obrunomota_

OPPOSITE: Anna Tillett | *Is Everything to Your Satisfaction?* | Acrylic on artist paper | Utah, USA | 2018 | www.annatillett.com | ⌾ annatinbot

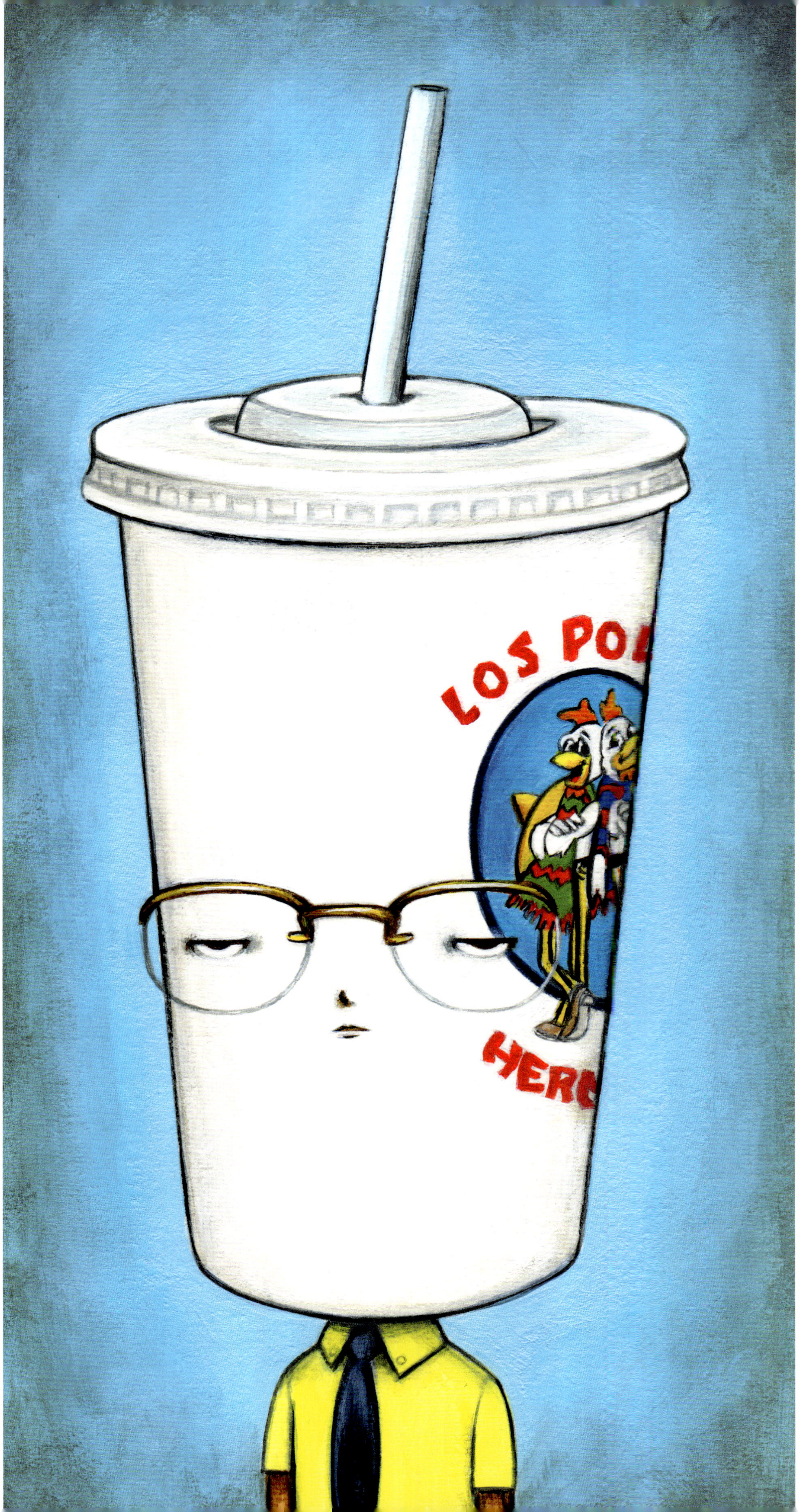
LOS POL
HERO

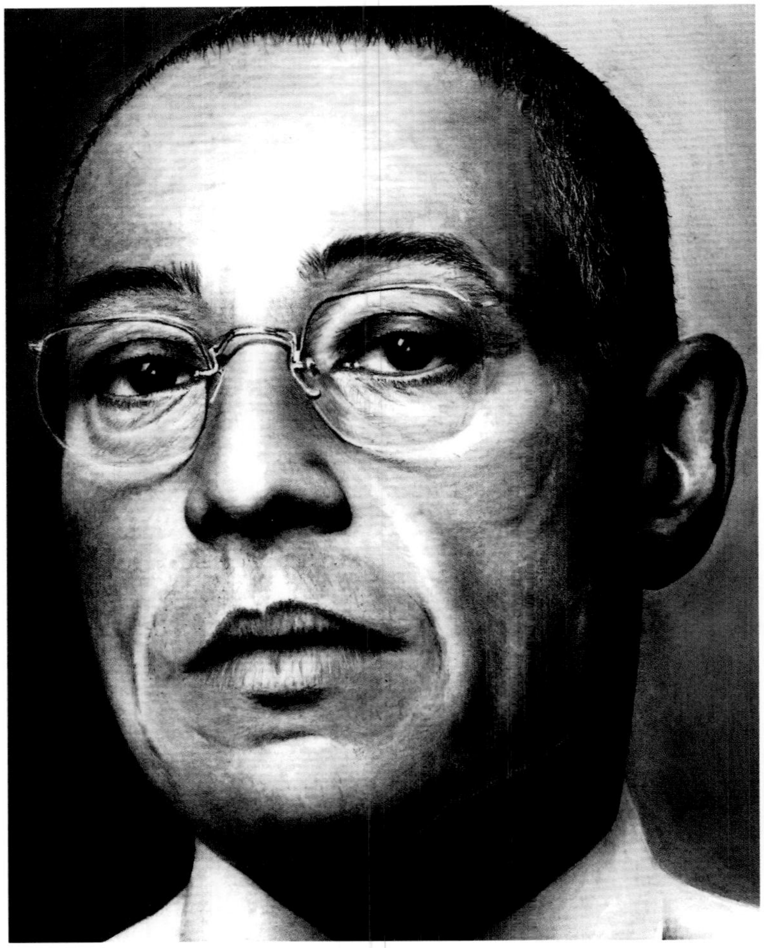

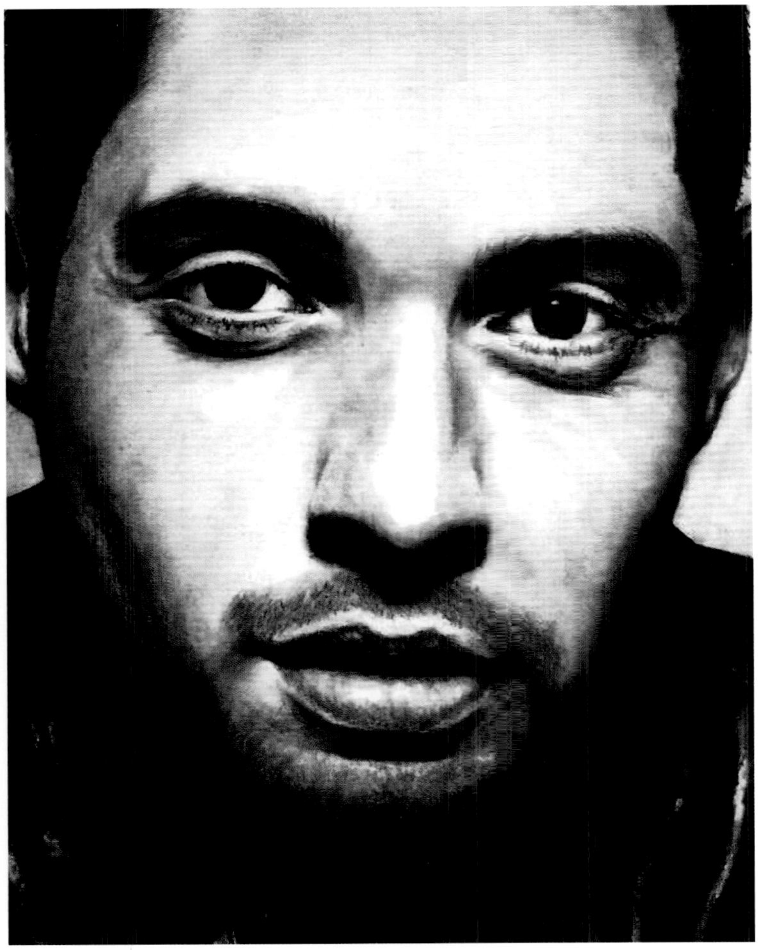

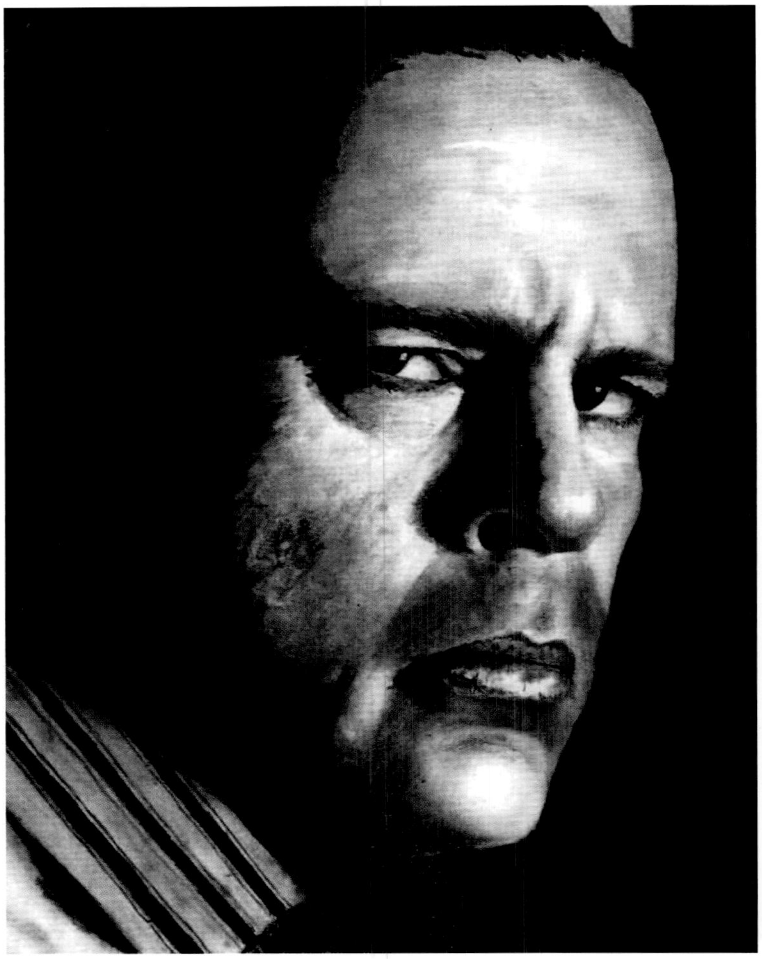

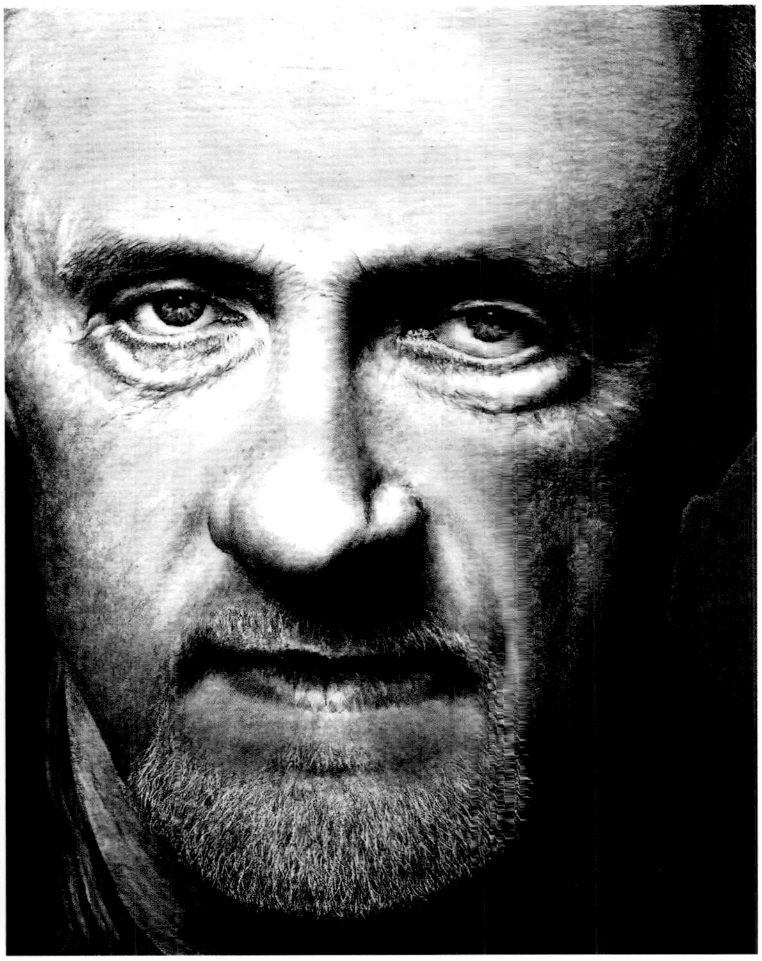

OPPOSITE (Clockwise from top left): Rick Fortson aka DrPencil | *Gus, Krazy-8, Mike,* and *Tuco* | Staedtler drawing pencils and Strathmore Bristol Smooth drawing stock
Chicago, Illinois, USA | 2010–2014 | www.DrPencil.com

OPPOSITE: Marc Valls Pla | *GUS* | Digital painting | Barcelona, Spain | 2013 | marc_valls_ | marcvallsanimation

PAGE 160: Rocco Tartamella, with paint and hair applied by Nathan Eckins | *Hector 2.0* | Wax/clay | 2013

PAGE 161 (Left to right, top to bottom): Rocco Tartamella | *Gus, Gus Face Off, Walter Beard, Saul, Hank, Tuco, Jesse, Mike,* and *Walter* | Wax/clay | Windermere, Florida, USA 2013 | www.roccotartamella.com

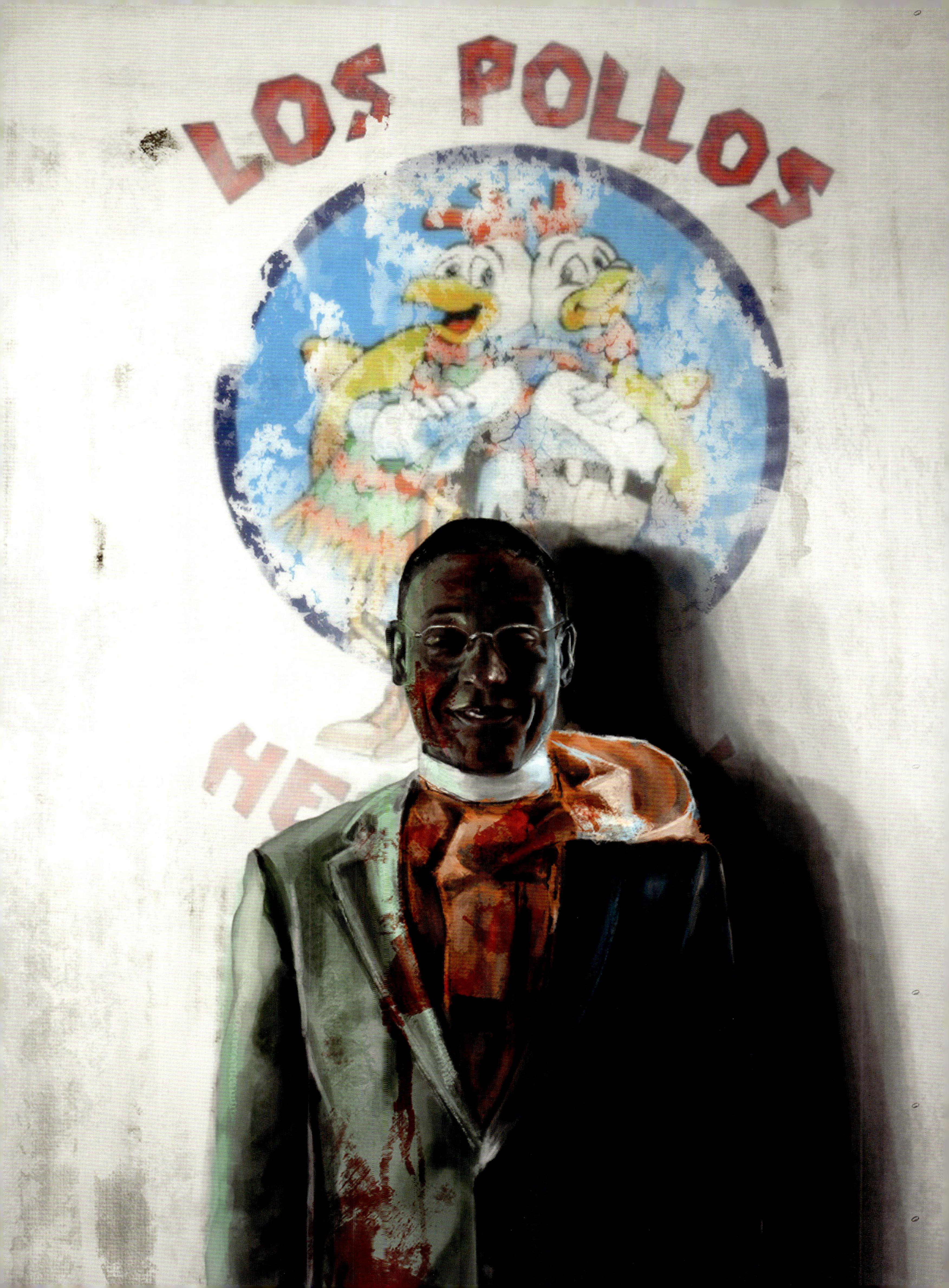
LOS POLLOS

160

161

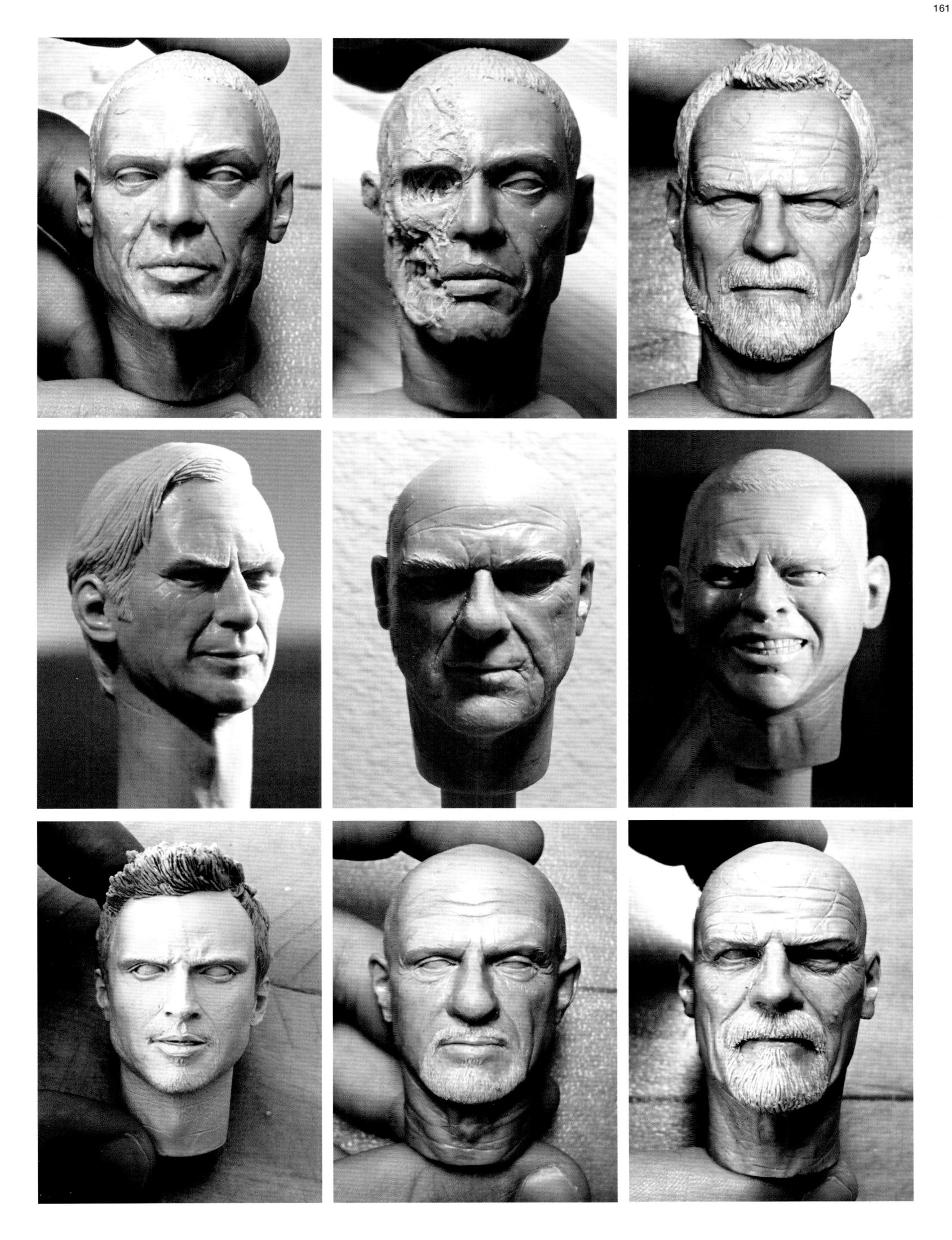

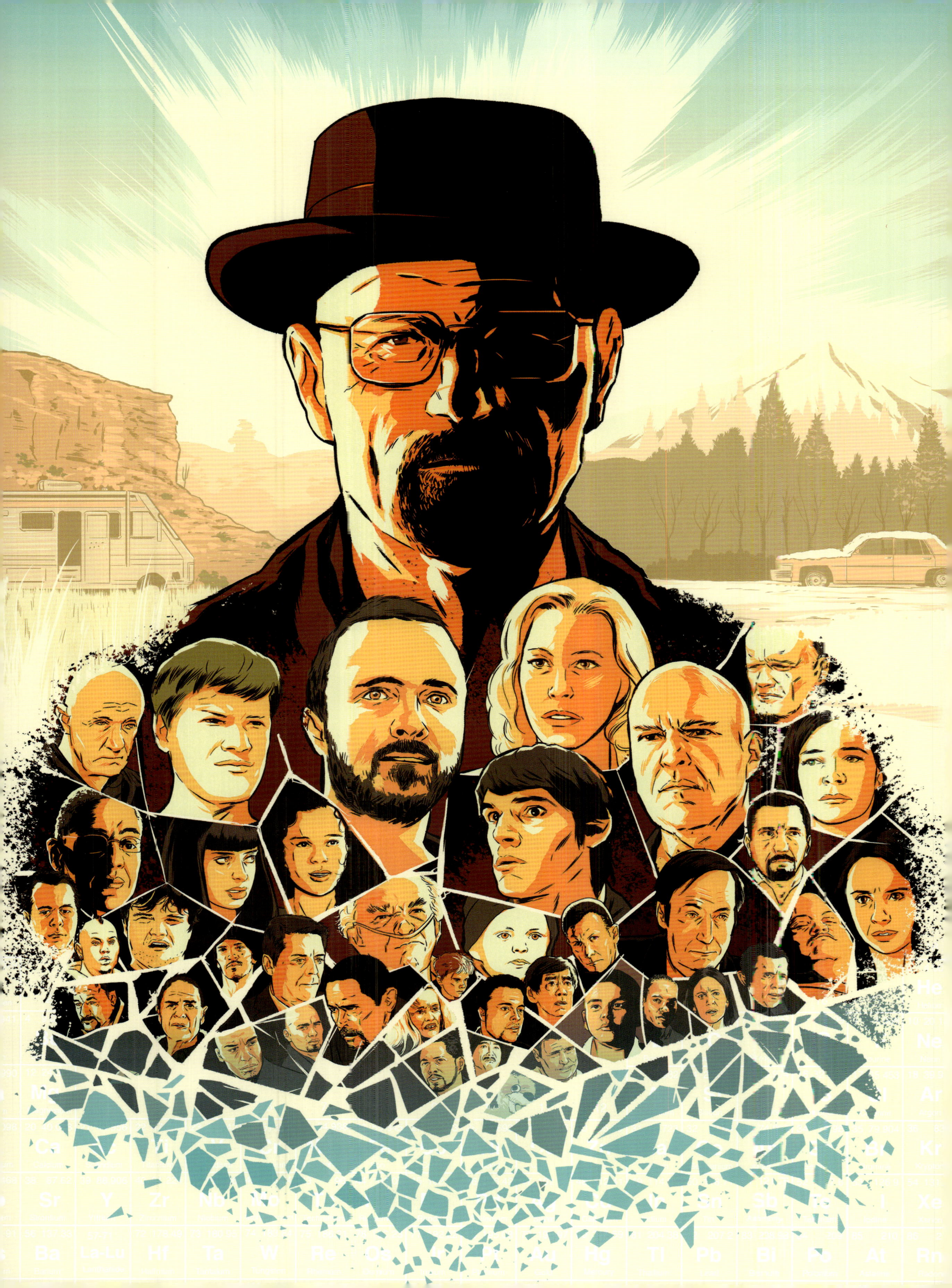

chapter 5
Land **O**f en**C**hantment

"Yo, yo, yo, 148, 3 to the 3 to the 6 to the 9, representin' the ABQ!" Jesse's answering machine greeting projected far past Albuquerque city lines, as *Breaking Bad* introduced audiences from around the world to the vibrant city Walt and Jesse called home and further deepened viewers' appreciation for the natural beauty of the Southwest. Indeed, sprawling desert vistas are among the distinct visuals—including a lone RV in the arid scrub, a dull green Pontiac Aztek, a one-eyed pink teddy bear, and a tray of shattered blue crystals—that have become virtually synonymous with the show.

THE ABQ AND BEYOND

***Breaking Bad* is inextricably linked to Albuquerque, the epicenter of the series and home to the majority of its characters.** London-based artist Phil Mamuyac commemorated the local ensemble in his *Nesting Bad* Matryoshka doll collection, consisting of fifteen customized nesting dolls ranging from Albuquerque's best-dressed criminal attorney, Saul Goodman, to Walt's former lab assistant and University of New Mexico graduate, Gale Boetticher. Mamuyac notes: "I was limited to a certain number of dolls, but this could've easily been a fifty-plus-character set." Casting director Sharon Bialy, who alongside partner Sherry Thomas was responsible for assembling the show's roster, explains that in selecting the supporting cast, the creative team prioritized "actors with great range [who were] not well known from previous work, so the audience would dive right into their world in Albuquerque."

Beyond its compelling cast, *Breaking Bad* has enthralled audiences with the singular desertscapes of New Mexico, otherwise known as the Land of Enchantment. "There is something immediately beautiful about the Southwestern landscapes depicted in the show, but their vastness and relative emptiness can't help but make you feel small and lonesome as well," ponders Boston-raised artist Scott Listfield. His oil-on-canvas painting *To'hajiilee* portrays an astronaut lost in the Navajo community of the same name, surveying a carefully arranged stack of vehicles from the show's canon.

French illustrator Aymeric Thevenot recalls: "When I first saw *Breaking Bad*, I was astonished by the atmosphere in the desert scenes." His piece *Dea.* re-creates the breathtaking high-plains backdrop where Walt, in the Season 3 finale, "Full Measure," meets with Gus Fring and Mike Ehrmantraut to negotiate his fate after killing two of Gus's men.

OPPOSITE: Guy Shield | *Breaking Bad* | Digital drawing | Melbourne, Australia | 2014 | www.guyshield.com | @ guyshield

Director of photography Michael Slovis, who also directed four episodes of the series, embraced the challenge of shooting in parched scrubland under an unrelenting sun: "I didn't fight it. I made it my friend. Ninety percent of the time, I had the actors backlit by the sun—which, to me, was beautiful." When capturing this exterior footage, he aimed "to convey the palette and grandeur that is New Mexico."

"As a Norwegian used to snow and mountains, the desert is foreign, strange, and exotic to me," says graphic designer Alvilde Gether, whose digital illustration *Fleetwood Bounder* shows Walt and Jesse's RV parked in the middle of an expansive wasteland. French artist Greg Fleurdépine is likewise intrigued. His piece *Desert Kitchen* captures the bleak wilderness where Walt and Jesse find themselves stranded after their RV battery dies in the Season 2 episode "4 Days Out." "Even though it's full of life, this desert is a dark, suffocating place," Fleurdépine muses. *Breaking Bad* executive producer Michelle MacLaren, the director of "4 Days Out" and many other episodes, "loved shooting New Mexico for New Mexico." "The gorgeous blue skies—filled with white fluffy clouds floating above the beautiful, endless, unforgiving desert with its stunning light" made for "a spectacular place to film," she reminisces.

ICONOGRAPHY

The Southwestern landscape is just one of the many powerful visuals that viewers associate with *Breaking Bad*. Arguably no desert shot is complete without at least a glimpse of Walt and Jesse's trusty Fleetwood Bounder. "The RV is for me a very significant symbol for the show—the small space known to most people as a mobile vehicle turned into something very different: the 'Krystal Ship,'" comments artist Alvilde Gether, referencing the nickname Jesse bestowed upon his meth lab on wheels.

Artist Scott Listfield's aforementioned piece *To'hajiilee* situates the RV under Walt's milquetoast Pontiac Aztek, which Listfield considers perfect for the character: "It epitomizes a sort of hopeless and generic blandness . . . It's impossible to look at a car like the Aztek and not yearn for an upgrade of some kind." *Breaking Bad* transportation captain Dennis Milliken adds that it's the "perfect vehicle for the way Vince wanted to show the fans how sad Walt's life was as the series began." In his piece *Blue Sky*, drawn in the throwback style of cartoons from the 1960s, Italian illustrator Ale Giorgini depicts the Pontiac Aztek with a newly replaced windshield. He surmises that Walt was constantly repairing the Aztek "in a very protective way, as he wanted to keep some link with his normal life."

The ragged pink teddy bear seen floating in Walt's pool is another icon: a stark reminder of the far-reaching consequences of Walt's failure to save Jesse's girlfriend Jane

Margolis from her heroin overdose in the Season 2 episode "Phoenix." Had Walt saved Jane, her father would not have been distracted at his job as an air traffic controller, thereby preventing the fatal Wayfarer 515 plane crash. In his watercolor piece *BKB BEAR*, Sicily-based tattoo artist Andrea Kroki suspends the one-eyed bear's head in a ring of black, pink, and blue paint splatter, representing the moment the stuffed animal landed in Walt's pool after the plane crash. Arkansas-based illustrator Timothy Lim reimagined the bear in the style of album cover art for "Fallacies," the single from Jesse's band, TwaüghtHammër, that premiered in a webisode to promote *Breaking Bad*'s second season. Lim views the damaged artifact as "a constant reminder of the piling guilt and consequences that Walter must contend with throughout the later part of the series."

Rather than limiting themselves to one iconic artifact from the series, UK-based Jordan Bolton and North Carolina–based Matt Stevens created compilation pieces entitled *Objects of Breaking Bad* and *Junk Drawer: White's Space*, respectively, with representations of Walt's journey through the series—for example, the box cutter with which Gus slashed Victor's throat, a vial of homemade ricin poison, and a pair of wire-rimmed glasses. In his piece *All I See Is Blue*, French illustrator Patrick Zédouard assembles three pairs of Walt's glasses along with his lab respirator on a background reminiscent of a sheet of blue meth. "It's funny how people recognize what it's about without even reading the description," he says.

OPPOSITE: Ale Giorgini | *Blue Sky* | Digital illustration | Vicenza, Italy | 2014 | www.alegiorgini.com | ⓘ alegiorgini

PAGES 168–169 (Clockwise from top left): Ryan Patrick Rapp | *52, Pink Bear, Broken, Box Cutter, Fly* | Digital | Lake Charles, Louisiana, USA 2013
www.ryanpatrickrapp.com | ryanpatrickrappart

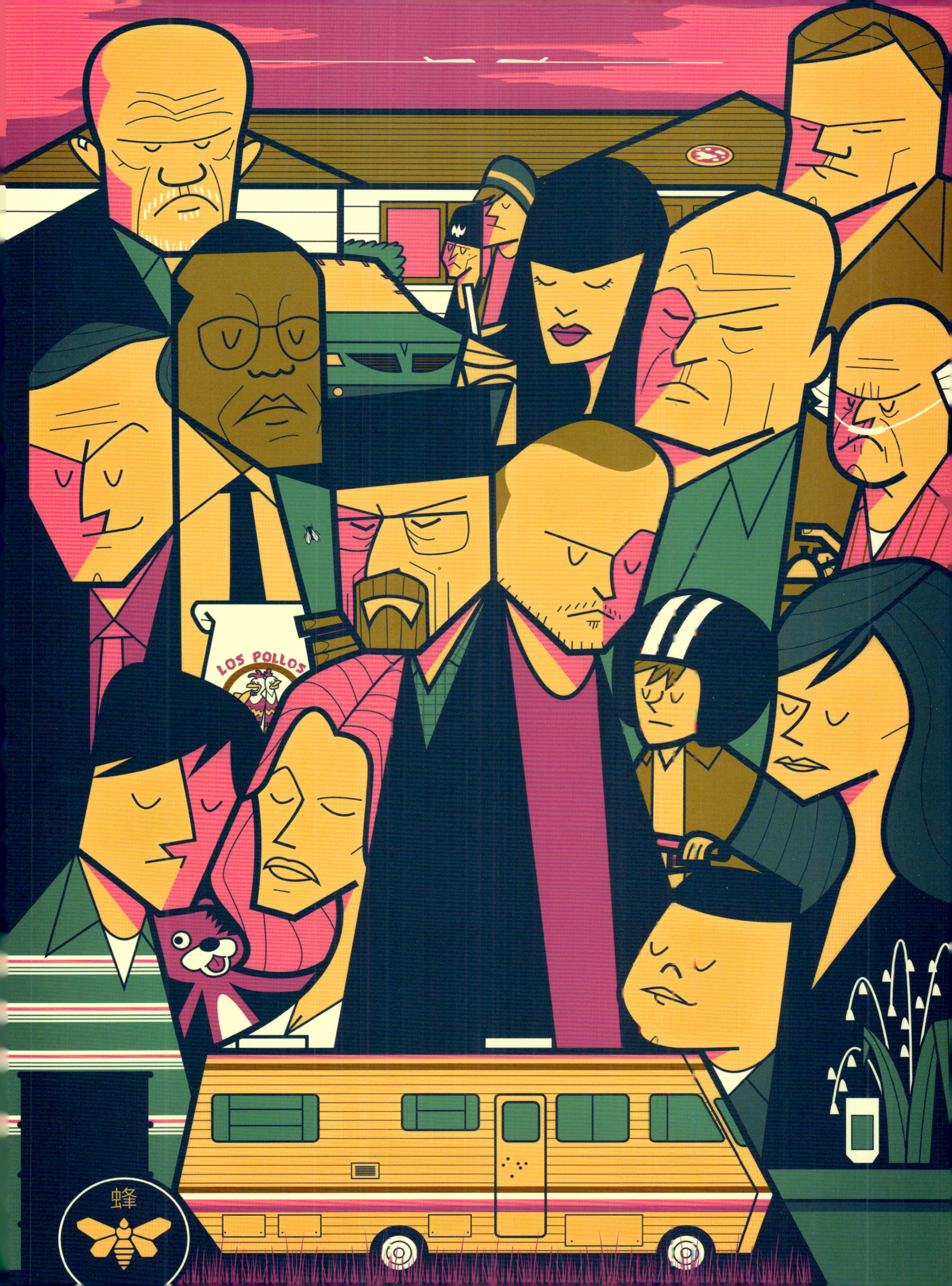
LOS POLLOS
蜂

168

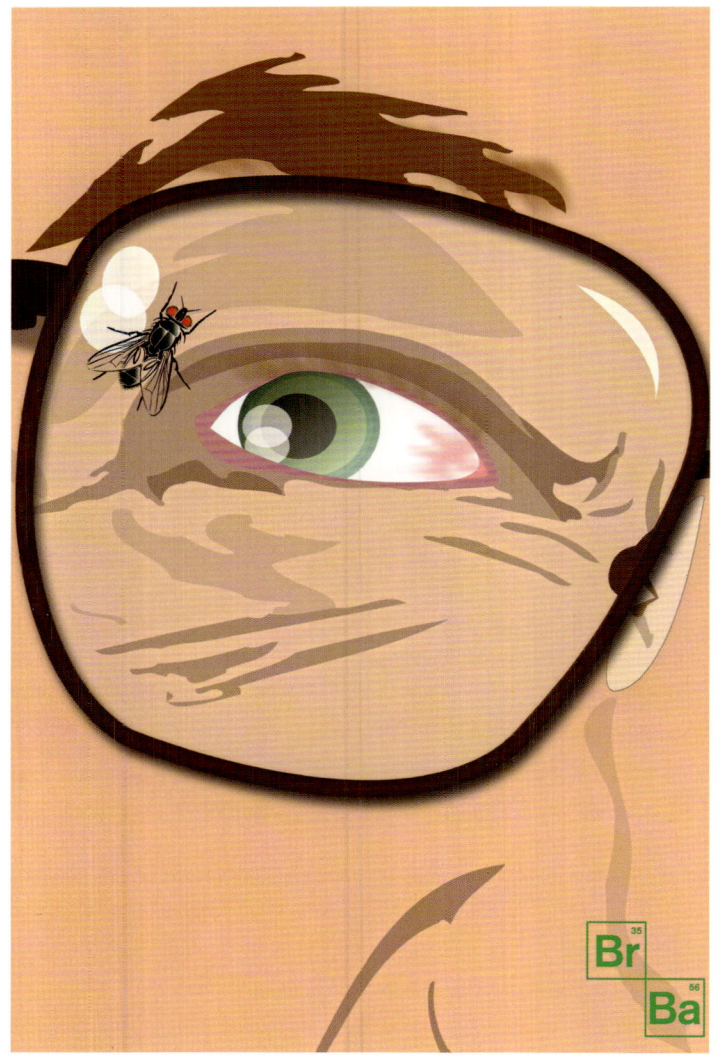

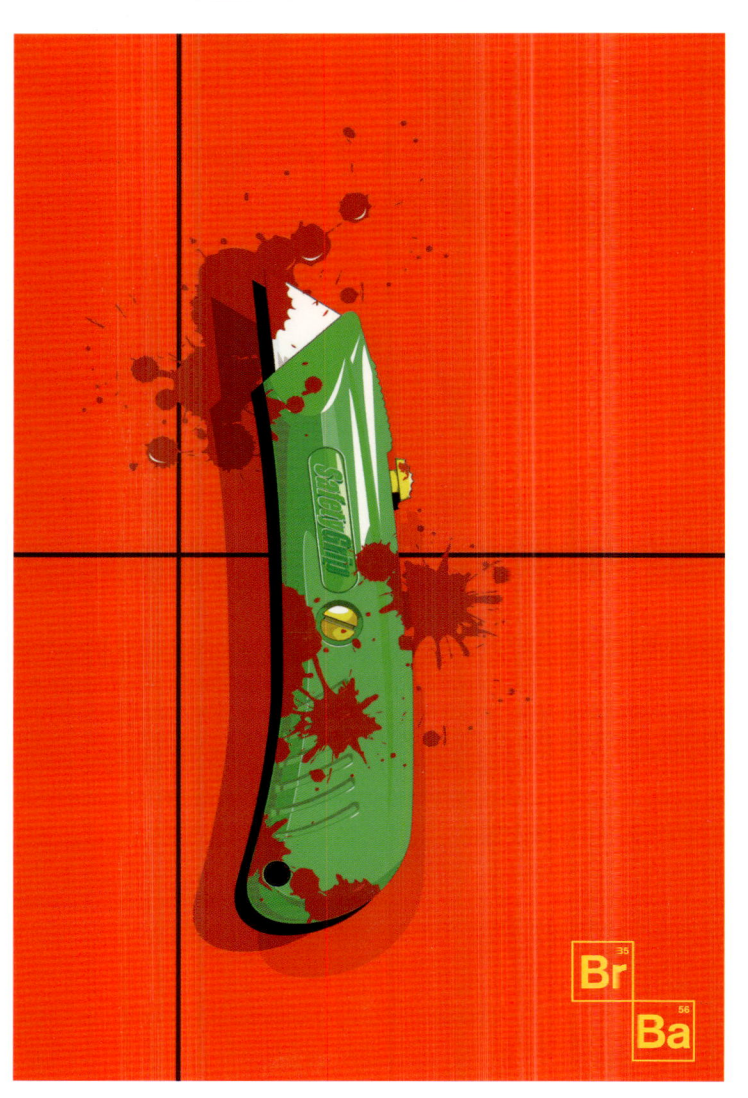

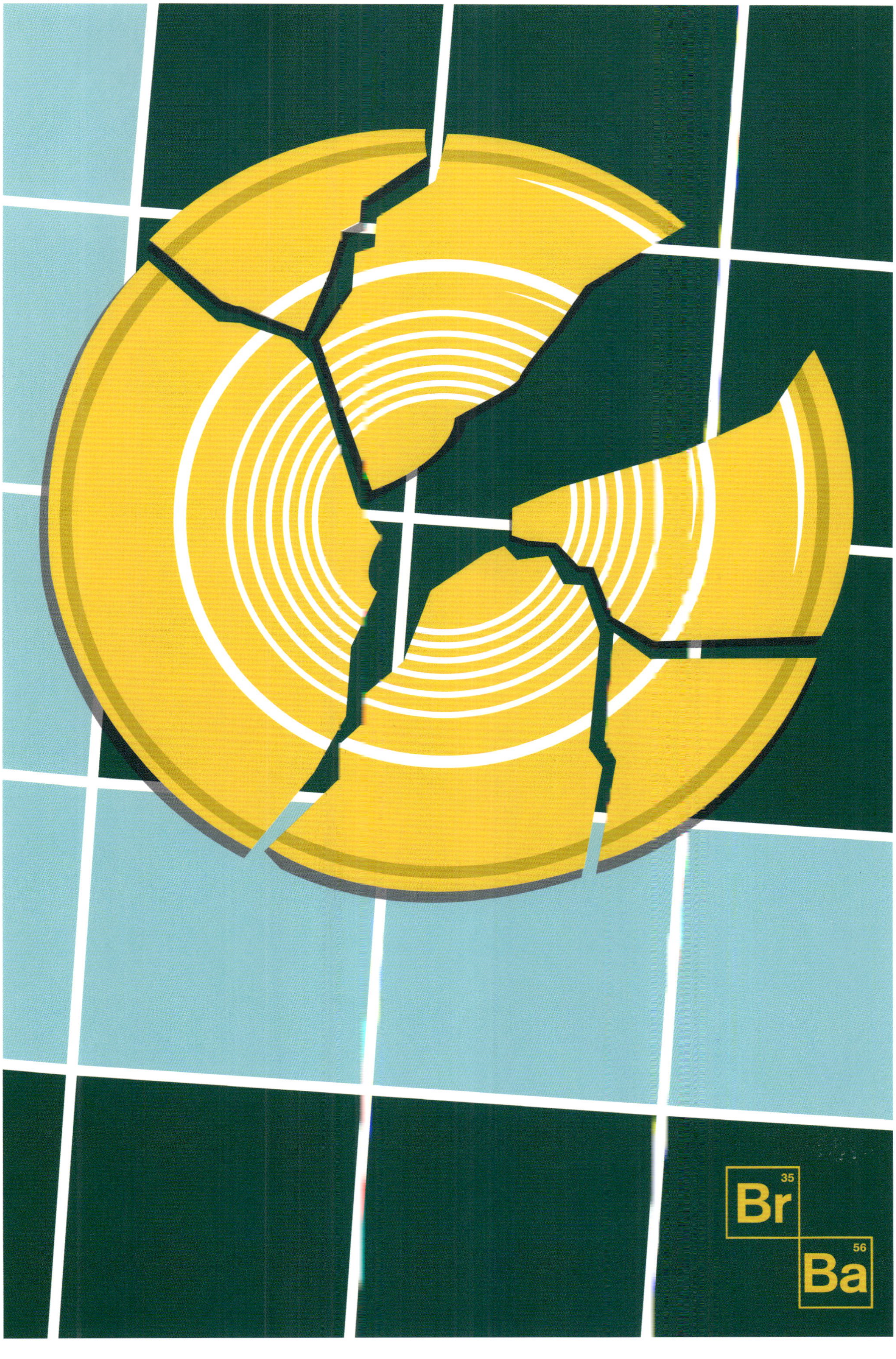
35
Br
56
Ba

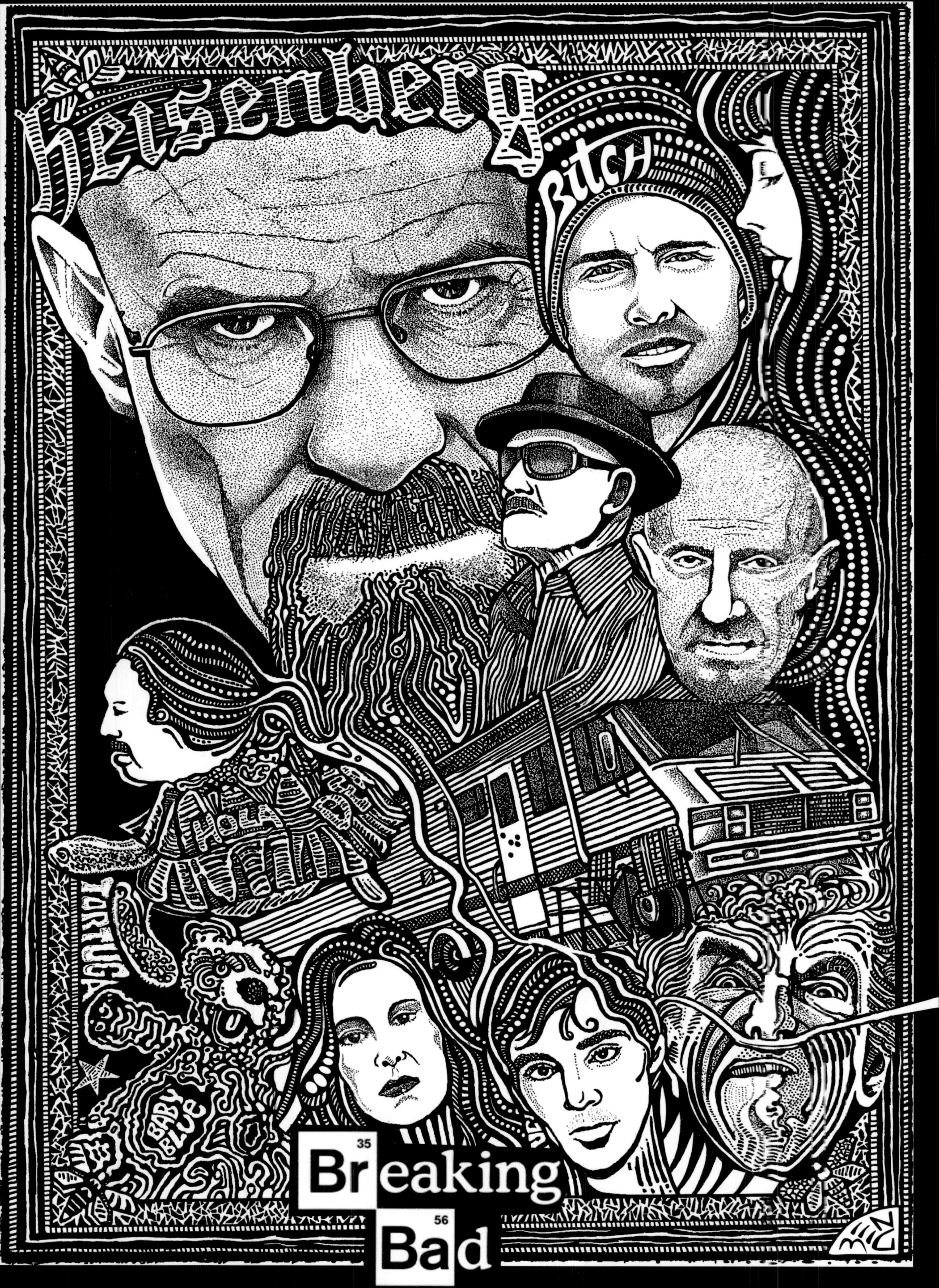
Heisenberg
Bitch
Tortuga
Baby Blue
35
Breaking
56
Bad

OPPOSITE: Ben Gormley | *Breaking Bad* | Pen and ink | Danbury, Connecticut, USA | 2014 | Posterography

BREAKING BAD CREATED BY VINCE GILLIGAN

BRYAN CRANSTON AARON PAUL ANNA GUNN RJ MITTE DEAN NORRIS BETSY BRANDT BOB ODENKIRK GIANCARLO ESPOSITO STEVEN MICHAEL QUEZADA KRYSTEN RITTER MATT JONES
CHARLES BAKER RODNEY RUSH JULIA MINESCI RAYMOND CRUZ MAX ARCINIEGA MARK MARGOLIS DANIEL & LUIS MONCADA CHRISTOPHER COUSINS STEVEN BAUER DAVID COSTABILE
IAN POSADA EMILY RIOS JONATHAN BANKS LAURA FRASER LAVELL CRAWFORD JESSE PLEMONS JESSICA HECHT ADAM GODLEY KEVIN RANKIN MICHAEL BOWEN ROBERT FORSTER

OPPOSITE: Claudia Vcrosio | *Breaking Bad – The Cast* | Digital illustration | London, UK | 2014 | Ⓑ clauciavarosio

ABOVE: Ali Hasen Didi (mrdr) | *Br35.Ba56* | Digital (Photoshop) | Malé, Republic of Maldives | 2013 | murdead | ⓘ kaanaabanana

OPPOSITE: Chris Morkaut | *Remember My Name* | Digital painting (Adobe Illustrator) | Queens, New York, USA | 2012

REMEMBER MY NAME

ABOVE: Aymeric Thevenot | *Deal* | Digital painting | Angoulême, France | 2016 | www.aymericthevenot.com
OPPOSITE: Derek Eads | *Heisenberg Headshot* | Digital drawing | Indiana, USA | 2015/2020 | derek_eads

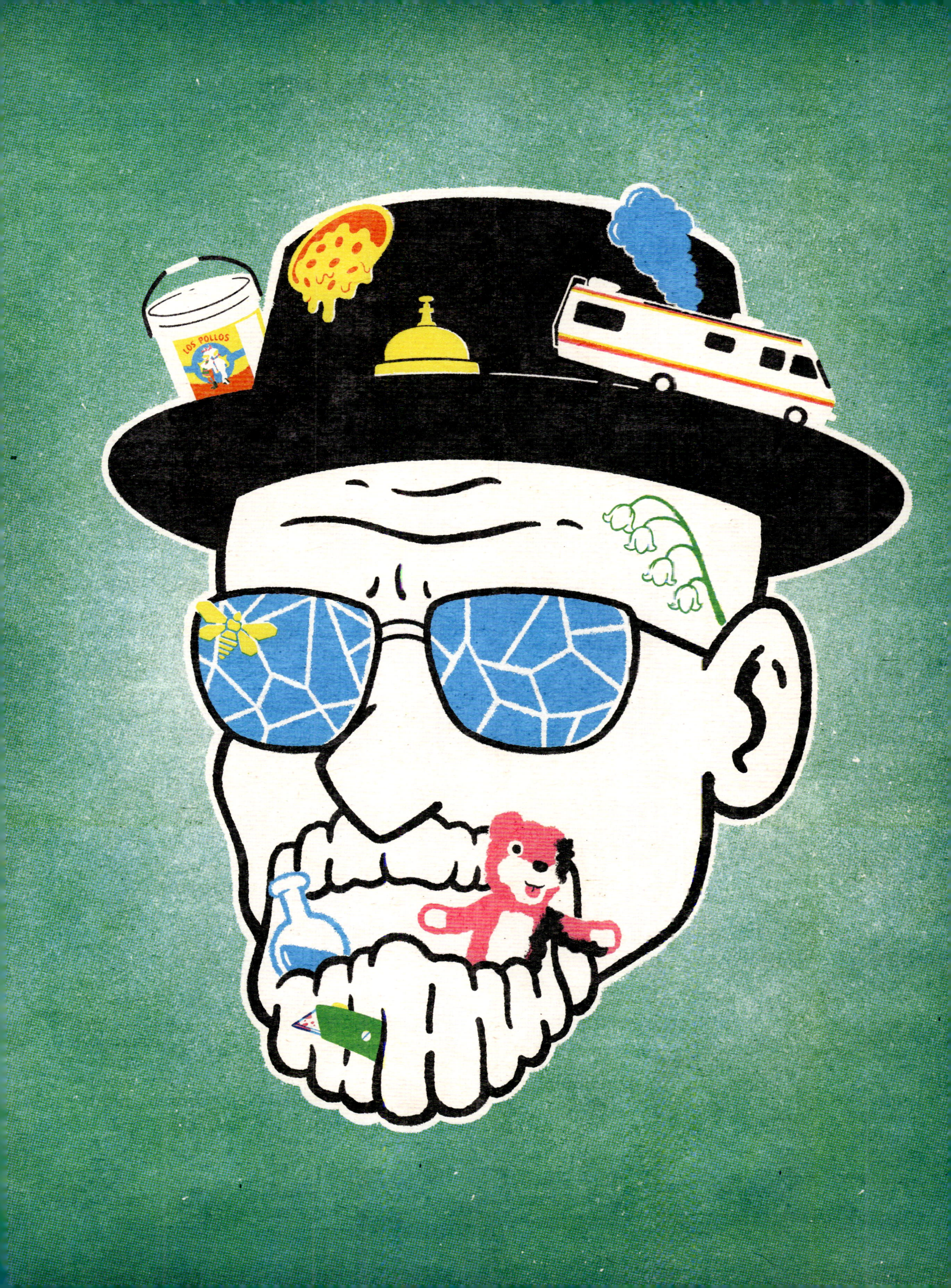
LOS POLLOS

ABOVE: Cyril Chambon | *Who's the Fly?!* | Ballpoint pen, watercolor, black felt-tip pen, white pen | Avignon, France | 2012 | @ moutch54

OPPOSITE: Brigid Fahy | *Crawlspace* | Watercolor | Belmar, New Jersey, USA | 2018 | @ b.a.fahy

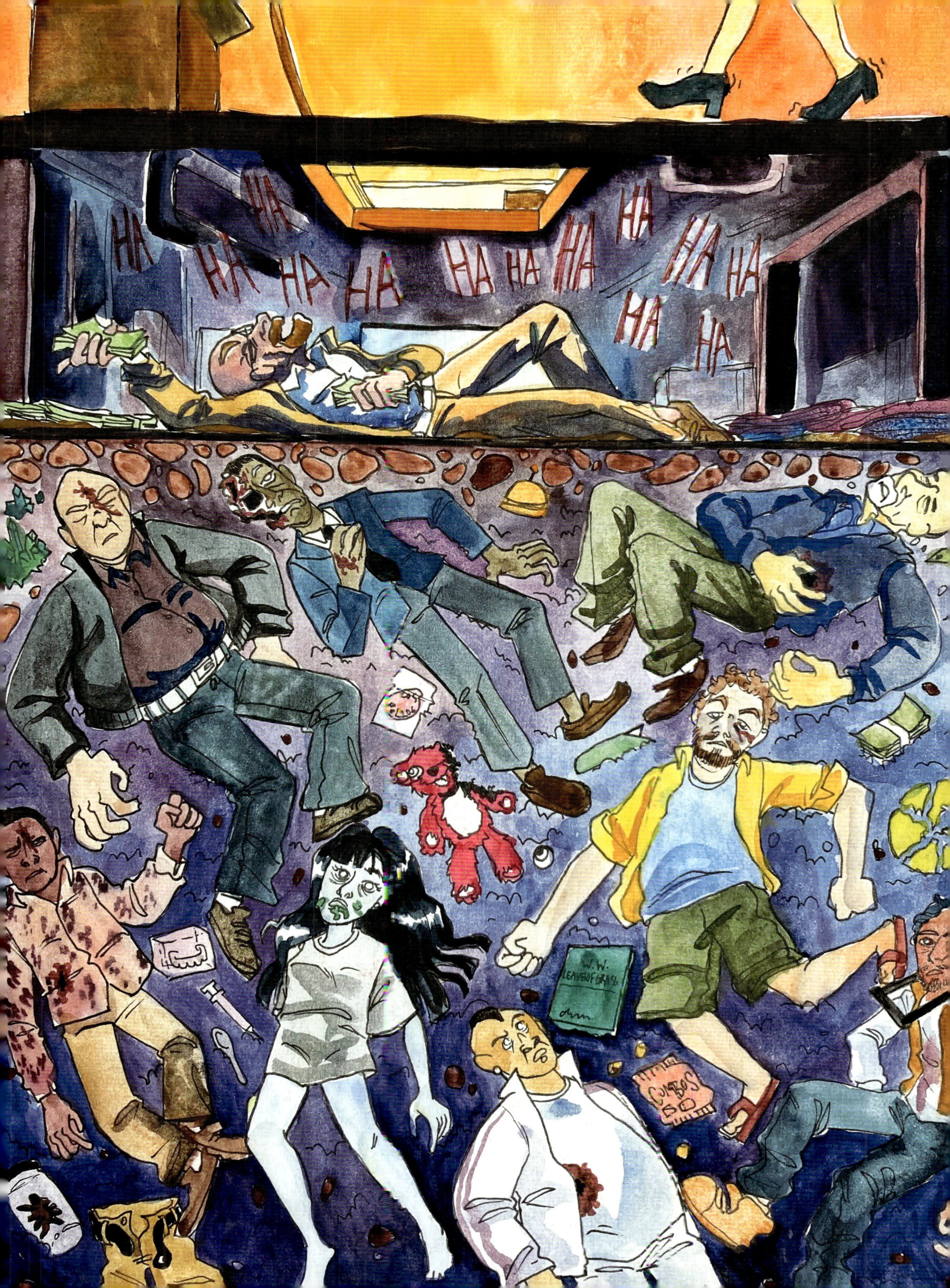
HA
HA
HA
HA
HA
HA
HA
HA
HA
HA
HA
HA
HA
W.W.
LEAVES OF GRASS
COMBOS

Jamie Sale | *Character Portraits* | Digital illustration | Braintree, UK | 2015 | toonjamstudios

Alvilde Gether | *Fleetwood Bounder* | Digital illustration | Bergen, Norway | 2014 | www.alvildegether.com

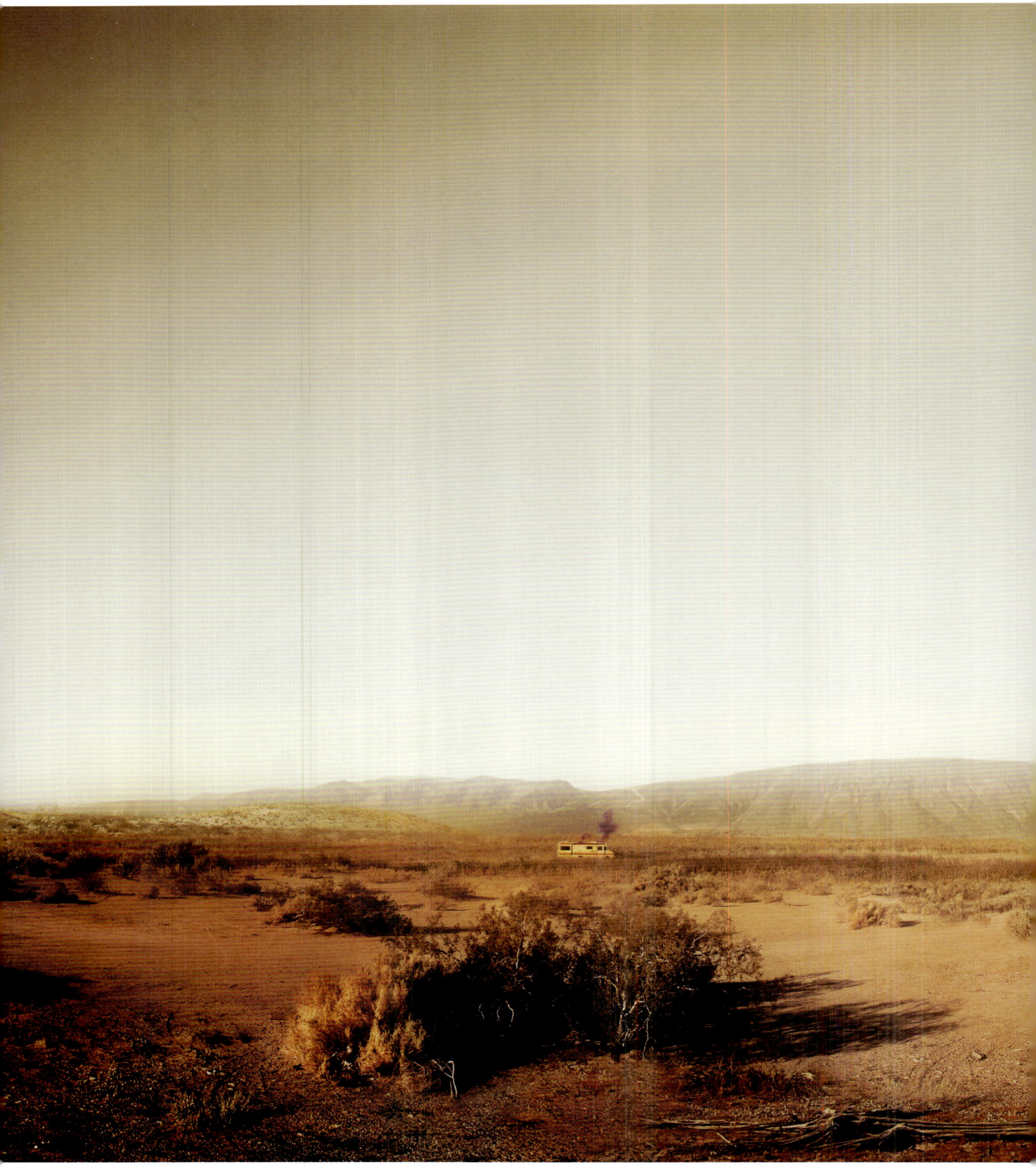

THESE PAGES: Greg Fleurdépire | *Desert Kitchen* | Digital matte painting | Lyon, France | 2015

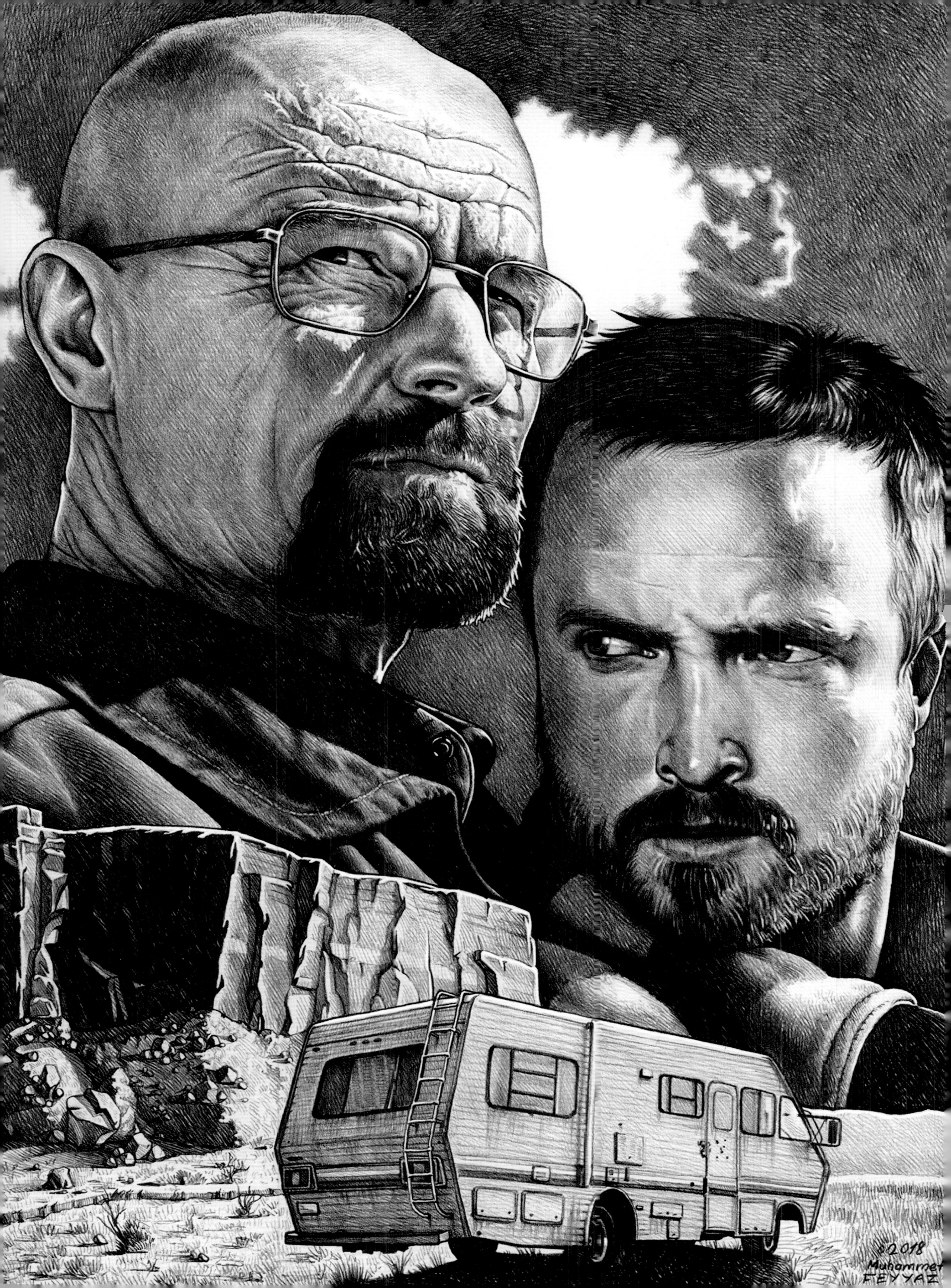
©2018
Muhammet
FEYYAZ

OPPOSITE: Muhammet Feyyaz | *Breaking Bad Poster Design* | Charcoal pencil on paper | Eskisehir, Turkey | 2018 | @ muhammetfeyyaz

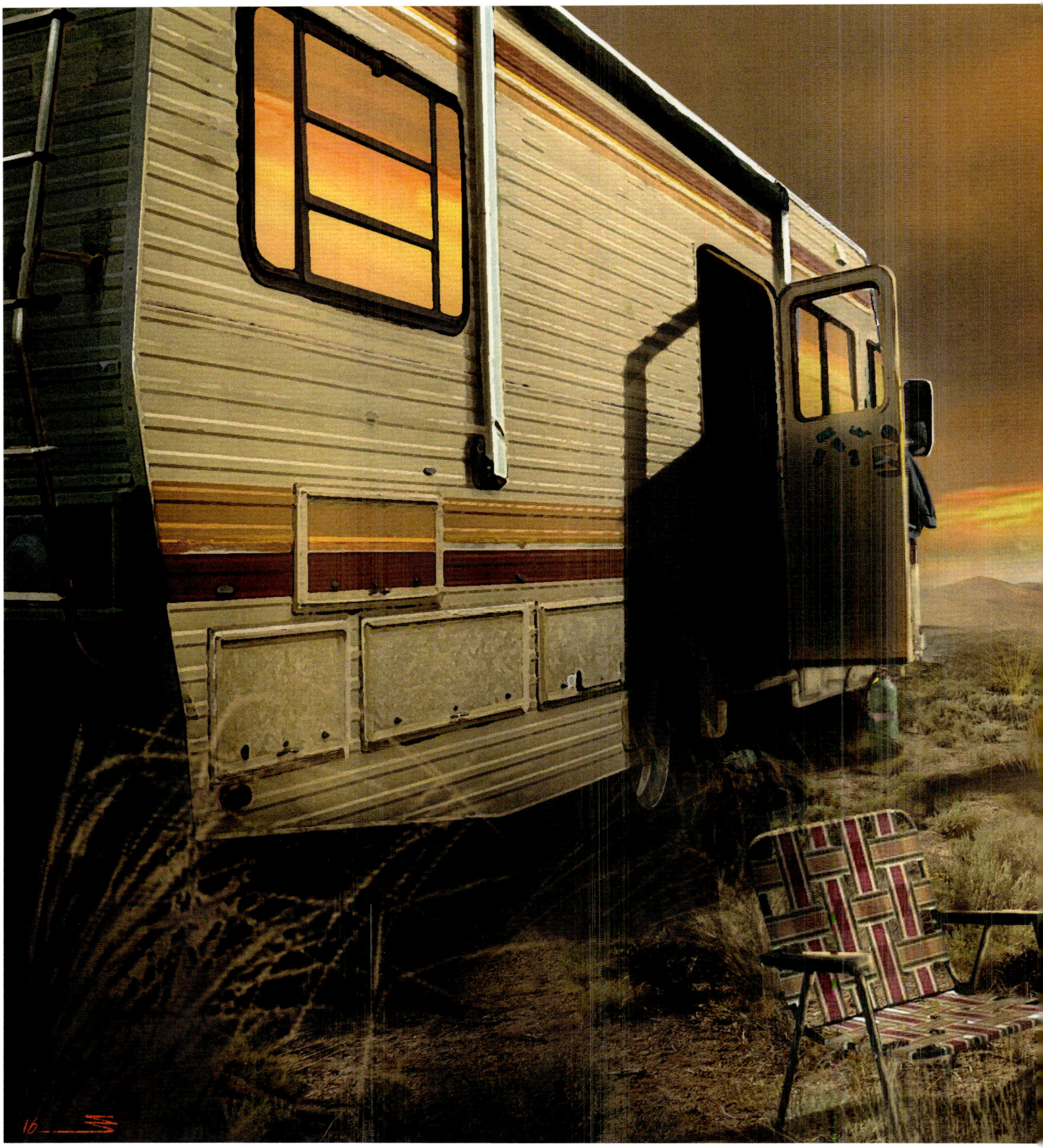

THESE PAGES: Omar Samy | *Breaking Bad Fanart* | Digital painting | Cairo, Egypt | 2016

AND THE
BAG'S
IN THE RIVER

CRAZY
HANDFUL
OF NOTHIN'

4 DAYS OUT

Caballo Sin Nombre

BOX CUTTER

38 SNUB

HAZARD
PAY

Dead
Freight

SEVEN
3
SEVEN

BIT
By a
DEADBEE

BETTER CALL
Saul

I F T

Sunset

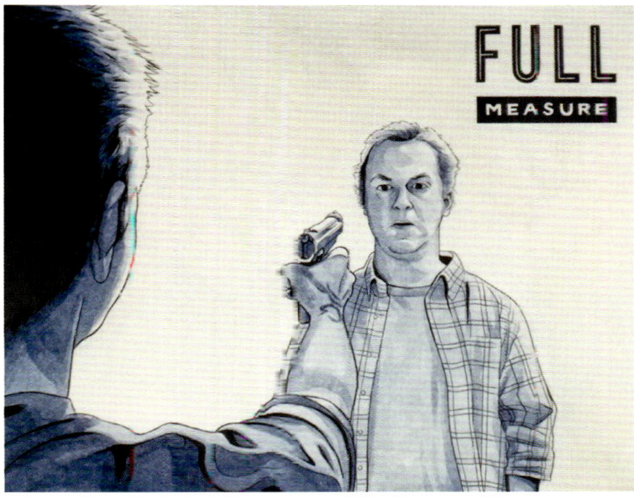
FULL
MEASURE

CRAWL
SPACE

Live Free
OR DIE

SAY MY NAME

RABID
DOG

PAGES 188–189 (Left to right, top to bottom): David Hildreth | *And the Bag's in the River, Crazy Handful of Nothin', 7 30 7, Bit by a Dead Bee, Better Call Saul, 4 Days Out, Caballo Sin Nombre, IFT, Sunset, Full Measure, Box Cutter, 38 Snub, Bug, Crawl Space, Live Free or Die, Hazard Pay, Dead Freight, Buyout, Say My Name, and Rabid Dog* | Ink and watercolor on Moleskine paper | Rochester, New York, USA | 2014–2015 | dhildreth36

OPPOSITE: Eliud Rivera Hernández | *Breaking Bad – Alternative Poster* | Digital painting, vector art | Santo Domingo, Dominican Republic | 2014 | eliud_rh

Breaking
Bad
HEISENBERG
HEISENBERG
LOS POLLOS
LILY OF THE VALLEY
CADENA ORIGINAL AMC AND SONY PICTURES TELEVISION
AND GRAND VIA PRODUCTIONS PRODUCTION A VINCE GILLIGAN
BRYAN CRANSTON AARON PAUL ANNA GUNN RJ MITTE
MICHAEL SLOVIS BETSY BRANDT
JONATHAN BANKS
Poster design by

A1A CAR WASH
CAR WASH
YOU'VE TRIED THE REST
NOW TRY THE BEST
Better call Saul!!
HEISENBERG

THESE PAGES: Antoine Corbineau | *Breaking Bad District* | Digital painting | Nantes, France | 2018 | www.antoinecorbineau.com

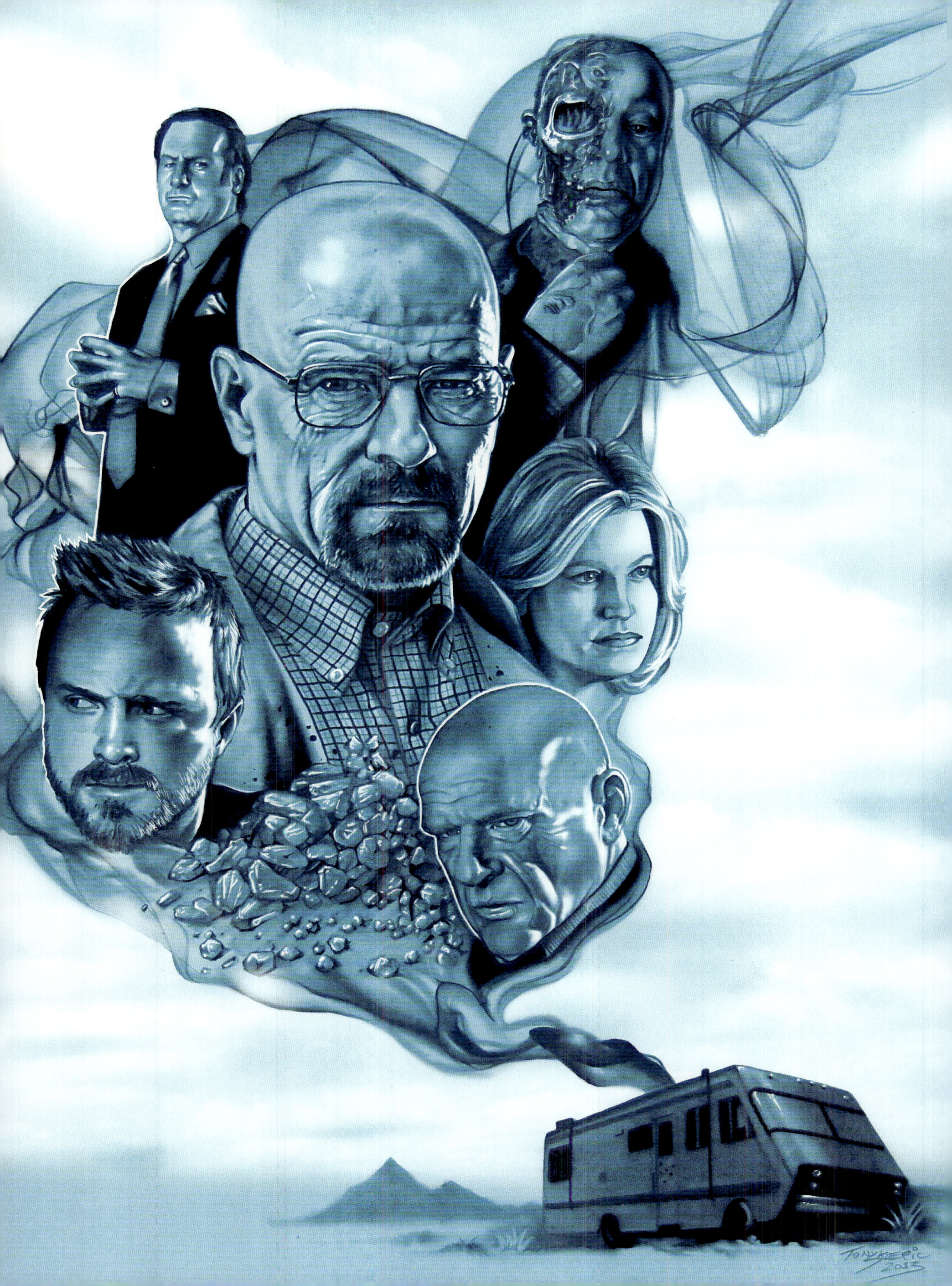
2013

OPPOSITE: Tony Sklepic | *Blue Sky* | Pencil with digital colors | Edmonton, Alberta, Canada | 2013 | ⓘ tonysklepictattoo

THESE PAGES: Matt Talbot | *Citizens of Albuquerque* | Digital | New Hampshire, USA | 2019 | www.mattrobot.com | mattrobot

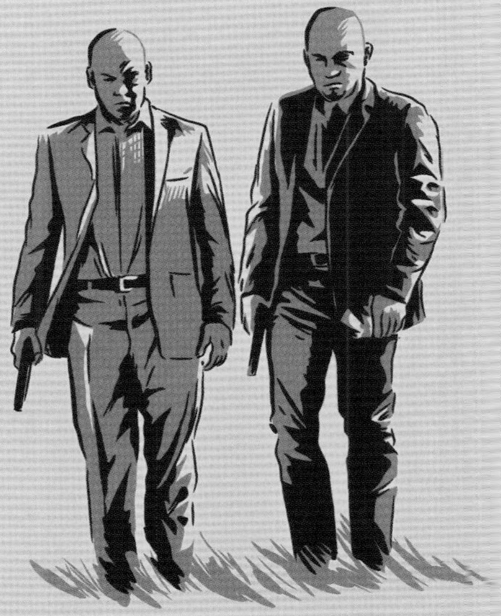

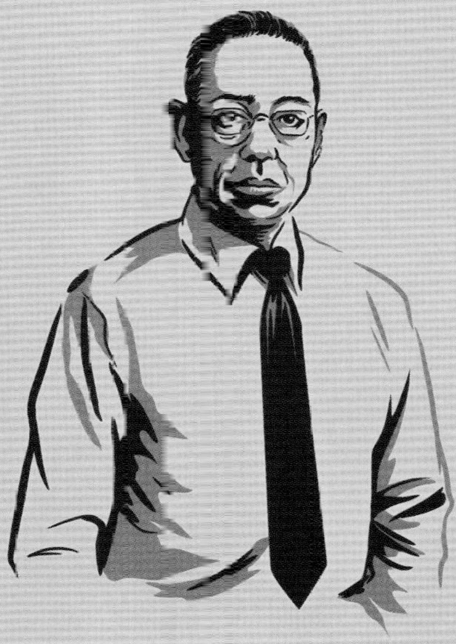

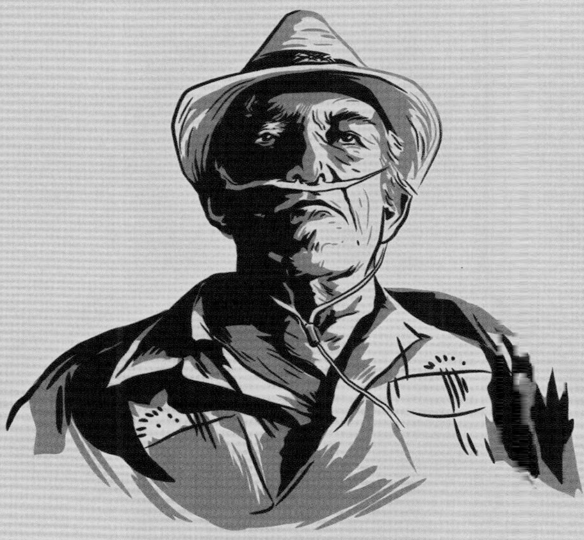

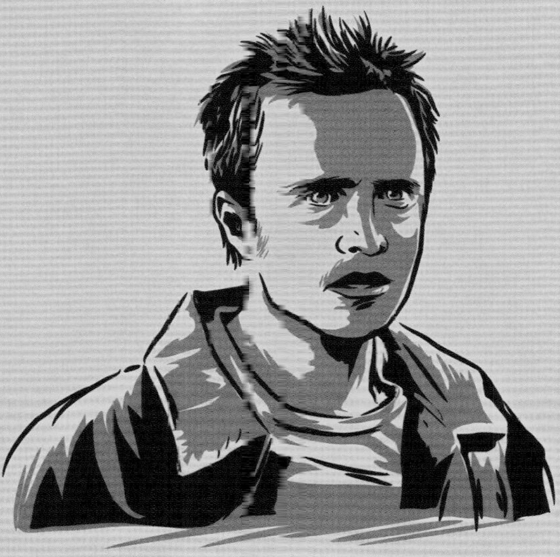

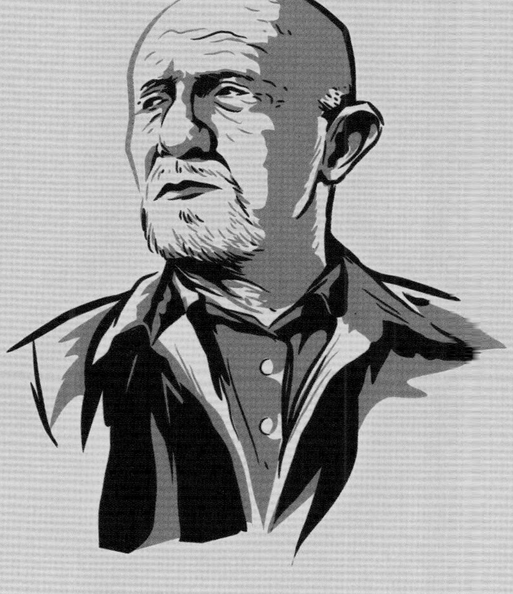

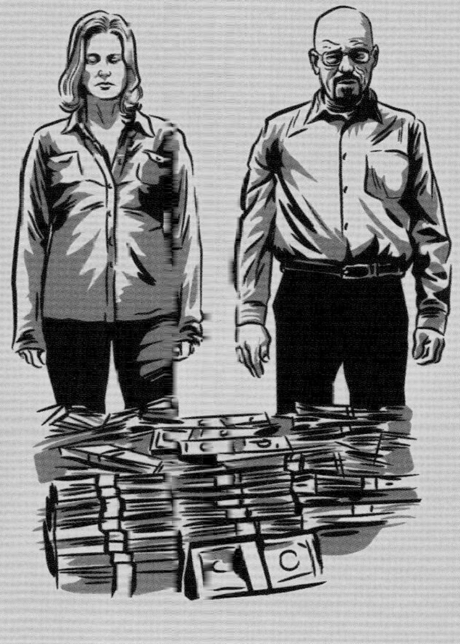

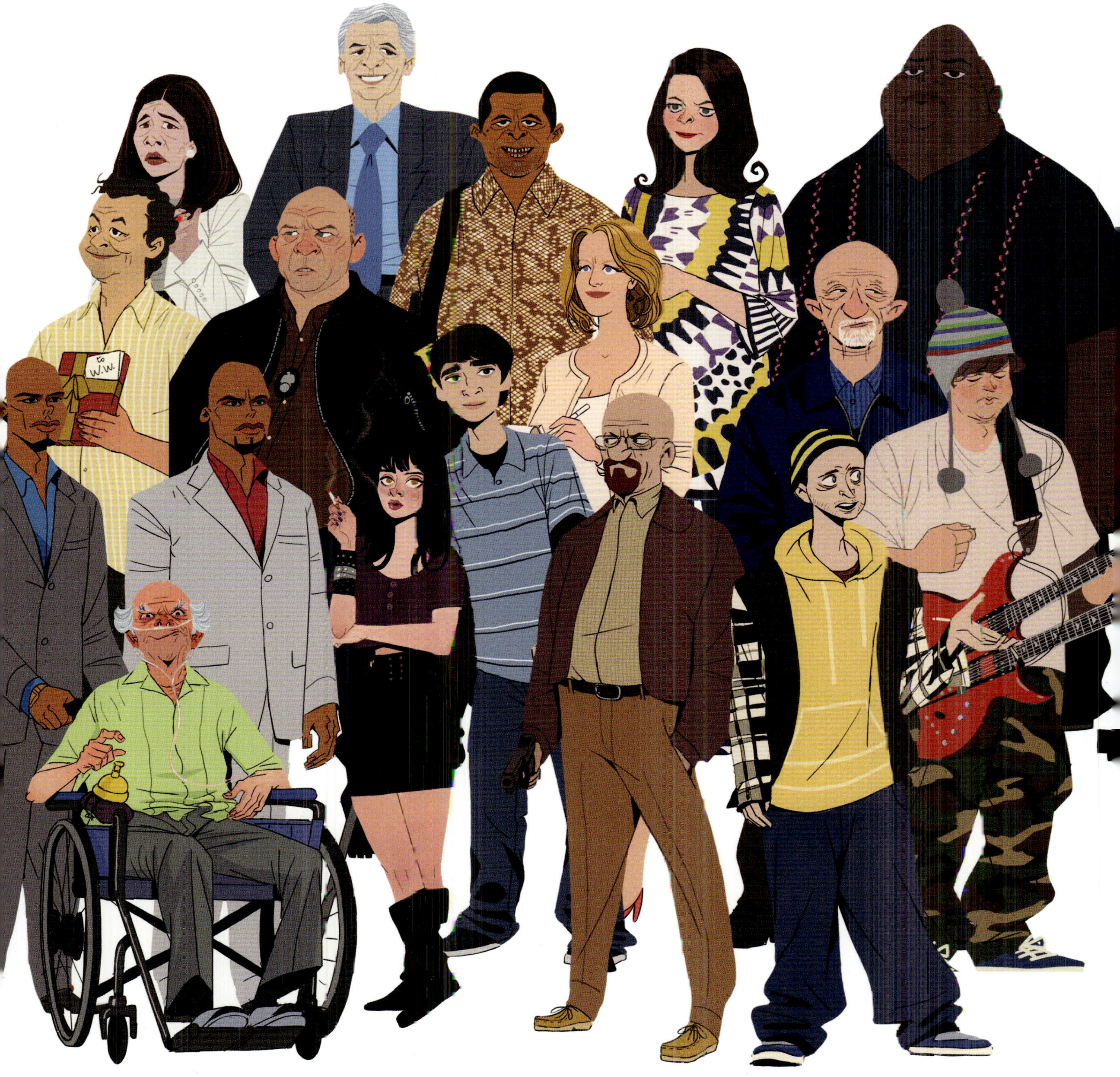
to W.W.

199

PAGES 198–199: Giulio De Toma | Photoshop CC | Bisceglie, Italy | 2018 | ciullit8888 | ciullit.ciullit

ABOVE: Santiago Landaburo | "I Won" | Digital Illustration | Buenos Aires, Argentina | 2014 | www.depalomita.carbonmade.com | depalomita

ABOVE: Studio 17 | *The 3rst Cube* | 3D modeling | Brazil | 2018 | www.studio17nj.com.br

PAGES 202–203 (Left to right, top to bottom): Kevin González | *Ancient, Ash, Bait, Build, Catch, Dragon, Enchanted, Frail, Injured, Freeze, Tasty, Husky, Wild, Pattern, Ripe, Ghost, Ring, Snow, Mistfits,* and *Swirl* | Digital painting | Miami, Florida, USA | 2019 | 🅾 🐦 KGeeDesign

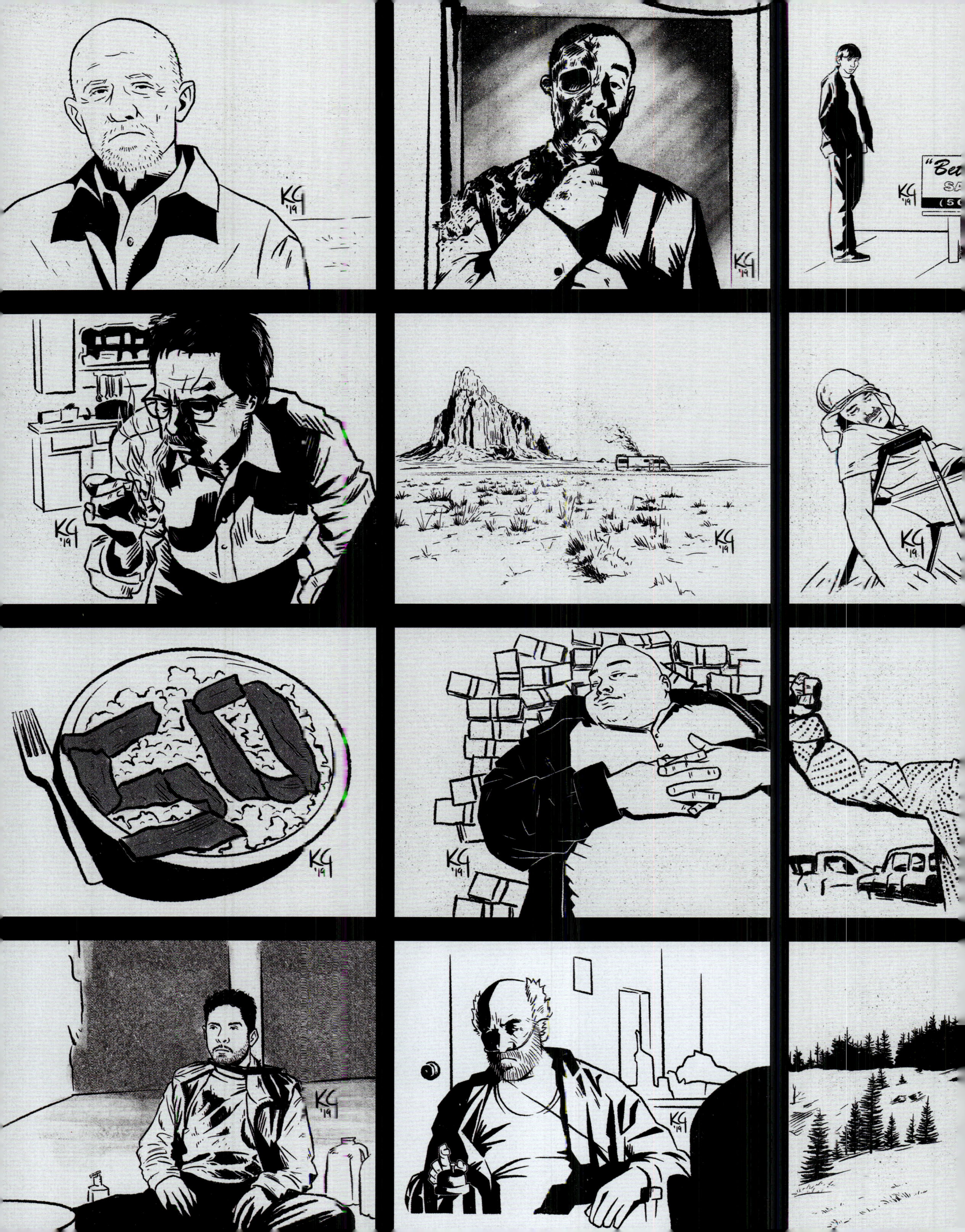

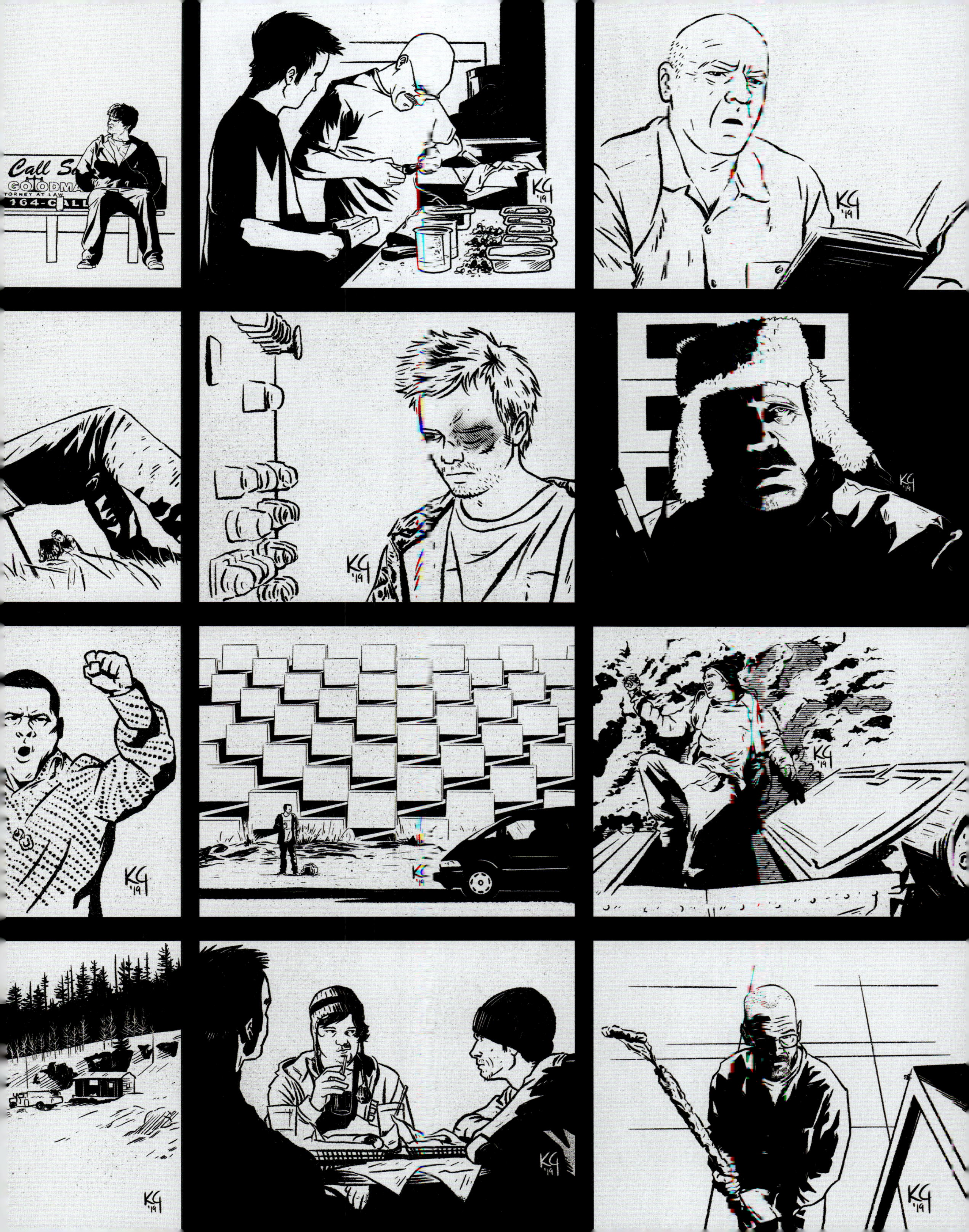
Call Sa
GOODMA
TORNEY AT LAW
164-CALL

THESE PAGES: Eugene Huang | *01x06* and *Season 5* | Digital painting | Los Angeles, California, USA | 2013 | www.thedukeofflies.com | ⦿ he_duke_of_flies

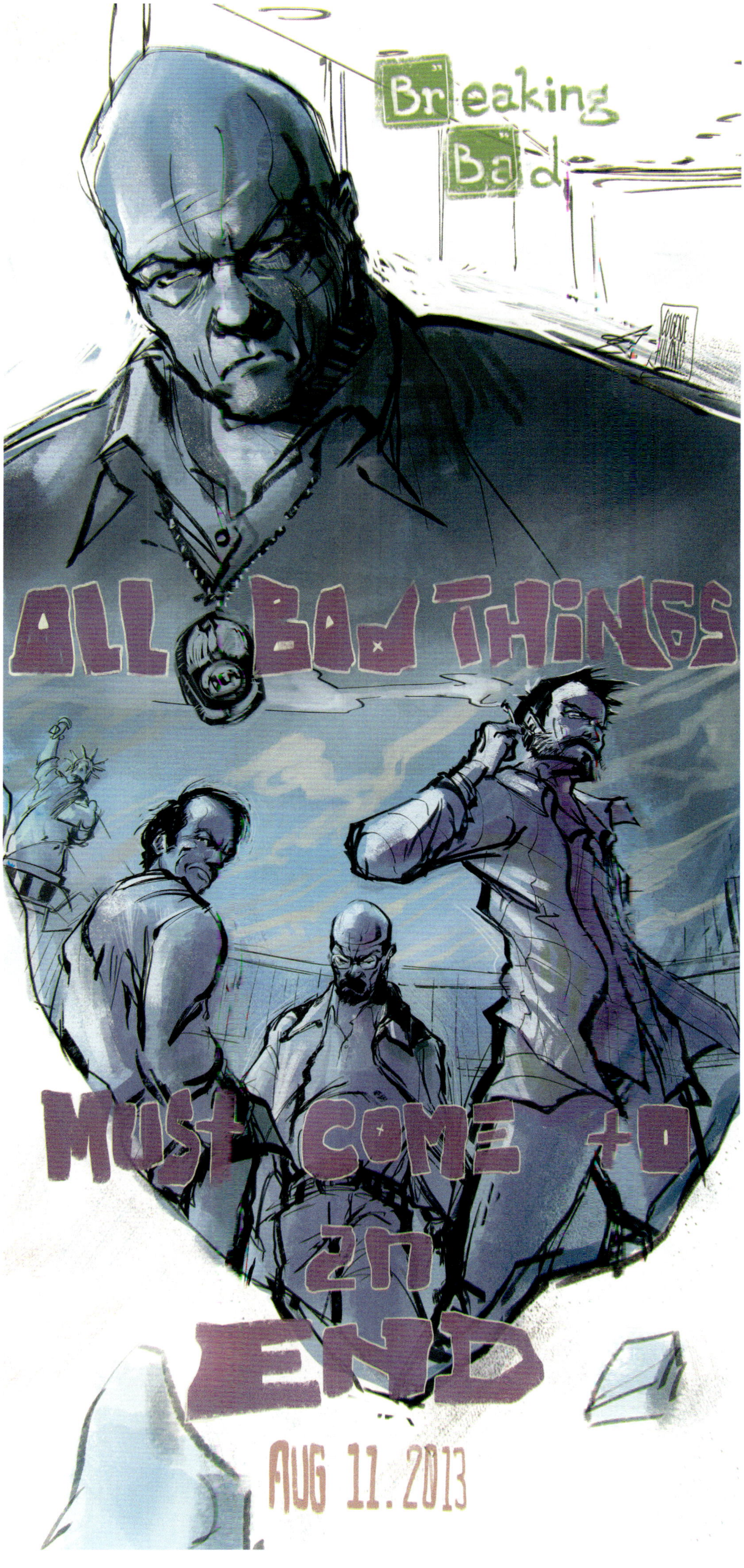
Breaking Bad
ALL BAD THINGS
MUST COME TO
AN
END
AUG 11.2013

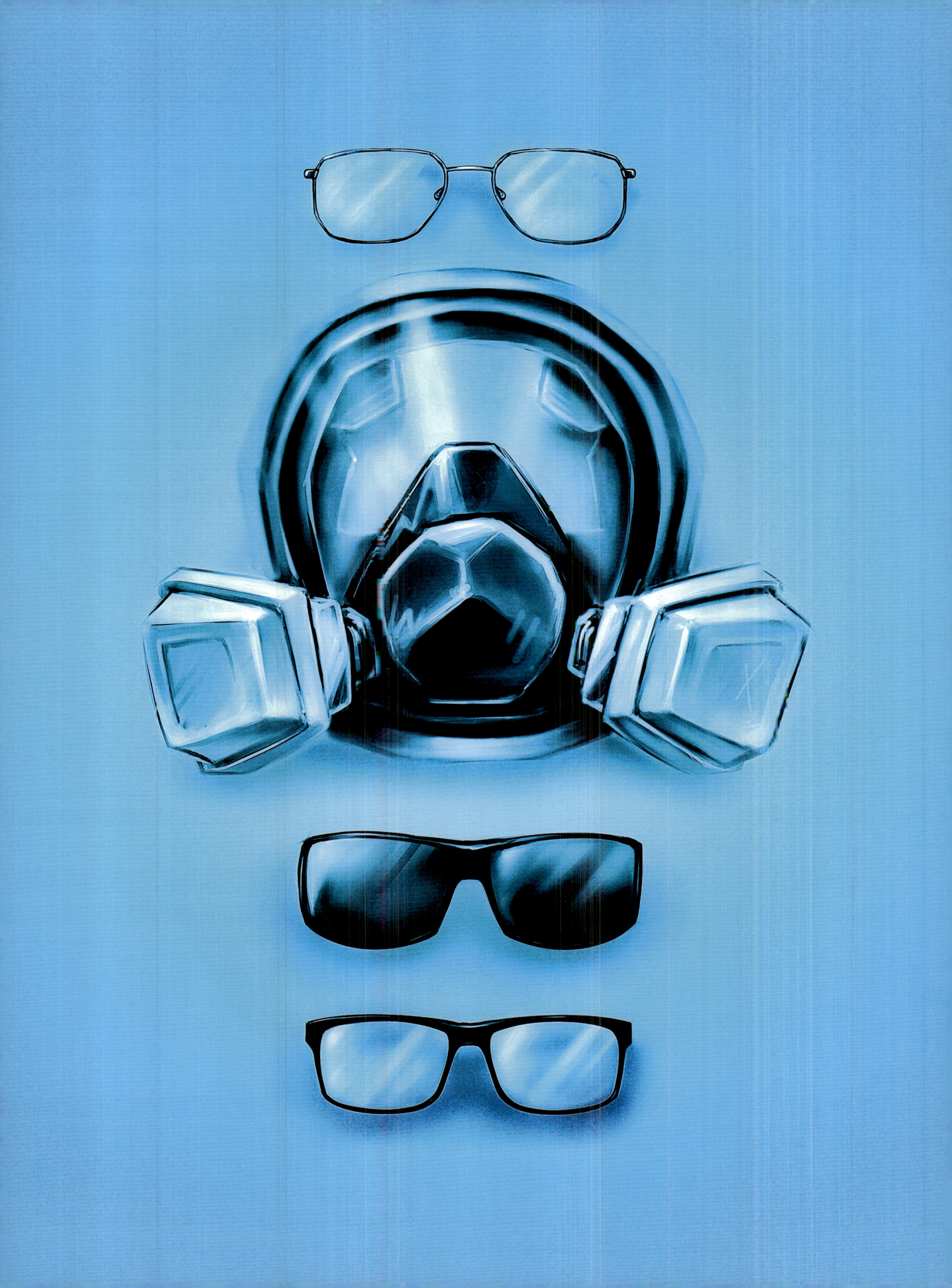

Breaking Bad

FAMILIA ES TODO
SALUD.
HEISENBERG
"Better Call Saul!"
515
YEAH SCIENCE!
A-1
RUN
THE CAPN
FUN-YUNS
COLD-A-FED
COLD-A-FED
COLD-A-FED
COLD-A-FED
ABQ
HYDROFLUORIC ACID
MISTER
WHITE
Schraderbräu
KAFKAESQUE
SANGRE POR SANGRE
LAB NOTES
I AM The One WHO KNOCKS
SAY MY NAME
Wilmington
W.W.
Felina
LOOK AT ME.
CORROSIVE

PAGE 206: Patrick Zédouard c0y0te7 | *All I See Is Blue* | Digital painting | Taverny, France | 2013 | www.c0y0te7.fr | 🅘 c0y0te7

PAGE 207: Jordan Bolton | *Objects of Breaking Bad* | Photography | Manchester, UK | 2017 | 🅘 jordanboltondesign

OPPOSITE: Kris Bicknell | *The_1_Who_Knocks* | Digital painting | Los Angeles, California, USA | 2016 | 🅘 closure_di

ABOVE: Timothy Lim | *Fallacies Album Cover Homage* | Digital painting | Little Rock, Arkansas, USA | 2014 | 🅘 ninjaink

OPPOSITE: Vanessa Harmel | *Colors of Breaking Bad* | Digital painting | Frankfurt, Germany | 2014 | nessasan

PAGES 212–213: Julian Birchman | *A Trip to Belize* | Ink and watercolor | Oakland, California, USA | 2013 | www.julian-birchman.com | julian.birchman

BREAKING BAD

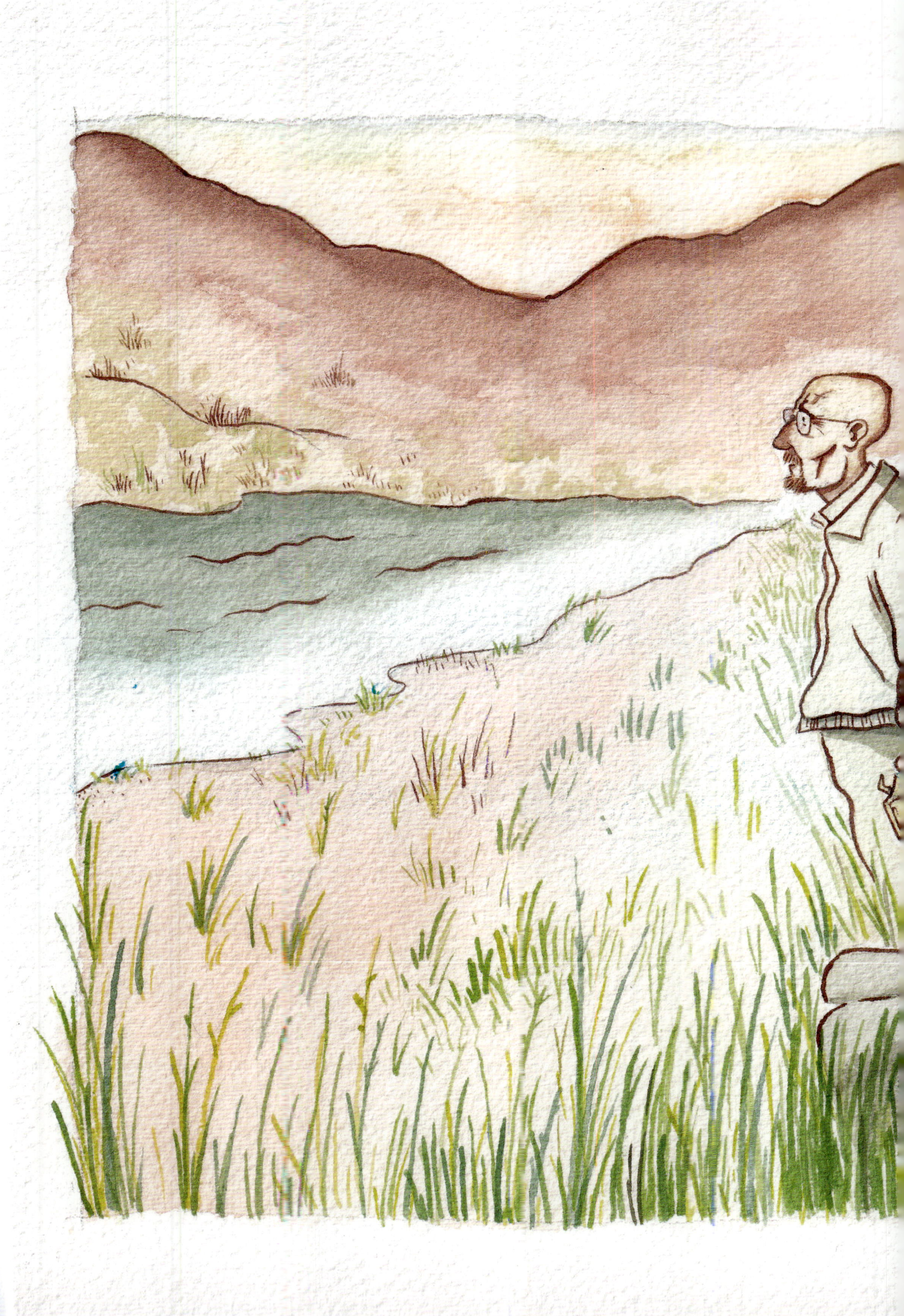

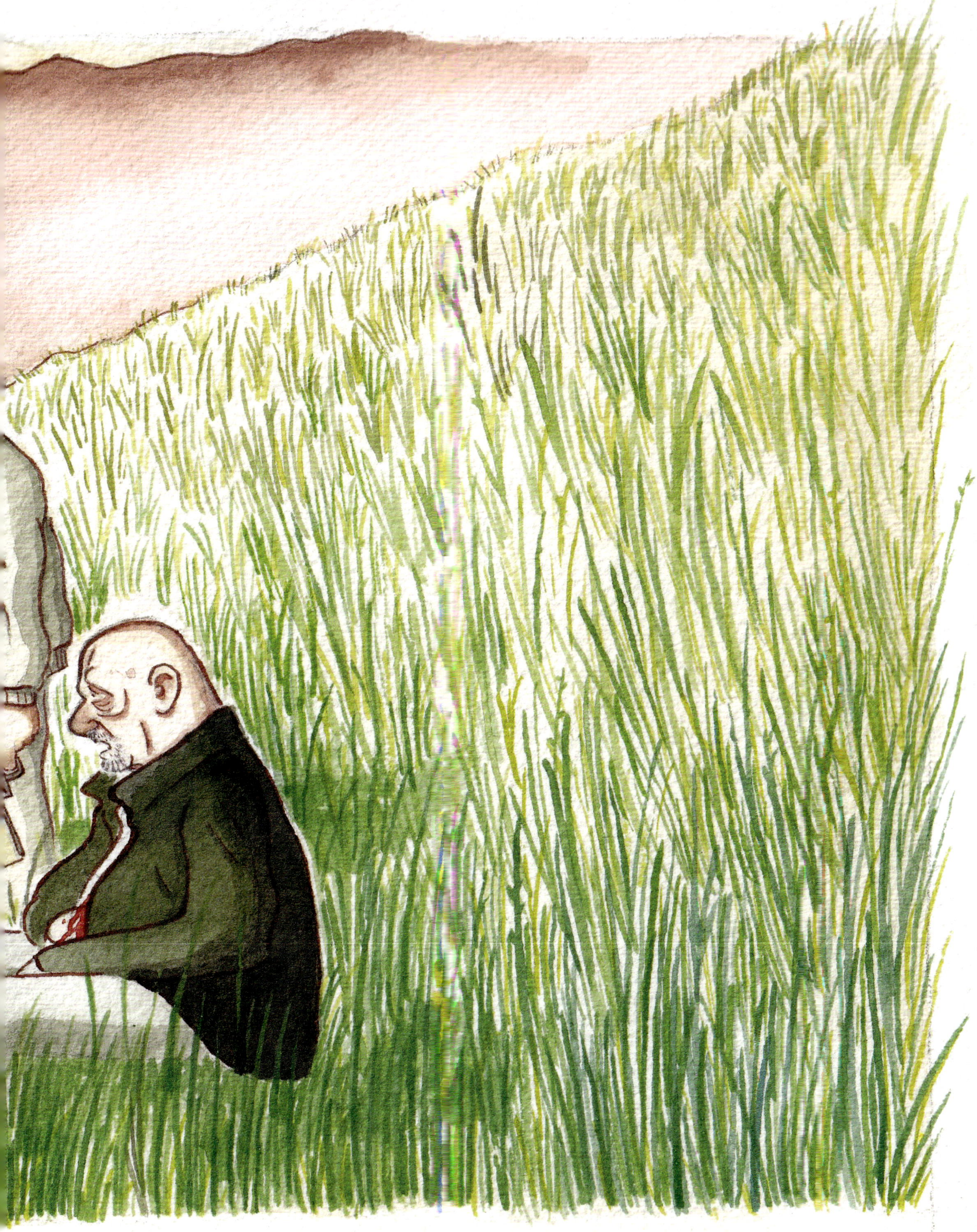

Schrauderbräu
LET HIM LIVE
KILL HIM
-ITS THE MORAL THING TO DO
-HE'LL KILL YOUR ENTIRE FAMILY IF YOU LET HIM GO
General Hospital
Collections Dept.
OPERATOR'S MANUAL
FOR
ONE CREDIT
LAZER BASE
VAMONOS
PEST
CROSSROADS
MOTEL
ROOFTOP PIZZA
MANAGERS SPECIAL!
4-ROOFPIE
ATTORNEY AT LAW
"BETTER CALL SAUL!"
WHITE, W.
Total: $6.00

SAY MY NAME

Breaking Bad
Serie estadounidense de Ciencia ficción mejor puntuada de la historia. **Cre**ada por **V**ince **G**illigan en 2008.

Magali Risoli

216

PAGE 214: Matt Stevens | *Junk Drawer: White's Space* | Digital | Charlotte, North Carolina, USA | 2012   www.hellomattstevens.com | mattstevensclt

PAGE 215: Magalí Risoli | *Say My Name* | Collage and photography | Buenos Aires, Argentina | 2019   magali_risoli

THESE PAGES: Phil G. Mamuyac | *Nesting Bad* | Matryoshka dolls and acrylics | London, UK | 2014 | www.killasauce.com | ArtPhilM

ABOVE: Andrea Kroki | *BKB Bear* | Base watercolors on paper 300g and digital details | Catania, Italy | 2016–2017 / 2020 | 📷 f andrea_kroki

OPPOSITE: Scott Triffle | *Elements* | Digital vector art | Melbourne, Australia | 2020 | www.striffle.com | 📷 striffle

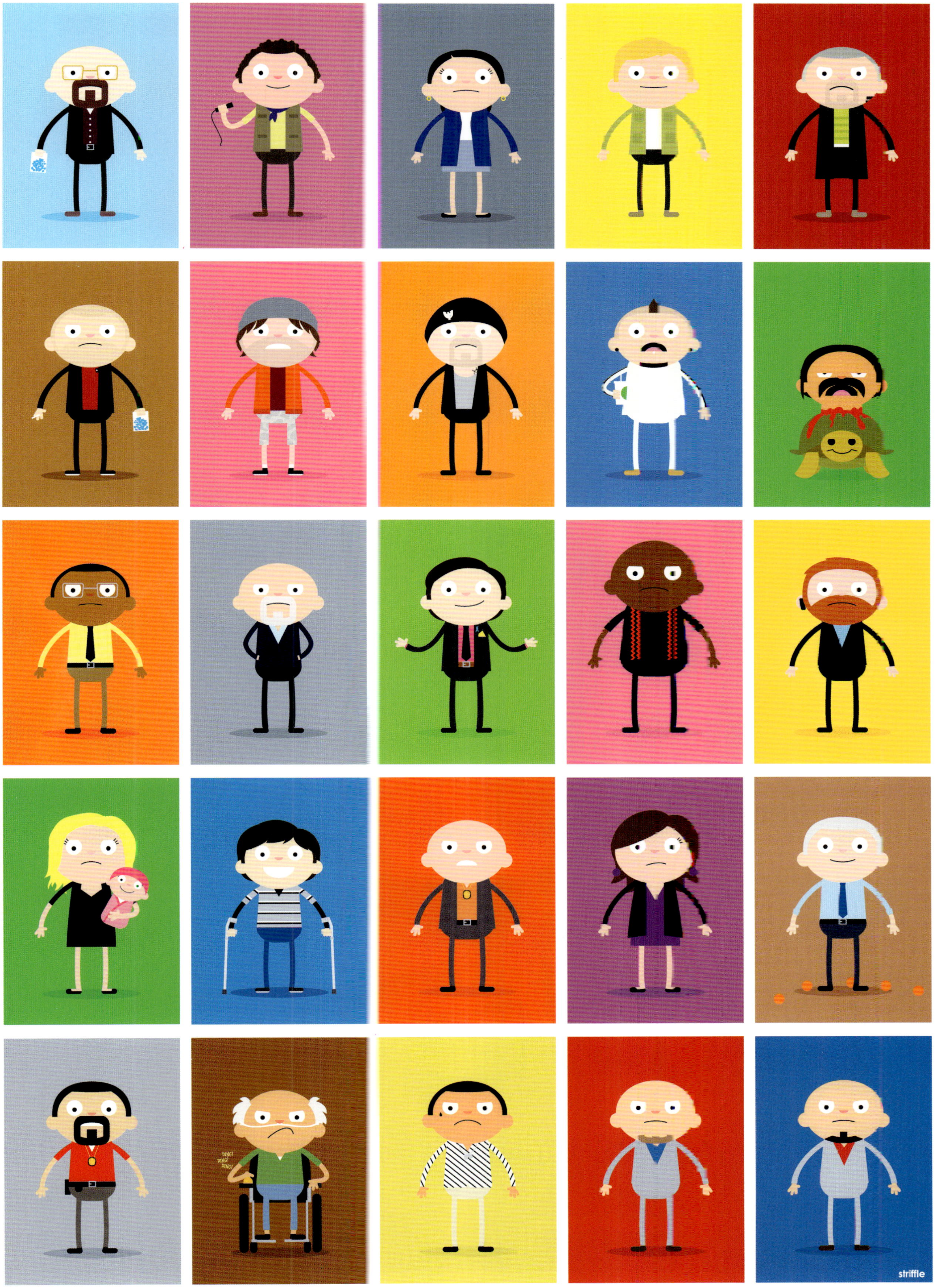
DING!
DING!
DING!
striffle

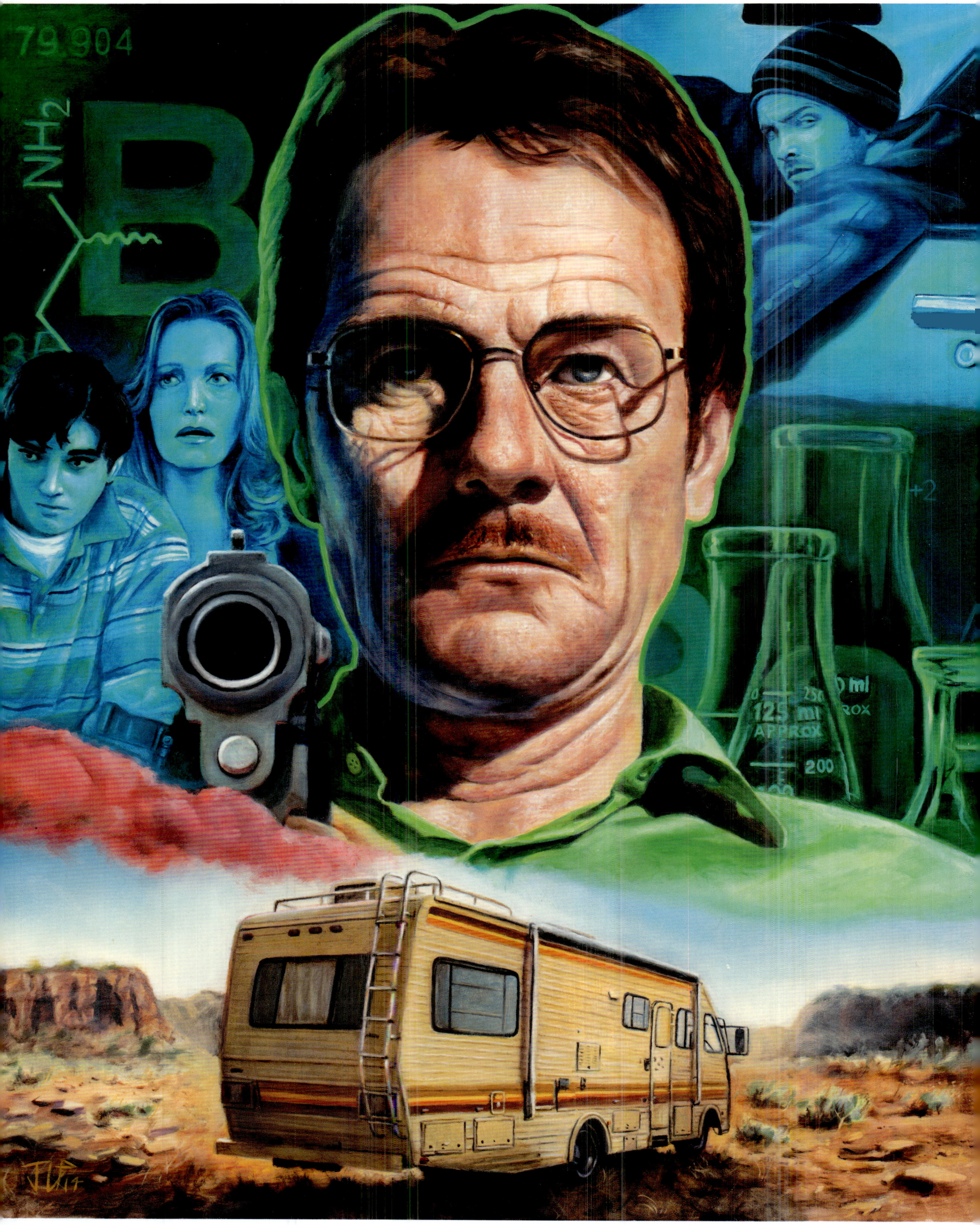
79.904
NH_2
B
125 ml
APPROX
200

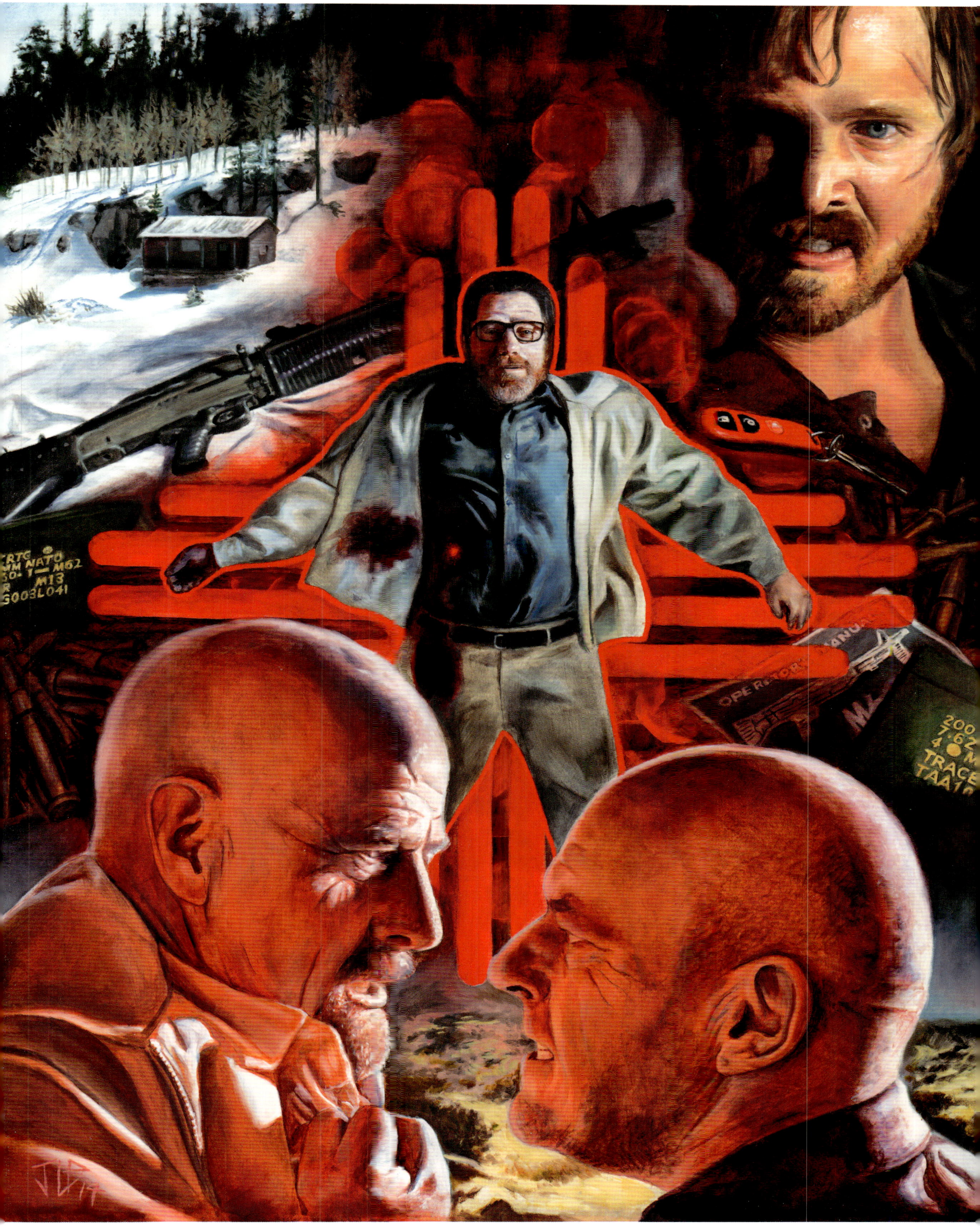
NATO
M62
M13
TRACE

PAGE 220 and PAGE 221: Jamie Lee Parker | *Season 1 and Season 5 Part 2* | Oil | Southern California, USA | 2014 | www.jamieleeparker.com | @ jamieleeparker

ABOVE: Ohab Tochukwu Bernard Johnbosco | *Ricinberg* | Digital illustration | Lagos, Nigeria | 2013 | www.ohabtbj.com | @ ohabtbj

OPPOSITE: Thobias Daneluz | *Breaking Bad: "The Animated Series"* | Digital painting | São Lourenço da Serra, Brazil | 2013 | @ thobiasdaneluz

223

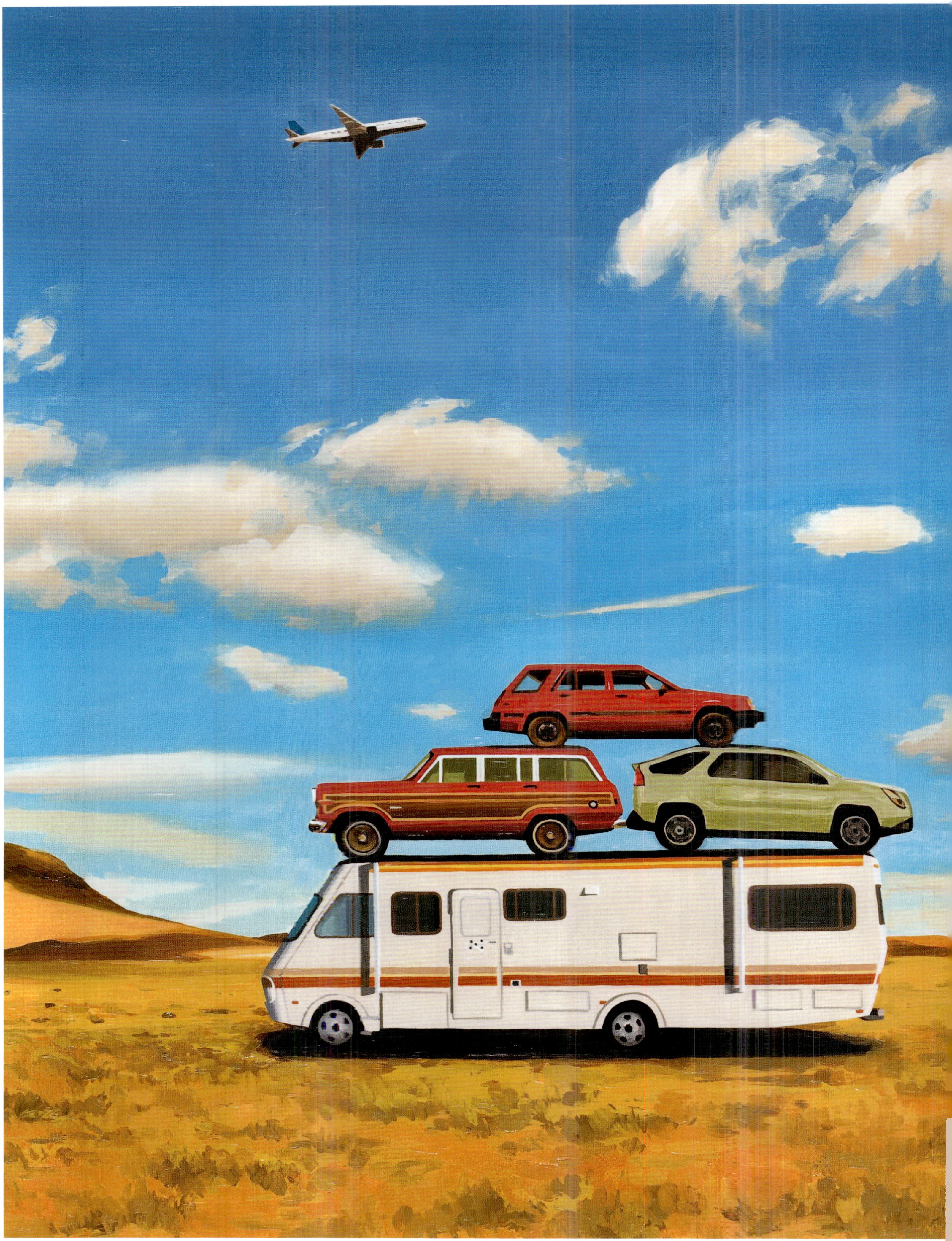

THESE PAGES: Scott Listfield | *To'hajiilee* | Oil on canvas | Somerville, Massachusetts, USA | 2014 | www.astronautdinosaur.com | scottlistfield

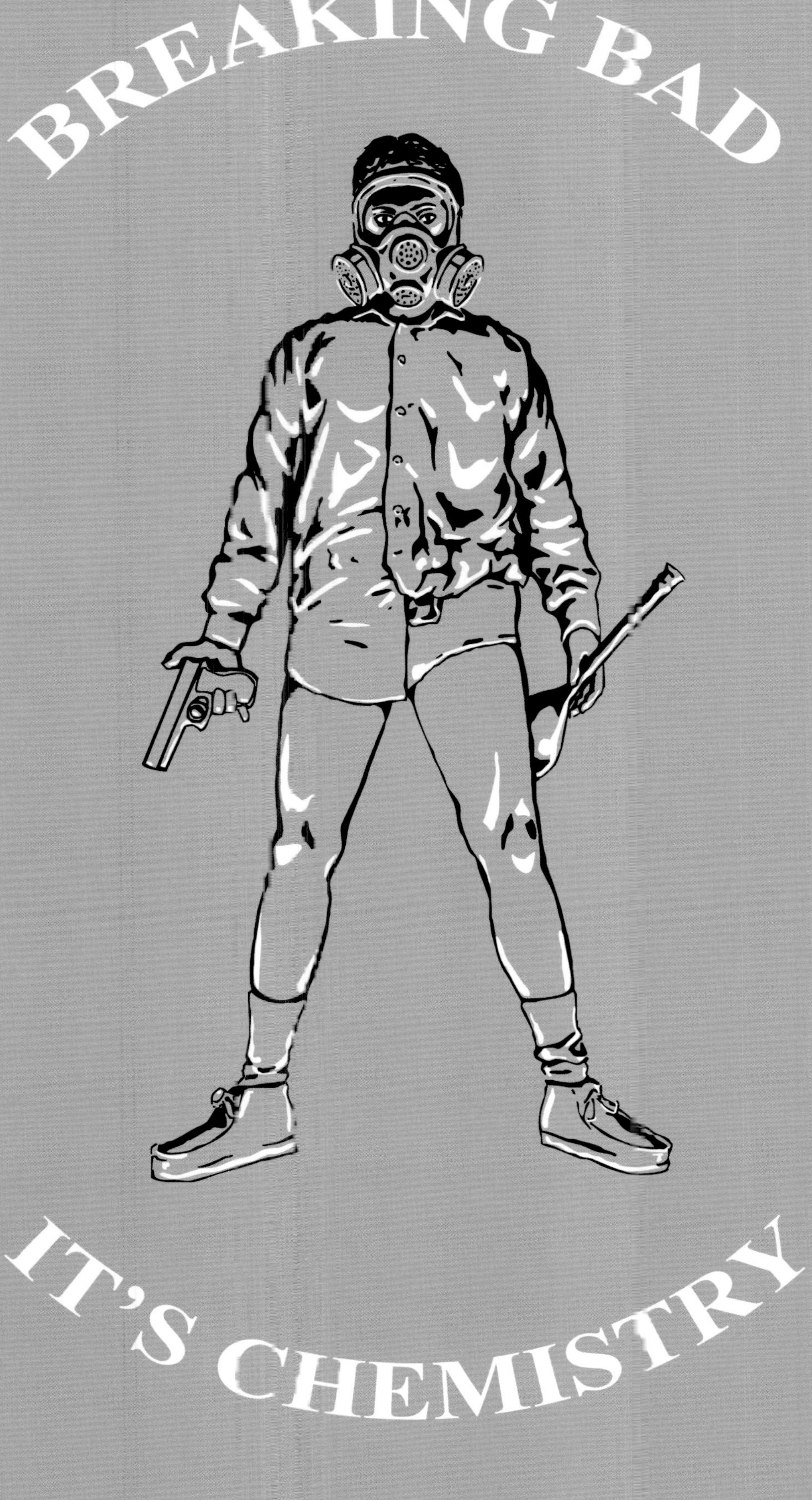
BREAKING BAD
IT'S CHEMISTRY

Epilogue

INSIDE JOB

"I am in love with the endless amount of fan art this beautiful show has received," says **Aaron Paul.** Since it first aired in 2008, *Breaking Bad* has inspired countless artists the world over, their works spanning a variety of mediums and disciplines. "These artists have taken key characters, moments, and themes and transformed them into incredibly impactful works of art that capture the essence of the show in unexpected ways," observes producer Diane Mercer.

Some of *Breaking Bad*'s biggest enthusiasts were members of the show's very own production crew, from location scouts to cinematographers. "It's wonderful to see the *Breaking Bad* crew's talent shine both on-screen and off," reflects Vince Gilligan. "What a testament to their investment in our series that so many members of the team have created their own works inspired by the show." Among this group is special effects technician Joseph Ulibarri, whose pieces include a neon skull-and-bones rendition of Heisenberg and an imposing illustration of Walter White in a gas mask and tighty-whities. "You never know what shows are going to be great and what shows are just shows, and to have landed working on such a gem like *Breaking Bad* so early in my career was very lucky indeed," says Ulibarri.

The creations of artists inside and outside the series serve as reminders of *Breaking Bad*'s enduring influence and the profound connection it has with its global audience. Music supervisor Thomas Golubić puts it perfectly: "It feels like a creative extended family."

OPPOSITE: Joseph Ulibarri / SFX technician
Breaking Bad Shirt | Digital art
Albuquerque, New Mexico, USA
2008 | eyebreakstuff

RIGHT: Marshall Adams / director of photography, Episode 501: "Live Free or Die"
Digital art | Albuquerque, New Mexico, USA
2018 | smadadp

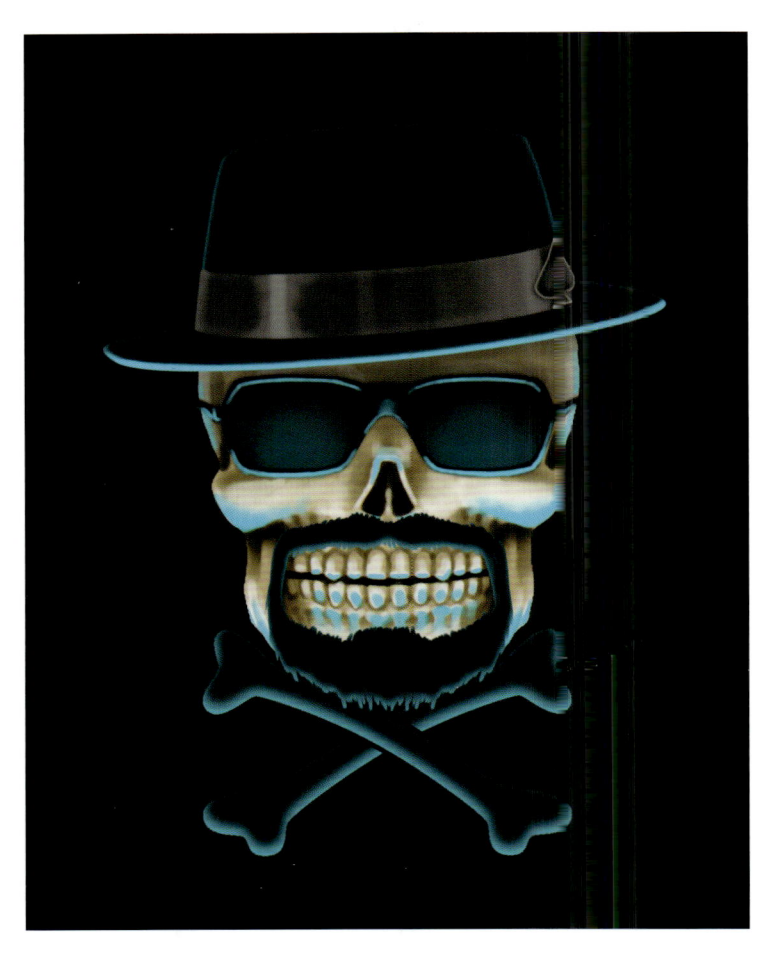

TOP LEFT: Joseph Ulibarri / SFX technician | *Skulls 'n' Stuff Blue Beard*
Digital art | Albuquerque, New Mexico, USA | 2012
⊙ eyebreakstuff

TOP RIGHT: Stephen Turselli / set production assistant, Michael Wiecow
I <3 NM | Screen-printed T-shirt | Albuquerque, New Mexico, USA | 2013
www.solanopictures.com | ⊙ stevetheno | www.metalthebrand.com
⊙ metal_the_brand

RIGHT: Luke Rancall / art department coordinator | *Episode 503 Tech Scout Concept* | Colored pencil, artist markers, and digital art
Albuquerque, New Mexico, USA | 2012

TOP: Alex Gianopoulos / assistant location manager | *Breaking Bad Characters* | Digital art | Albuquerque, New Mexico, USA | 2013 | @ alexgnop

BOTTOM: Joseph Ulibarri / SFX technician | *Breakin' Bad Logo* | Digital art | Albuquerque, New Mexico, USA | 2007 | @ eyebreakstuff

PAGES 230–231: Rocío Fernández Lorca | *W. W.* | Ink on paper | Parma, Italy | 2017 | www.fernandezlorca.es | @ 26medio | @ 26ymotion

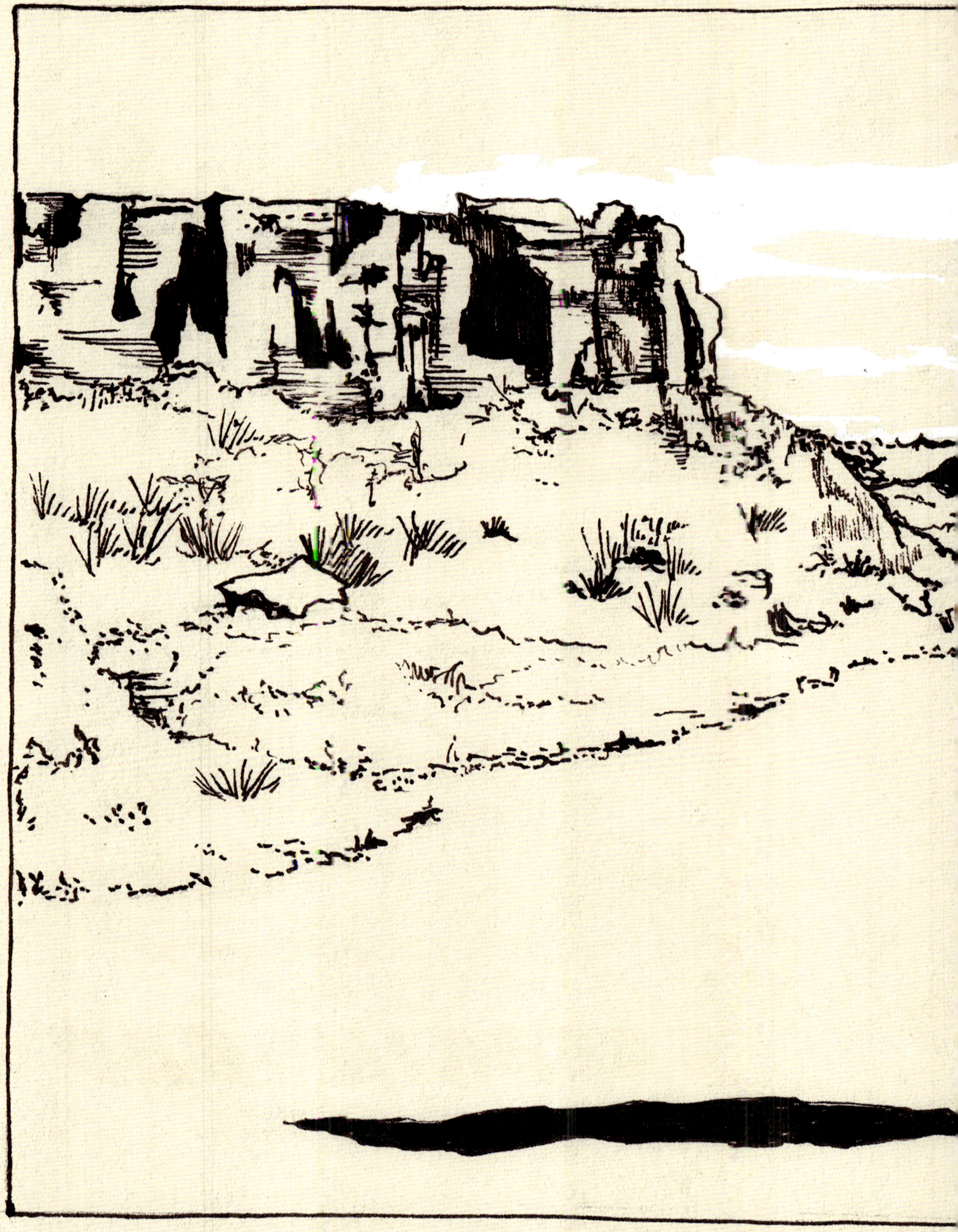

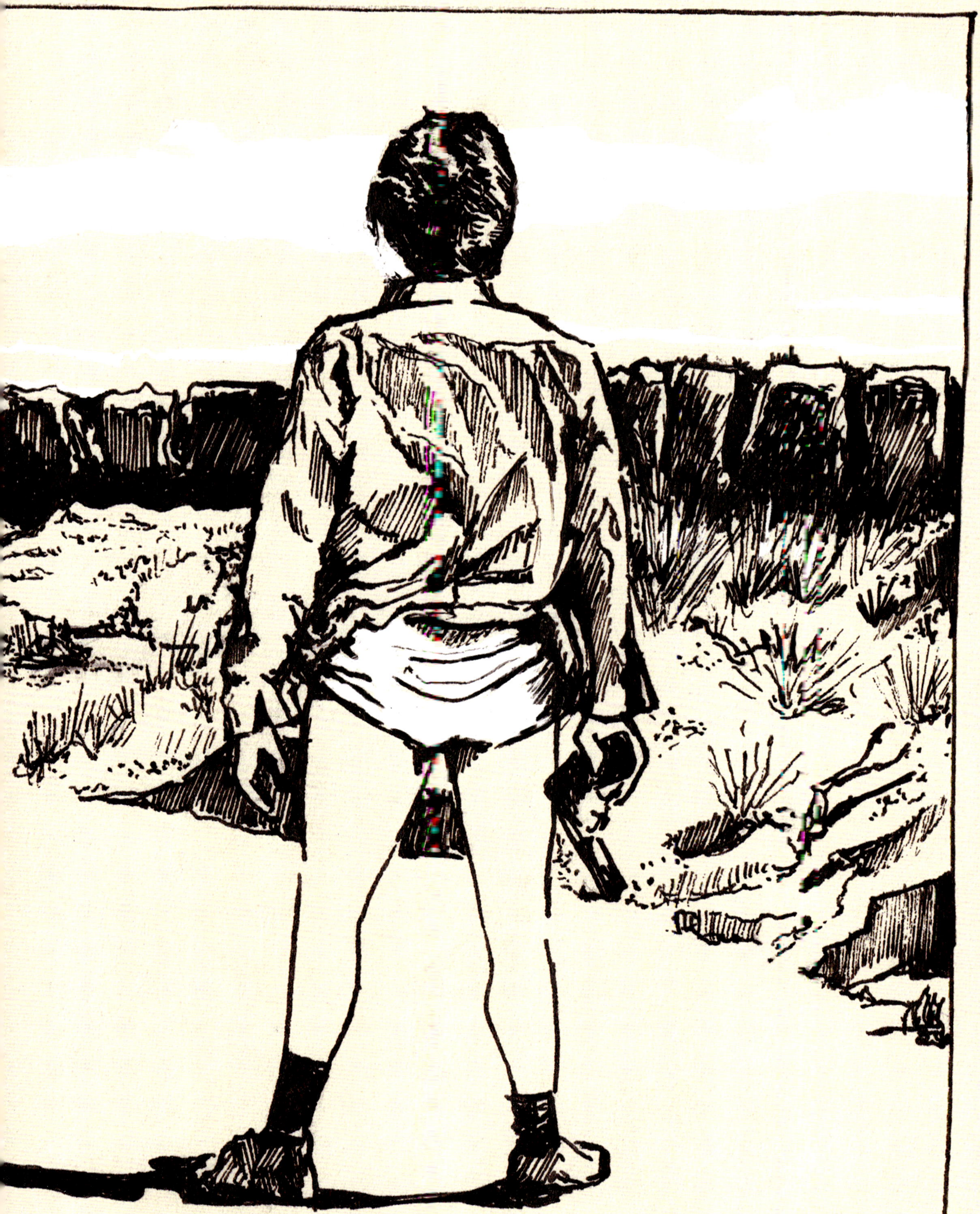